The Best Ever Notes & Queries

edited by

Joseph Harker

FOURTH ESTATE • *London*

First published in Great Britain in 1996 by
Fourth Estate Limited
6 Salem Road
London W2 4BU

A catalogue record for this book is available from the British Library.

ISBN 1-85702-559-8

Typeset by Palimpsest Book Production Limited,
Polmont, Stirlingshire

Printed in Great Britain by Clays Ltd, St Ives plc

The contents of this volume were originally published in the *Guardian* newspaper between 1990 and 1996. Any legal, medical and technical details included here may now be out of date, and readers should not rely on their accuracy or that of any other information herein.

INTRODUCTION

How does one introduce a book like this? Unfortunately, that's not one of the 2,000 questions which have been answered since the Notes & Queries column began in the *Guardian* one Monday morning in November 1989.

Over the past seven years, the pool of knowledge contained within the daily's one million readers has been called on to answer queries as deep as 'What is the meaning of life?', as domestic as 'Why are dusters yellow?', and as daft as 'Did Adam and Eve have navels?' Queries which have tormented ordinary folk for years have now been solved.

But, as the column has proven, there are more questions than answers. Notes & Queries still receives around 100 missives per week from inquiring minds. Not surprisingly, some of these are posed more than once (for example, during each Wimbledon fortnight we are asked why the tennis scoring system is 15, 30, 40). So, having previously emulated the movie industry with Notes & Queries I to VI, we now aspire to be like those top pop bands with our first 'Best of . . .' volume, combining our most commonly asked questions with the most bizarre answers. Many of these were first published during the term of the column's founder editor, Brian Whitaker, who built Notes & Queries into one of the most popular sections of the paper. Its enduring popularity is largely down to him, and has taken further leaps worldwide with its inclusion in the *Guardian Weekly* – available across the globe – and, this year, the creation of an Internet web site.

The column succeeds above all probably because it allows argument. Readers may believe that an expert has given the definitive response one week, but in the next issue another specialist may well disagree. Why is water wet, for example. Well, after eight competing replies, we now know . . . I think.

It all leaves one agreeing with Descartes, who said: 'The only truth is the existence of doubt.' But, then again, how could he be so sure?

Joseph Harker
September 1996

QUESTION: What are the origins of the expressions 'Cloud nine' and 'Cloud-cuckoo-land'?

☐ 'CLOUD-CUCKOO-LAND' is a translation of the Greek *Nephelo-kokkugi* (*Nephele* = cloud, *kokkux* = cuckoo) which is to be found in Aristophanes' comedy, *Birds*, first performed in 414 BC in Athens. The play concerns two Athenians disillusioned with life in the city who go to seek somewhere better to live. Eventually they conceive to build a city in the air with which they can intercept the sacrificial smoke which nourishes the gods. The birds, under the two Athenians, build the city which is to be called Cloud-cuckoo-land.
John Hudswell, London EC1.

☐ 'CLOUD NINE' is an advance on 'cloud seven', a pictorialisation of the Seventh Heaven (or Heaven of Heaven), the abode of God Himself in both Jewish and Mohammedan tradition; it seems to be an example of the inflationary tendency of the 1960s.
D. W. R. Whicker, Wimborne, Dorset.

QUESTION: Who was the composer of 'Happy Birthday'?

☐ WORDS and music were by an American nursery teacher called Patty Hill. She wrote it so her children could sing it when someone had a birthday.
Chloe Walker (aged 7), Bristol, Avon.

☐ IT IS, I understand, the world's most sung song. Written in the 1890s, it was not copyrighted until 1935 and is still in copyright. In 1988 the firm which had owned the song since 1935 put it up for sale. This company had been collecting about a million dollars a year in royalties. It was acquired by Warner Communications in a $25 million deal.
Leslie Jerman, Epping, Essex.

QUESTION: What is the origin of the phrase 'to have a chip on one's shoulder'? It sounds American, but where or when?

□ THIS does seem to be of American origin and derives from a custom once common to bar rooms. A man who felt like a fight put a woodchip on his shoulder and defied anyone to knock it off. The challenge was rarely refused. An Anglo/Irish analogue was (is?) 'trailing the coat'. Here, the would-be gladiator trailed his coat behind him in the hope that someone would tread on it. The formal customs have long ceased but the attitudes remain. Today the allegation that some stranger has merely looked in the wrong direction is deemed sufficient to justify assault. The older usage now seems positively chivalrous.
Alan W. Smith, Chigwell, Essex.

□ TO ANY North American the origin of the phrase 'a chip on one's shoulder' can be a painful memory. My first experience of it, more than 60 years ago, was as an English child in a Canadian playground. The school bully picked a chip of wood from the ground, placed it on his shoulder, and invited me to knock it off. I did so, and was felled by his fist. In time I learnt that the best method of avoiding an unwanted fight, or the taint of cowardice in refusing the challenge, was to place another chip on my own shoulder and dare my opponent (who was sometimes my friend) to knock that off first. This usually succeeded, and the affair ended painlessly in taunting shouts and honours even.
John Prebble, Kingswood, Surrey.

QUESTION: Who was Gordon Bennett?

□ JAMES GORDON BENNETT (1841–1918) was an American journalist, editor of the *New York Herald* (in succession to his less well-known father, also James Gordon Bennett) and sports enthusiast. He is probably best-known now for being the man who commissioned Henry Morton Stanley to search for Dr Livingstone (thus presumably occasioning a telegram which began 'Gordon Bennett – I've found Livingstone!'). Bennett also introduced polo to the United States and was involved in horse-racing (Leopold Bloom spends some time in *Ulysses* contemplating a bet upon a horse in the Gordon Bennett Handicap, actually run that day in Dublin).
Nicholas Graham, Teddington, Middlesex.

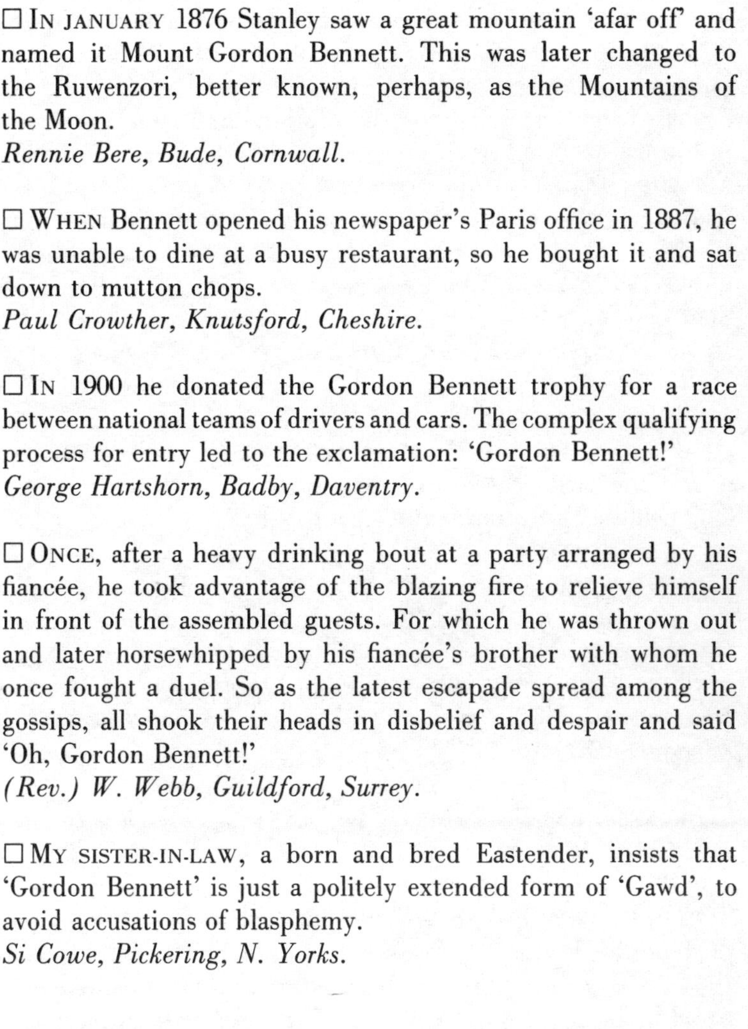

□ In January 1876 Stanley saw a great mountain 'afar off' and named it Mount Gordon Bennett. This was later changed to the Ruwenzori, better known, perhaps, as the Mountains of the Moon.
Rennie Bere, Bude, Cornwall.

□ When Bennett opened his newspaper's Paris office in 1887, he was unable to dine at a busy restaurant, so he bought it and sat down to mutton chops.
Paul Crowther, Knutsford, Cheshire.

□ In 1900 he donated the Gordon Bennett trophy for a race between national teams of drivers and cars. The complex qualifying process for entry led to the exclamation: 'Gordon Bennett!'
George Hartshorn, Badby, Daventry.

□ Once, after a heavy drinking bout at a party arranged by his fiancée, he took advantage of the blazing fire to relieve himself in front of the assembled guests. For which he was thrown out and later horsewhipped by his fiancée's brother with whom he once fought a duel. So as the latest escapade spread among the gossips, all shook their heads in disbelief and despair and said 'Oh, Gordon Bennett!'
(Rev.) W. Webb, Guildford, Surrey.

□ My sister-in-law, a born and bred Eastender, insists that 'Gordon Bennett' is just a politely extended form of 'Gawd', to avoid accusations of blasphemy.
Si Cowe, Pickering, N. Yorks.

QUESTION: It's (now) officially admitted that MI5 and MI6 exist. During the Second World War there was, I believe, MI9 and MI14. But what did MIs 1–4, 7, 8, 10, 11, 12 and 13 do?

□ This question shouldn't really be asked – or answered – but basically it seems probable they did nothing, but drew pay for it. It is believed that MI1 and MI11 were eliminated long ago because of confusion between Is and 1s in the accounts department. As to the rest, it is said that out of the huge sums voted as 'contingencies' modest amounts are transferred to MI2 and MI3

and allocated to the Prime Minister and Home Secretary to reward their alleged responsibilities for the non-existing MI5 and MI6. Further amounts, charged to MI4 account, may be offered either to the Chancellor of the Exchequer or to the Foreign Secretary to compensate for loss of tied week-end cottages – and similar. The large balance (charged to MIs 7, 8, 10, 12 and 13, which are 'notional' only) is used as necessary to bump up 'invisibles' in specially bad months to keep Balance-of-Payment deficits below the £2 billion mark, where possible. But please note, this is off the record.
A. I. Pottinger, Edgbaston, Birmingham.

QUESTION: To, either out of ignorance or boldly and with malice aforethought, insert words into a verb's infinitive form is considered grammatically sinful. Why?

☐ LOST for appropriate models, 18th-century grammarians turned to Latin when a need was felt to regularise or standardise English. In Latin, of course, it is not possible to split an infinitive – it's one word. Arbitrarily this 'rule' was applied to English.
Bob Jope, Head of English and Drama, Sydenham High School, London SE26.

☐ BECAUSE the question has to be read twice to be understood.
Andrew Mackay, London N1.

☐ IN DEFENCE of bad syntax, every child should be able to quote the following heroes of 20th-century culture . . . Raymond Chandler wrote to his English publisher: 'When I split an infinitive, god damn it, I split it so it stays split.' There can be few people who don't know the major contribution of Captain James T. Kirk to the English language ('. . . our five-year mission – to boldly go where no man has gone before').
Arabella McIntyre Brown, Liverpool 17.

☐ SHAKESPEARE did it, the *Guardian* regularly does it, and I for one will continue to happily do it without any anxiety over its supposed incorrect or even 'sinful' nature. Of course the rule is to pedantically be observed when, as in this sentence, it leads us into ugliness.
Sean Barker, Moss Side, Manchester.

QUESTION: How did the newt, a graceful and agile creature, come to be regarded as an index of inebriation?

☐ IT WAS a mistake, a mishearing of 'an Ute', as used by US Army personnel in Britain during the Second World War. The celebrated drunkenness of the Ute Indian tribe on their reservation forced the US Government to ban the sale of alcohol there.
Harold Smith, Bradford-on-Avon, Wilts.

☐ THE phrase actually comes down to regional accent in the days of Henry VIII. Half-way through a banquet the king inquired as to what brew one young reveller had been partaking of, to be begged by the young man's father to 'forgive him, Sire, he is but a youth and as for wine he is new to it!' Hence he was p----- as a 'new to it.'
Lesley Robertson, London, SW4.

☐ NEWTS, like many other small creatures which were easily found in the countryside around places where beer was being brewed or cider pressed, were often added to the barrels of drink to improve flavour and strength. An article in *Tenth-Century Studies* by David Parsons remarks that the medieval practice was to put mice or weasels in beer to flavour it, but it was considered sinful to do this deliberately and cruelly drown the beasts, so the English got the priest to bless the beer first. This absolved them, since the animals were going into a holy liquid. Cider-makers in Somerset have been known to add lumps of beef to the fermenting juice, and stories circulate about rats floating in barrels of scrumpy. The newt as an amphibian would survive in liquid longer than mouse, weasel and rat, and presumably would pass so much alcohol through its gills that it would soon reach that happy state wherein its grosser bodily functions would be a matter of complete indifference to it.
Angela Costen, Axbridge, Somerset.

☐ AMAZED that three people could supply different but equally mistaken answers, we feel it our duty to provide the correct answer. Abraham Newton (1631–1698) of Grantham, the presumed author of the first known treatise on the medicinal properties of the beer of Burton-upon-Trent (now unfortunately lost), was such a well-known tippler that, in his lifetime, even Londoners would

use the expression 'Pissed as Abe Newton'. He was so famous that when his fellow townsman, Isaac Newton, achieved prominence, people would say of him, 'No, not that Newton.' The confusion reached its height in the early 1700s, so it was probably around this time that 'pissed as a Newton' sprang into being, only to be gradually contracted into the phrase we all know so well.
M. and B. Gidley, Exeter.

QUESTION: I believe that it is possible to avoid junk mail by writing to an organisation that will remove your name from mailing lists. Do any readers know of such an organisation?

□ THERE ARE two addresses that one can write to to prevent junk mail being delivered. They are: Mailing Preference Service, Freepost 22, London W1E and Office of the Data Protection Registrar, Springfield House, Water Lane, Wilmslow SK9 5AX. If you write to these two bodies they will remove your name from the lists.
Mark Peters, c/o Royal Mail Letters, Harrow, Middx.

□ THE Mailing Preference Society can only control mailings from organisations affiliated to the scheme, and addressed to you personally at home (i.e. items addressed to 'the occupier' or 'householder' are outside its scope). Additionally, you can use the scheme to receive more unsolicited mailings should you feel you are not getting a sufficient supply of 'Win a Car'/'Your Lucky Number Is . . .' type correspondence.
Barry Mills, London SE6.

QUESTION: What did William Blake have in mind when he used the expression 'dark satanic mills'?

□ THE PHRASE was used in the preface to *Milton* (1804) and refers not to the new cotton mills or factories but, as David Erdman suggests (Blake: *Prophet Against Empire*), to the 'mills that produce dark metal, iron and steel, for diabolic purposes.' At the time London was 'a major war arsenal and the hub of the machinery of war' – the war against the French had been renewed in 1803 after a brief peace – and Blake's symbolism

was part of what Erdman calls Blake's 'determination to forge counterarms of art'.
Keith McClelland, London N4.

QUESTION: My wife maintains that the final two pages of *The House at Pooh Corner* by A. A. Milne comprise the most poignant passage in English literature. Can anyone suggest alternative candidates for this title?

☐ THE last page in Charles Dickens' *A Tale of Two Cities*: 'It is a far far better thing that I do . . .'
(Miss) Lucinda Powell, London W6.

☐ THE last page of *Wuthering Heights*: 'I lingered around them . . .'
Diana Johns, King's Langley, Herts.

☐ I CAN strongly recommend *Where's Master?* by Caesar, the King's Dog. Caesar belonged to Edward VII and walked immediately behind the gun-carriage at the King's funeral on 20 May 1910. Hodder & Stoughton published the book on 13 June that year and it reached its ninth edition on 30 August. Having bought a copy at a book fair, I made the mistake of reading it on the train back. Quite what the other passengers made of an unshaven 35-year-old snivelling over a second-hand book, I am unable to say, but I wish I'd had a handkerchief on me.
John Whiteley, Altrincham, Cheshire.

☐ THE most poignant passage in English (or, perhaps, any other language) is surely the last two pages of *Watership Down*, particularly the third-from-last paragraph, which contains this sentence: 'It seemed to Hazel that he would not be needing his body any more, so he left it lying on the edge of the ditch, but stopped for a moment to watch his rabbits and to try to get used to the extraordinary feeling that strength and speed were flowing inexhaustibly out of him and into their sleek young bodies and healthy senses.' Never fails to make me sniffle.
C. Sullivan, East Dulwich, London.

☐ I NOMINATE 'The Piper at the Gates of Dawn' chapter from

The Wind in the Willows by Kenneth Grahame. Regrettably, some editions omit this chapter as irrelevant to the plot, so if buying a copy make sure it is unabridged.
Pete Clinch, Dundee.

☐ THE part of the prologue to Evelyn Waugh's *Brideshead Revisited* where Charles Ryder compares his feelings to the Army to that of a husband caught in a failed marriage.
Gillian Kempster, Chobham, Surrey.

☐ AT the end of Malory's *Morte D'Arthur*, after 20½ books of cartoon fighting, knights bashing each other about, and it all being jolly fun, the mortally wounded Arthur lies in a chapel near the field of the last battle, and hears cries and shrieks from the field. He sends Sir Lucan to investigate and Lucan sees 'pillours and robbers' picking their way among the dying men on the field, looting from them, killing them for their jewels if they're still alive. Real life has arrived after the golden age of Arthur.
Ian Lewis, Farnham, Surrey.

☐ SURELY the final paragraph of Emily Bronte's *Wuthering Heights*, by many a tear.
Hilary Cripps, Worthing, W. Sussex.

☐ WHETHER at school, in the Army, earning a living or now, 70 years on, the pith of poignancy was ever exemplified for me by the words of Charles Lamb: 'I have had playmates, I have had companions, in the days of childhood, in my joyful school-days. All, all are gone, the old familiar faces.'
Frank Carpenter, N. Walsham, Norfolk.

☐ THOMAS HARDY is surely the master of poignancy. My choice would be the final three paragraphs of *The Woodlanders* (but read the rest of the book first!).
Andrew Foster, Wickford, Essex.

QUESTION: Why are the police referred to as 'the Bill' or 'the Old Bill'?

☐ THE 'Old Bill' seems to be a piece of word play combining the

Old Bailey where you went for the more serious offences, with the sought-after Bill Bailey of the popular song. The TV series *The Bill* circulated the shorter phrase among those lacking the proper cultural background.
A. W. Smith, Chigwell, Essex.

☐ NOTHING to do with Bill Bailey/Old Bailey. Old Bill pre-dates Robert Peel's peelers to the days of the Townman or Watchman – 'Three o'clock and all's well' – who patrolled the streets of London at night carrying a lantern and a halberd. The halberd, a long-shafted axe with a hook on the back of the blade, was an early army weapon from the 15th century which later became the symbol of authority and denoted the rank of sergeant. Ex-army halberds were handed on to the Townmen to impart an appearance of officialdom. As usual with army issue, the halberd had a nickname in the ranks: the bill. The cockneys of the time, to show their derision and lack of respect for the Townmen, and also to let it be known that the Townman's symbol of authority was in fact nothing more than a bit of second-hand army surplus, called the Townman 'Old Bill'.
Red Daniells, London SW2.

QUESTION: Why are dusters yellow?

☐ AS an office and industrial cleaner for many years, I offer these suggestions: one of the duster's great attributes is its use for polishing. In the past, before the advent of pressurised canisters and the dreaded CFCs, this was done with beeswax. The manufacturers of such may have decided to make and sell its necessary accompaniment – dusters. Wishing to keep an identification with their main product they would naturally have dyed them yellow. Early dusters were not the bright ones of today, but a more ochre colour – indeed, some were pastel green. Alternatively: an enterprising marketing director of yesteryear may have attempted to corner the market by using most people's association of the colour yellow with springtime, through an increase in sunshine and daylight hours. He would have realised that sales of dusters would be increased enormously by using the appropriate colour especially during the annual spring cleaning season. There are many examples of how the colour has become connected with spring, such as daffodils and the expression 'to be as busy as a (yellow) bee'. Spring cleaning with (yellow) wax and duster is an almost symbolic gesture of spreading sunlight around the home.

P. Millard, Bristol, Avon.

□ IF, as P. Millard suggests, dusters were originally coloured yellow in order to work upon the public's association of the colour with the season of spring, then the ploy will probably have been unsuccessful. Despite the increase in sunshine hours and various other yellow connotations, green and not yellow has been shown to be more commonly linked with this particular season. This was proved by the psychologist, P. H. K. Seymour, in 1976. In order to test a phenomenon of perceptual confusion known as the Stroop effect, Seymour's version of the phenomenon involved the linking of seasons and colours. In order to lay the groundwork for such an experiment, extensive testing found that the majority of people link yellow with summer, brown with autumn, white with winter, and green with spring. So if, in a few months' time, you find yourself automatically reaching for some green dusters, beware the mind-games played by *Guardian*-reading marketing directors.

Michael A. Martin, London SW20.

□ I HAVE despaired of reading a sensible explanation. Here is my theory instead. In the first half of the 19th century a large quantity of bright yellow cotton cloth was imported from Nanking in China, and subsequently imitated and produced in Britain, from which highly fashionable trousers (Nankeens) were made. After the garments wore out, the remaining cloth was recycled as polishing rag in the hands of the thrifty. Yellow buckskin breeches had been fashionable earlier and they were made of leather, cotton or wool. White linen and cotton rag was usually recycled for high quality paper, and there was never enough. I do not know if two senses of 'buff', that is (1) yellow ox-leather and (2) to polish with a piece of the same, have anything to do with the matter, but see *OED*. The traditional association between a yellow material and polishing may have reinforced the use of Nankeen cloth for dusting and cleaning after the fashion for the trousers ceased.

Charles Newton, London N22.

QUESTION: Who was the first man to do what a man's gotta do, when did he do it and what was it when he'd done it?

☐ THE words are often, wrongly, attributed to John Wayne. They were, in fact, uttered by Shane (Alan Ladd) in the film of the same name. What Shane has to do, in the conscious sense, is kill Wilson (Jack Palance) *et al.*, and pave the way for a peaceful existence for his friends, the homesteaders. However, there is an undercurrent, touched on in the movie but camouflaged by the superb action scenes and atmospheric location. It is more fully developed in the novel, *Shane*, by Jack Schaeffer, which shows that Shane is obviously in love with his friend's wife (Jean Arthur). There is also a hint that she may be falling in love with Shane while retaining her love for her husband, Joe (Van Heflin). Therefore Shane must do two things for his friends: he must rid the range of villains, at the cost of his life perhaps; and he must take himself out of their lives for ever. This is what a man has to do, and do it he does.
R. A. Southern, Wigan, Lancs.

☐ I DON'T think your correspondent is quite right in attributing the phrase to Alan Ladd in *Shane*. He uses similar expressions like 'A man has to be what he is' and 'I couldn't do what I gotta do', but never the exact words. The expression does occur in John Steinbeck's *The Grapes of Wrath* in Chapter 18 (p. 206 of the Penguin edition) when Casy says 'I know this – a man got to do what he got to do'. This was published in 1939, which predates *Shane* anyway. Yours pedantically.
Stephen Collins, Ripon, Yorks.

QUESTION: What is the origin of the phrase 'as sick as a parrot'?

☐ TO AVOID United States quarantine and livestock importing restrictions, people smuggling parrots from South America into the US dope the birds on tequila as they near the Mexican border. Careful timing of the binge will ensure that the birds are sleeping it off through the border crossing formalities and will not greet the officials with a mouthful of verbals as is the

breed's wont. Having thus avoided detection, the downside for the exotic loudmouths is coming to with the mother and father of a hangover. This queasiness manifests itself in the origin of the expression.
F. L. O'Toole, London SW19.

☐ THE phrase originates from 1926 when the previously obscure disease of bird psittacosis became a pandemic of clinical importance, involving humans in 12 countries with more than 800 cases. The association of respiratory infections in man and contact with parrots was soon recognised.
(Dr) F. W. A. Johnson, Liverpool.

☐ IT IS a corruption of 'sick as a pierrot' and refers to the typically pale and miserable face of that French pantomime character.
Peter Barnes, Milton Keynes.

☐ ANOTHER theory (but a quite erroneous one) is that the Amazon parrot – a large green bird with yellow cheeks – was the most sickly looking creature imaginable.
(Mrs) Jane M. Glossop, Pwllheli, Gwynedd.

☐ I FIRST heard this simile shortly after the Monty Python 'Norwegian Blue' sketch. Whether this is relevant, or whether it is just another example of people finding non-sequitur expressions of this type amusing, I know not. My mother always used to be as sick as a cowboy's 'oss. The interesting thing is that being sick as a parrot is not the same as being sick as a dog.
Alex Wilson, Billingham, Cleveland.

QUESTION: Why are British elections always held on Thursdays?

☐ UNTIL 1918, polling at General Elections took place over several days and at one time different constituencies could complete polling on different days, thereby – it was alleged – creating a bandwagon effect for a successful political party. The 1918 Representation of the People Act restricted polling to one day (except for Orkney and Shetland until 1929). Since 1918 a General Election

has always been on a Thursday, except for 1918, 1922, 1924 and 1931. The reason for choosing Thursday, it is said, was as follows. On Fridays the voters were paid their wages and if they went for a drink in a public house they would be subject to pressure from the Conservative brewing interests, while on Sundays they would be subject to influence by Free Church ministers who were generally Liberal in persuasion. Therefore choose the day furthest from influence by either publicans or Free Church clergymen, namely Thursday. Although these influences are much less significant today, the trend towards Thursday becoming a universal polling day has continued, because Urban District Councils and Rural District Councils all polled on a Saturday until they were abolished under the 1972 Local Government Act. Their successor, District Councils, poll on a Thursday and the Parish Council polling day was changed from Saturday to Thursday at the same time.
E. M. Syddique (Research and Information Department), Electoral Reform Society, London SE1.

□ BRITISH elections aren't held only on Thursdays. General elections have been held on a Thursday only since 1935: before then, any weekday was used – or even a Saturday, as in 1918. By-elections, too, can be held on any day except a Sunday, although there have been only two since 1965 not held on a Thursday; Manchester Exchange in 1973 and Hamilton in 1978 (because the World Cup started on the Thursday), both on a Wednesday. Using Thursday is a convention, rather than a rule, so the reason for it is open to argument. I've always presumed it had something to do with Friday being pay-day, giving voters an incentive to go out and do their civic duty and get 'rewarded' for it the next day. Of the 74 post-war by-elections not held on a Thursday, only two were held on a Friday, two on a Saturday and three on a Monday, compared to 29 on a Tuesday and 38 on a Wednesday. If pay-packets were conventionally delivered on a Thursday, Wednesday would doubtless be the convention for elections.
L. Raphael, Kilmaurs, Strathclyde.

QUESTION: What is a rostrum camera and why, judging by the credits on all TV channels, does only Ken Morse have one?

☐ KEN MORSE is almost certainly too busy to explain, so I'll try to do it for him. Ken has a solid bench ('rostrum') with a camera (film or video) firmly mounted above it. Both bench and camera can be moved in relation to one another, sometimes in quite complex ways, and often under computer-control. This arrangement allows precision cinematography of all kinds of things a director might find useful: for example, a slow and elegant move from a wide-shot of a music score to a huge close-up of Beethoven's scribbled '*Muss es sein? Es muss sein.*' This sort of thing is often difficult to shoot on location – either because you didn't know the precise timing needed; or because you hadn't even thought of it. The reason everyone goes to Ken Morse used to be that he had a parrot. Now it's simply because he's good, fast, and doesn't rip you off. He also exercises a certain degree of editorial control. I once hired him to shoot 12 transparencies of Mayan hieroglyphics on loan from the British Museum, and he filmed only six. When I phoned to ask about the others, he told me that six was enough for any TV programme. I used four.
Christopher Sykes, London SW13.

☐ NO, Ken Morse does not have the only one.
Millard Parkinson, Rostrum Camera Dept, Granada TV, Manchester.

QUESTION: Does the Rubicon still exist?

☐ THE RUBICON is a small stream rising in the foothills of the Etruscan Apennines to enter the Adriatic Sea at the resort of Gatteo a Mare, some ten miles north of Rimini. It formed the southern boundary of the province of Cisalpine Gaul with the Roman Republic, and so its crossing by Julius Caesar in January 49 BC was effectively a declaration of war on his rival, Pompey, who commanded the armies of the Roman senate. The stream's identity was once a source of some dispute, the Uso, the Piscatello and the Fiumicino di Savignano all being the subjects of rival claims. The Uso was awarded the name by a Papal Bull of 1756, but a comparison of distances with the accounts of Suetonius, Plutarch and Lucan led to the Fiumicino being officially renamed the Rubicon in 1932.
James Elliot, British Library Map Library, London WC1.

□ NOWADAYS travellers in this part of the world are better catered for than Julius Caesar was in 49 BC when he crossed the Rubicon, as they can stop off for a snack at the Rubicone service station on the A14 *autostrada* between the Cesna and Rimini interchanges.
Keith Spence, Tunbridge Wells, Kent.

QUESTION: Can anyone explain why sex had to enter into some languages? Why, for example, do the French sit on a masculine bench at a feminine table?

□ THE original Indo-Europeans classified things into male objects, which act on other things or change them; female objects, which bring other things into existence; and childish (that is, neuter) objects, which have no effect on other things but only have things done to them. Thus the earth and the sea are feminine, weapons and tools masculine. In German, diminutives are neuter. Because neuter objects could not do anything they could never be the subject of the sentence and could not have a nominative case. Even now the nominative is the same as the accusative. The Germans regard the sun as feminine because in northern Europe it is a gentle entity which appears in the spring and coaxes the plants out of the ground. The moon is a masculine object that tells the mighty ocean to come and go. In Italy, on the other hand, the sun is much more like Ra, and will frizzle your brain if you go out without your hat. And in the Mediterranean there are no tides. I suppose the French bench is masculine because it carries the diners and the table is feminine because it is thought to produce the goodies thereon.
John Ward, Bristol, Avon.

□ SEX does not really enter into the question of gender in French and similar languages. Most European languages put nouns into either two or three genders, and the real world category that is most nearly related to gender is that of sex. English tends to make females feminine, males masculine, and sexless items neuter. It comes closer to a one-to-one correspondence than other natural languages. However, even English can still treat any powerful or fast-moving machine as feminine, and some animals have obligatory genders, disregarding their sex (Jenny

wren and Robin redbreast, Jack daw and Mag pie). German, as Mark Twain pointed out, has neuter for 'young lady' (*das Fräulein*), and feminine for 'turnip' (*die Rübe*). Latin, the parent of French, had three genders with the same sort of 'fits where it touches' match as has German today. As French evolved from Latin, the endings of words were 'eroded', and neuter singulars ceased to be distinguished from masculine singulars, neuter plurals from feminine singulars, leaving only two genders, so that – regardless of sex – all nouns must be either masculine or feminine. 'Table' comes from 'tabula', which was already feminine in Latin. '*Banc*' (bench) is derived from the same Germanic word that gives us bench, which was (and is) feminine, but like many foreign borrowings was taken as masculine.
W. S. Dodd, Language Centre, University of Exeter.

□ ONE theory is that man's fantasy personalised and personified everything, and hence bestowed on every object, even inanimate ones, the qualities of a man or woman. The great and powerful was seen as possessed by male attributes, and smaller and weaker seen as possessed by female ones. Eventually this notion survived in modern language. A second theory is that it was the sex of the pronoun which accompanied the noun, i.e. his or hers, which became transferred to that noun. A third theory has also been advanced, based on the recorded fact that among some primitive people (for instance, Latin American tribes) two languages existed side by side, a male and female one. Thus an object would be called by a different word depending on whether a man or woman spoke of it. With the passage of time the two languages became merged but the idea of gender survived. A question that arises is why did men and women have separate languages in the first place? It is quite likely that the tribes' females came from another part of the country or another tribe altogether. Their presence might have been due to them having been captured as the spoils of war. The language that they spoke would have been foreign to the men and impregnated with their sex. Similar events would evolve due to the practice of marrying women from another tribe.
Alan Willmott, Cheltenham, Glos.

QUESTION: Who was Riley and why does living his life sound so desirable, in spite of dissolute overtones?

☐ THE saying comes from a comic song, 'Is That Mr Reilly?' (*sic*), which was popular in the US in the 1880s. There was also a music-hall song in England at about the same time: 'Are You The O'Reilly?' One was probably a variant of the other. The latter includes the lines 'Are you the O'Reilly they speak of so highly? Cor blimey, O'Reilly, you are looking well.'
Stephen Pratt, Twyford, Berks.

QUESTION: Why do the British drive on the left and other countries on the right?

☐ THE left is the natural side to ride if you are on horseback. Mounting a horse is done from the left, so that a sword (worn on the left by right-handed men) will not get in the way. If you mount from a mounting block or the verge on the left, it is natural to set off on the left-hand side of the road.
Christine Moore, London SW4.

☐ THERE IS a theory that the change to the right came about with firearms, which are fired from the right shoulder, thus aimed to the left. Certainly a major proponent of keeping to the right was Napoleon Bonaparte who, whether for military reasons or personal custom, imposed keeping to the right wherever he went. In the 20th century it was another dictator who imposed keeping to the right, wherever he went: Adolf Hitler. In his birthplace in Austria and in Czechoslovakia signs reading '*Rechts fahren*' (drive right) were put up when the Nazis moved in. So by keeping to the left we are sticking to our British independence.
Noel Ellis, London SE15.

☐ IMPLICIT in the question is the suggestion that Britain is alone in this particular practice. In fact, over 40 countries drive on the left.
Nicholas Pritchard, Southampton.

QUESTION: Who was the first April Fool?

☐ THE tradition of the trickster in northern Europe goes right back to our pre-Christian religion. In the Norse mythology, the

prankster-god Loki can be disruptive towards the other gods but able to carry out tasks no other can. He represents the need to question and challenge authority so that patterns of thought and behaviour do not become stale or accepted uncritically. Loki is traditionally thought of as patron god of April.
Andy Lawton, Chesterfield, Derbys.

☐ WHEN Vasco da Gama arrived in Calicut in March 1498 (not in May as is commonly thought), he could not have known that he was creating the first documented April Fool. He was invited to the Feast of Huli, on the last day of March. The chief amusement was the be-fooling of people by sending them on fruitless and foolish errands. As any fool knows, Vasco da Gama was sent by the Hindu Rajah of Malabar inland looking for cloves and pepper in any area where they did not grow, but the event is not always attributed to the date of his return – the morning of April 1.
A. J. G. Glossop, Pwllheli, Gwynedd.

QUESTION: Who was Kilroy when he was here, and where is he now?

☐ THE original Kilroy was an inspector at one of the inland shipyards in America where they built 'Liberty Ships'. Inspection is a responsible job, with lives depending on it. Each weld of the hull has to be inspected as it is completed, because quite often the next step will build some structure internal to the ship that will mask the weld and leave it inaccessible to later inspection. It was Kilroy's peculiar custom to record his approval of each weld by writing on the weld itself. Along decks and gangways subsequent traffic soon removed his marks, but where internal structures hid them they remained. The result was that among every crew who eventually sailed one of his ships, his became a name to conjure with, an invisible presence among them. Nobody ever met Kilroy face to face, yet he must surely be there, hiding himself away, because whenever you looked into an unused locker or enclosed space, no matter how small or inaccessible (provided only that it backed on to the hull), he had been and gone just before you, leaving his message freshly chalked on the wall 'Kilroy was here'.
Daniel Lowy, Sutton, Surrey.

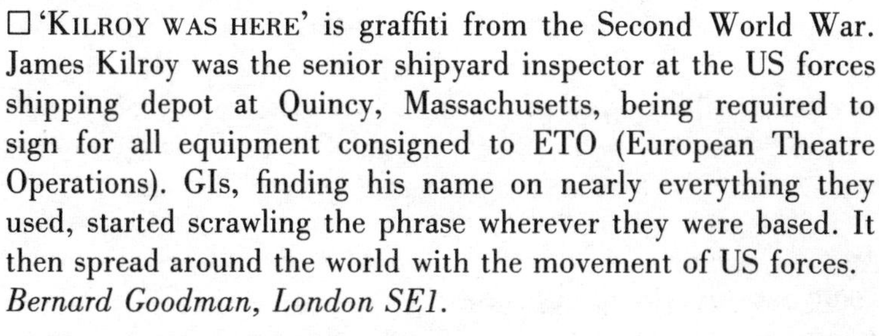

□ 'KILROY WAS HERE' is graffiti from the Second World War. James Kilroy was the senior shipyard inspector at the US forces shipping depot at Quincy, Massachusetts, being required to sign for all equipment consigned to ETO (European Theatre Operations). GIs, finding his name on nearly everything they used, started scrawling the phrase wherever they were based. It then spread around the world with the movement of US forces.
Bernard Goodman, London SE1.

□ ACCORDING to an article by an American journalist, Susan Ulbing, he was an infantry soldier who got tired of hearing the air force brag that it was always first on the spot. Kilroy specialised in being the first and only one to show up in outrageous places, like the bathroom reserved for Truman, Stalin and Attlee at the Potsdam Conference.
John Idorn, London W8.

QUESTION: The leader of the British military mission to Russia in 1939 was Admiral Sir Reginald Plunkett-Ernle-Erle-Drax. Is this the longest hyphenated surname in the UK, and how does a man aspire to have such a surname?

□ THE name of the explorer, Sir Ranulph Twisleton-Wykeham-Fiennes, contains more letters (33) than that queried (32), but with only three barrels to Sir Reginald's four. As to how the name was acquired, many complex names (not necessarily hyphenated) are the result of marriages, alliances and so forth. The Fiennes family was given the name Wykeham in the Civil War, as a reward for preventing the desecration by the Roundheads of William of Wykeham's tomb in Winchester Cathedral.
Arabella McIntyre Brown, Liverpool 17.

□ OUR formal family name just beats Plunkett-Ernle-Erle-Drax (21 letters) viz: Hovell-Thurlow-Cumming-Bruce (25 letters). Needless to say, we all abbreviate it. When I was up at Trinity College, Cambridge, it was a curiosity much appreciated by tourists passing the hall doors at the foot of the staircase to my rooms to see the whole rigmarole, prefaced 'Hon. A. P.' painted upon the lintel, and followed by 'The Earl Kitchener' and 'The Earl Jellicoe.' There's class! This dotty accumulation derived from the 18th/19th

century usage of a husband's hyphenating his wife's name if she was heiress to landed property. In our case H-T also then elected to marry C-B.
Alec Cumming-Bruce, Durham.

□ In the event that you do not receive a suitable explanation from a member of the Drax family, perhaps the chauffeur's daughter can outline the cause of all the hyphens. The Admiral's ancestors were far better at breeding daughters than sons, so that when Miss Plunkett (a relative of Lord Dunsany – the eminent author) married Mr Ernle their daughter was Miss Plunkett-Ernle. She married Mr Erle; their daughter, Miss Plunkett-Ernle-Erle, married Mr Drax and Reginald got all the surnames. After four or five daughters Reginald begot a son, who is known as plain Mr Drax. He has dismally failed to maintain the family tradition and has four or five sons. His eldest son is married to the Princess Royal's former Lady-in-Waiting, Zara (yes, that's where the name came from) Something-Something. If she threw in her maiden name, her children would be Something-Something-Plunkett-Ernle-Erle-Drax. Of more value than the admiral's abortive mission to Stalin was his pioneering interest in solar heating (for his swimming pool).
(Ms) V. E. Troy, Chatham, Kent.

□ My own name comfortably exceeds that of the gallant admiral.
(Brigadier) Dermot Hugh Blundell-Hollinshead-Blundell, BFPO 26.

□ The longest multi-barrelled surname on record in England is: Major Leone Sextus Denys Oswolf Fraudatifilius Tollemache-Tollemache-de-Orellana-Plantagenet-Tollemache-Tollemache (1884–1917). If you insist on non-repetitious ones, try this for size: Lady Caroline Jemima Temple-Nugent-Chandos-Brydges-Grenville (1858–1946).
Steve Arloff, Watford, Herts.

QUESTION: Why is water wet?

□ Water isn't wet. Wetness is a description of our experience of water; what happens to us when we come into contact with water

in such a way that it impinges on our state of being. We, or our possessions, 'get wet'. A less impinging sense experience of water is that it is cold or warm, while visual experience tells us that it is green or blue or muddy or fast-flowing. We learn by experience that a sensation of wetness is associated with water: 'there must be a leak/I must have sat in something.'
Jacqueline Castles, London W2.

☐ ANY fluid could be said to be wet if wetness is a result of the sensation caused by the movement of a fluid over the skin. Have you ever noticed that you can't feel wetness if you hold your hand perfectly still while it is submerged, or that a drop of water on the skin doesn't feel wet?
Chris and Shevvy Ould, Chesterfield, Derbyshire.

☐ THE wetness of water is thought to be due to its high moisture content.
(Dr) Jason A. Rush, Dept of Mathematics, Edinburgh University.

☐ WATER is wet to make it a more marketable commodity.
Sam McBride-Dick, Colchester.

☐ THE questioner will be little enlightened by the previous replies and you must surely give him or her another chance. Two answers were humorous; two were just wet. As an amateur photographer, I am familiar with what is, I think properly, called wetting agent, which is added to water – to the final washing after developing and fixing – to make it wet with respect to the surfaces of photographic film. Without this agent the water resides on film in blobs, resulting in drying marks; with it, most of the water drains off and the rest dries evenly. So in response to the query I would say (a) water isn't always wet; wetness is always relative to a given substance and/or type of surface and (b) as to why it is wet when it is, presumably the answer is in terms of surface tension.
Laurie Hollings, Brighton.

☐ WATER is wet, in the sense of being a liquid which flows easily, because its viscosity is low, which is because its molecules are rather loosely joined together. The sensation of wetness is largely due to the cooling caused by evaporation, and water has a rather

high latent heat of vaporisation, which is the amount of heat it removes from its surroundings in order to convert liquid water into water vapour.
John Geake, Handforth, Cheshire.

□ NONE of the answers given to this question so far quite gets to the chemical explanation for water's 'wetness'. Wetness is here synonymous with 'clingingness' – water wets because it clings. Water, of course, is molecularly H_2O and this compound of hydrogen and oxygen is electrically neutral. However, there are also in water many free charged hydroxyls (-OH–, negatively charged) and hydrogen ions (H+, positively charged). These charged particles retain the ability to attract other charged particles (with the opposite charge) just as magnets do. In this way they stick or cling, involving other neutral H_2O molecules at the same time. If water was made up entirely of neutral particles it would not cling, or wet, because the component elements would 'prefer' to stick to each other rather than to make bonds with other substances.
Ian Flintoff, London SW6.

□ IAN FLINTOFF has surely misrepresented the chemistry behind water's properties. Hydroxyl ions and hydrogen ions in water, far from being 'many' are very few (pure water contains some 556 million water molecules for every hydrogen ion). Water molecules are indeed 'electrically neutral' but are highly polar molecules, that is they have a positive 'end' and a negative 'end', though neither 'end' carries a full unit of charge. It is this polarity which causes water molecules to 'stick to' one another and, given the chance, to other molecules of a polar nature. Other liquids can be wet, even those which contain molecules which are entirely non-polar (e.g. octane, benzine and even liquid nitrogen – don't try 'em!), but only in relation to another substance because wetness is to do with surface tension and that implies an interface between two substances. For this reason water is rather poor at wetting things: try washing your hands without soap! The molecules of water do prefer to stick to one another than to molecules of other substances but this effect is easily overcome by introducing another substance which interferes with the interactions between the water molecules. This allows the water molecules to interact with the molecules in the other surface instead.
C. A. Mitchell, Reading, Berks.

QUESTION: What are the origins of the common surnames White, Black, Green and Brown? Why are there no Reds, Blues, Yellows, etc.?

☐ WITH the exception of yellow, all the colours may be found in one form or another today. Yellow seems to have fallen out of use quite early, though a Widow Yellowe of Suffolk was noted as late as 1674. Yellow's lack of favour might well be because of its pejorative meaning, 'cunning, duplicitous, hypocritical', which dates from as early as the 14th century. Among others in current use are: **Black** – Blache, Blatch, Black, Blake, Colley, Collie (coal black). **Blond** – Blunt, Blout, Blondel, Blundell. **Gold** – Golden, Goolden, Goulden. **Yellow** – Faugh (pale brown, reddish yellow), Favell (fallow or tawny), Flavell. **Red** – Read, Reed, Red, Rudd, Rous, Russell. **Sorrell** – (reddish brown), Soar, Sanguine, Sangwin. **Grey** – Gray, Grey, Hoar, Hore, Biss, Bissett, Grice, Griss, Girson, Grissom (grey hair). **Brown** – Brownett, Brunet, Brown, Dunn, Burnett, Burall, Borell, Nutbrown, Brownnutt, Brownutt, Brownhutt, Perbrun. **White** – White, Snow. **Blue** – Blewett, Bluett, and probably Blowe, Blaw. **Green** – Green. As is obvious from the above, many of these colour-names relate to hair colour or some other physical characteristic like complexion or clothing. There are numerous others which have Celtic origins, like the range of Welsh names with derivatives of 'gwyn/gwen – white', usually in the metaphorical sense of 'pure.'
Derek Shields, Staffordshire Polytechnic, Stoke-on-Trent.

QUESTION: Does scratching your head really help?

☐ INDEED it does. While contemplating the action of scratching your head, your subconscious mind has time to insert an answer into your conscious mind and bingo – the solution appears. For more profound problems either brew tea and/or raise the Titanic.
Zina Kaye, London SW6.

☐ I SCRATCHED my way through eight O-levels and passed only three of them. The answer is no.
C. Leach, Cambridge.

☐ ANIMAL behaviourists have guessed this to be a form of displacement activity: 'inappropriate' behaviour following indecision or conflicting interests. Another example is the stickleback at the edge of its territory. Torn between pursuit and defence, it stands on its head.
R. B. Taylor, London SW19.

QUESTION: What is the origin of that maddening rhythm, 'Pom tiddly-om-pom pom-pom'?

☐ ACCORDING to *The Book of World-Famous Music* by James J. Fuld, the phrase first occurs in 'Hot Scotch Rag' by H. A. Fischlet (1911). It was later used in several songs, with a variety of words added. One possible forerunner is Sullivan's setting of the words 'Shall they stoop to insult? No! No!' in *HMS Pinafore* (1878). After several bars of austere harmony, the last two words are preceded by an open octave played by a full orchestra – a strikingly bathetic cadence.
Tom McCanna, Dept of Music, University of Sheffield.

☐ THE origin is said to be the sound of the coaches of the Chicago elevated railway (the El') running on the overhead track. Even more maddeningly they say 'shave 'n a haircut, two bits'.
(Prof.) Robert Moore, Holywell, Clwyd.

QUESTION: What is the reason for the little white square in the top right-hand corner of the picture on a TV screen? Why does it appear and disappear?

☐ THE dot is seen on ITV and Channel Four. It alerts the 15 regional ITV companies to get ready to play in the commercials on both networks. It appears about a minute before the break, and disappears with five seconds to go.
Steve Perkins, Regional Officer, Independent Broadcasting Authority, Norwich.

☐ IT IS known in the trade as a 'cue dot'. When it appears, it signifies 30 seconds before the next programme. It disappears at 10 seconds to go. It is vital for getting the following programme

on air on time – and without gaps in between. For BBC employees in Birmingham, it is London's sign (for that is where it originates) to us to wake up.
Jane McLean, Production Assistant, BBC, Birmingham 5.

QUESTION: Why must the letter Q always be followed by U in English?

□ THE first European alphabet was Greek, which was an adaptation of Old Phoenician. This contained the letters gamma (T or G), kappa (K) and qoppa (Q). These last two represent the 'K' sounds in 'keep' and 'coop' which the early Semites distinguished (and I believe some of their descendants still do). The Greeks made no such distinction and soon dropped the Q. Before they did, the Etruscans took over the alphabet. The Etruscans had no 'G' sound in their language, so they used the gamma as yet another 'K'. The gamma, which by now looked less like an inverted L and more like a C, was used before E and I; the kappa before A and the qoppa before U and O. This is why the letters are called cee, kay and quoo. The Romans took over the Etruscan alphabet and had to re-invent a 'G' letter by adding a small stroke to the C. They eventually dropped the K, using the C before all vowels except U, which is still the case today. Contact with Greece and the introduction of Greek loan words made it necessary to reintroduce the K at a later date.
John Ward, Knowle, Bristol.

□ SIMON MCCARTIN was a bit too *qick* with his *qestion*, and my *qery* is how can he pronounce these words without pronouncing the essential 'U'? Until we have a symbol for a combined consonant and vowel, we can only continue to use two such. Now perhaps he can tell us *hwy* he did not ask *hwat* is the reason for spelling '*hwich*' as we do, and *hwen* it started?
W. W. Bloomfield, Camberley, Surrey.

QUESTION: Do the living now outnumber the dead?

□ THE answer is no; the living population forms about 9 per cent of the total population who have ever lived, so the dead outnumber the living by about ten to one.
John Haskey, Statistician, Office of Population Studies, London.

QUESTION: Why is it that when you see a person yawn you want to yawn yourself?

☐ THE function of yawning is poorly understood. It is a common behaviour in a wide range of animals but contagious yawning has only been observed in humans. One hypothesis is that in humans yawning has a paralinguistic function in communicating the subject's state of wakefulness to other members of his social group. According to this hypothesis, yawning is contagious because it is part of a mechanism which serves to synchronise wake/sleep cycles among different members of the social group. (Reference: Provine *et al.*, *Ethology*, 1987, vol. 76, p. 10.)
(Dr) A. T. Chamberlain, Department of Human Anatomy, University of Liverpool.

QUESTION: What are the rules of the game 'Mornington Crescent'?

☐ I HAVE no proof, but I believe that 'Mornington Crescent' is derived from the game 'Finchley Central' which was invented by John Conway (now Professor of Mathematics at Princeton University, but then a lecturer in Cambridge) around 20 years ago. 'Finchley Central' was invented as an example of a game with extremely simple rules which defies conventional game-theoretic analysis, and its rules are as follows: two players alternately name stations on the London Underground, and the first one to say 'Finchley Central' is the winner. However, in order to achieve a perfect win (which is worth infinitely more than an ordinary win), you must say 'Finchley Central' immediately before your opponent was going to say it. It seems quite probable that this game evolved into 'Mornington Crescent' as played on 'I'm Sorry, I Haven't a Clue' but I have no information about the route by which it got there.
(Dr) P. T. Johnstone, Dept of Pure Mathematics and Mathematical Statistics, Cambridge.

☐ THE origins of 'Mornington Crescent' have been most reliably traced to the old Gerry's Club in London's West End (now under new management). Among the regulars to whom Gerry's in the

Sixties was not so much a haunt as a home, the writer John Junkin has claimed authorship of the game. Nowadays, however, even Junkin is slow to divulge the rules, and the determined enquirer must have time and money on his side (about £20 ought to do it). For those who will stop at nothing, N. Stovold's *Rules And Origins* may be begged or stolen; but it has been out of print for years, and the British Library has drawn a blank on it. More fruitfully, though, the regulars of 'I'm Sorry, I Haven't a Clue' on Radio 4 can still be heard playing the original game to a high standard of elegance and cunning. Indeed, William Rushton's lethal mastery of Junkin's Parallel remains a joy to behold. I fear, though, that this is as much as can be said in print. The truth is that 'Mornington Crescent', like poker, can be played but seldom explained; its rules can be learnt but never taught; and its beauty should be noted but never queried.
Jon Magnusson, Producer, BBC Radio Light Entertainment, London W1.

□ WHEN playing the underground version of 'Mornington Crescent' it is vital to remember that it was quite difficult to alight at 'Mornington Crescent' as most trains did not stop there.
C. S. Mence, New Malden, Surrey.

□ THIS question is really too tiresome to bother with a full answer, and in any case Samantha (the scorer) is probably the only person fully qualified to answer it in full. The questioner must just listen more carefully and work out the rules for himself.
Justin Downing, Sheffield.

QUESTION: Who first faded out at the end of a record, rather than having a proper ending?

□ THE first person to fade the end of a piece of music was Gustav Holst. In the last movement of his *Planets* suite he used the gradually fading sound of a female choir to evoke the immensity of outer space. As this was written in 1915 before the introduction of electrical recording, he asked his singers to walk slowly into the distance while still singing, or for a door to be gradually closed between them and the audience. In this astonishing movement Holst anticipated the later electronic fade-out, but had in fact

already used the idea as early as 1905 in his settings of songs from Tennyson's *The Princess.*
Michael Short, Bradford-on-Avon, Wiltshire.

☐ JOHANN STRAUSS (father) composed the 'Radetzky March' in 1848, in honour of Field Marshal Radetzky who put down Italian patriots in Milan in the same year. The fifes fade out at the end, marching away into the distance. Other members of the Strauss family use the same device (e.g. '*Perpetuum Mobile*').
G. H. Shackleton, Reading, Berks.

☐ ACCORDING to Nick Tosches in his book, *Country*, the first record to have a fade-out was 'The New Call of the Freaks', recorded by Luis Russell, the jazz musician, on 6 September 1929. This version of a tune previously recorded by Russell fades out on the added chanted refrain: 'Stick out your can, here comes the garbage man.'
David Rothon, London SW12.

☐ DUKE ELLINGTON'S 'Showboat shuffle' (from 1935) fades away at the end but I think it was Count Basie, in the late 1930s, who started the fashion. I assume it caught on because it was a convenient way around the problem of how to end a piece. And perhaps some jazz records were faded out simply because musicians exceeded the 3- to 3½-minute time limit of the old 78s.
Sidney Evans, Chirk, Clwyd.

☐ FADE-OUTS became widespread in the United States as the result of a trade survey in the early Fifties. This showed that when records were played on juke-boxes, people felt more inclined to replay a record that faded out because it left a subconscious feeling that you hadn't completely heard it. The importance of the 'juke-box factor' has never been as potent in Britain, but in the States its earning capacity has always been considerable. After the creation of the fade-out ending, the only other innovation to stimulate juke-box plays was pioneered by the Chess-Checker Record Company of Chicago, who developed a new groove-cutting technique for their 45s, which ensured that when played on juke-boxes, they were one-third louder than all other records in the machine.
Dave Godin, Sheffield.

□ THE fade has been used as an effect for many years, but it is especially suited to pop numbers, which usually consist of, or develop into, repetition of a single monotonous phrase. In consequence, the device was seized on by the groups, most of which were able to produce (one hesitates to say compose) such phrases but lacked the musical talent to bring them to an end.
David Carlé, Guildford.

QUESTION: Why do we hear the sound of the sea when we hold a shell to our ear?

□ WHEN we hold a shell to our ear, we hear our own blood rushing through the blood vessels in our ear. The shape of the shell provides a simple sort of echo chamber, and the opening in the shell allows other sounds to be almost shut out when we hold the shell to our ear. It is not just sea-shells that allow us to hear the 'sea'. We can achieve the same effect with hollow animal horns, tin cups, and . . . pyramids. The King's chamber in the Great Pyramid of Cheops at Giza, Cairo, acts as a large echo-chamber, and is also incredibly well sound-proofed. If ever you could spend some time alone in the chamber and in the pyramid, you would, after about 15 minutes of total silence, hear a very loud rushing noise, like the sound of a waterfall at the end of a deep, quiet valley. This sound is the sound of the blood in your body, especially close to your ears.
Andrew Weston-Webb, London SW8.

QUESTION: Is there any reference in authentic Jewish historical records to the massacre of male infants up to two years of age between 8 BC and AD 6?

□ THERE is no trace of this story anywhere except for the one reference in Matthew's gospel. It is not mentioned, for example, by the Jewish historian Josephus. The story is not historically impossible. Herod was a ruthless killer who murdered a number of his own children. Had he heard rumours of a child destined to supplant him it would have been entirely in character for him to have acted in this way. Since the number of children

involved would have been quite small, the lack of reference to this story in other sources is not of itself decisive. On the other hand Matthew, in his stories about the infancy of Jesus, seeks to present the truth about Jesus through what are closer to being meditations on Old Testament texts rather than simple bald historical statements. Throughout his gospel he seeks to show that Jesus is the New Moses. Here, just as Pharaoh slaughtered the children before the birth of Moses, so now Herod does the same before the birth of Jesus. In both cases, however, God foils the plans of tyrants and proceeds to liberate his people. In probability therefore the origin of this story is not history but reflection on an Old Testament text.
(Rev.) Martin Camroux, Birkenhead, Wirral.

☐ THE Jewish-Roman historian, Josephus, gives a fascinating, if partisan account of Herod's career in *The Jewish War*. Herod is portrayed as a brilliant ruler but a ruthless and brutal man who ordered the execution of his favourite wife, Mariamne, in a fit of jealously. He had no compunction in torturing and murdering anyone he believed was implicated in real or imaginary plots against him. No one was safe – brother, mother-in-law, sisters-in-law, brothers-in-law. His relationships with his numerous family (10 known wives and 15 children) were so troubled that it was said that it was safer to be Herod's pig (in view of his conformity to Jewish dietary law) than his son. His two sons by Mariamne were strangled and he ordered the execution of his eldest son and heir only five days before his own death. Herod was obviously aware of how unpopular he was with his subjects and Josephus describes how he planned one last monstrous outrage. As he lay dying in agony, he locked up the leading men from towns and villages all over Judaea in the hippodrome with instructions that they were to be butchered as soon as he died. He thus hoped to ensure that there would be weeping and mourning at his death instead of the expected wild rejoicings. Happily, his sister made sure the prisoners were released before they could be murdered. A man as callous as this would not hesitate to massacre a few baby boys in an insignificant little village if he thought one of them might be a threat to him.
Linda Holmes, Cottingham, N. Humberside.

☐ THE story is part of the myth that grew up around the concept

of Jesus as the Messiah, the destined King of Israel. A similar slaughter was rumoured to have been carried out by King Arthur, and there are parallels in African traditions. The idea, a very ancient one, is that the Old King, hoping to be immortal, goes to any length to prevent the conception, birth and survival of his successor. Behind this, no doubt, is the subterranean enmity of fathers towards the sons who will grow to manhood as they themselves decline towards death.
C. C. Wrigley, Lewes, E. Sussex.

QUESTION: Why 15, 30, 40 (not 45) in tennis?

☐ ORIGINALLY, a points scoring system was introduced, based on the quarters of a clock, in minutes, probably to avoid confusing point scores with game scores. This provided a neat, cyclic '15–30–45–game' system. However, the three-syllable '45' proved too much of a mouthful, and was soon abbreviated to '40', and has stayed as such ever since. (Ironically the estranged 'five' has made a comeback at club level, as an abbreviation itself, for '15' when the players themselves are keeping score.)
Peter J. Phillips, London E6.

QUESTION: Why are the largest insects only a few inches long? Is there any reason why they should not evolve into creatures the size of elephants?

☐ INSECTS are one of several classes of animals belonging to the major group, the Arthropoda (the jointed legged ones). All of these animals have an external jointed skeletal skin which is rather like a hard armour. In order to increase in size, arthropods must periodically shed their skin, a process which renders them vulnerable until the new stretched skin can harden to function again as a skeletal support. Some arthropods are able to survive many such growth spurts because they live in water which supports the floppy vulnerable stage. But insects which live in air would risk desiccation and collapse under these circumstances. For this reason, most accomplish their growth during a special larval stage and are severely limited in growth once they are adult. Insects do not have conventional lungs but breathe instead with a system of microscopic pores through which gases diffuse in and out of their bodies. This system would be hopelessly inefficient with much larger body sizes. The reason is because of relative rates at which surface area and volume increase. Consider a one-inch cube which has a surface area of six square inches and a ratio of 6:1. Double the size to a two-inch cube (eight cubic inches) which has a surface area of 24 square inches and a ratio of only 3:1. It becomes clear that the body volume of the animal would be increasing at a rate too fast for the maintenance of an efficient surface-related respiratory mechanism. This same principle would cause 'design problems' in connection with other aspects of their life processes. Mouth parts of insects are 'designed' specifically according to feeding habit. Enlarging these parts would render them unsuitable for the insect's diet, while keeping them at constant size would prevent the larger animal from acquiring sufficient food. Consider the amount of sap an elephant-sized aphid would need to take through its 'hypodermic' mouth nozzle! To grow a mouth tube with a bigger bore would render it quite unsuited for precision plant puncturing, not to mention the effect on the plant on which the aphid depends. It is difficult to imagine how some insects could fit a substantially greater growth phase into their lifespan. A butterfly, for example, forms its wings in a once-and-for-all process at the end of metamorphosis. There is no mechanism by which it could grow further, so a larger version would require an already elephant-sized caterpillar which would collapse under its own weight. Some moths are simply a non-feeding, egg-laying stage in the life-cycle of the organism. Their 'purpose' in life is simply to reproduce and ensure the continuity of the species. Apart from the fact that there is no feeding mechanism to provide the necessary energy for growth, there would be no evolutionary advantage since the animal dies after fulfilling its brief reproductive function. There are more problems. There is a finite limit to the size of any structure constructed out of a given material. This can be illustrated very easily with aluminium kitchen foil. It is easy to construct quite rigid small-scale objects with folded foil but when, with increase in size, the total weight of the structure is too great for the strength of the foil, it will collapse unless a thicker gauge of foil is substituted. Translated into insect terms, a stage would be reached when (say) legs would need to be so thickly built that they would become a clumsy hindrance.

John W. Stanley, Keele University.

□ I THINK John Stanley has tended to sell Mother Nature a bit short. Certainly, elephant-sized insects are out, but evolution might well have produced a viable lobster-style land insect, 30 inches long, with a type of air-lung (scorpions have pulmonary sacs with 'lung-books'), and feeding lobster-wise by tearing up flesh with its claws and stuffing it into its mouth (might have made a jolly good watchdog?). Of other insects, way back, there used to be dragonflies big enough to give a modern kestrel a fright, and arthropoda in the sea (although probably not much good on land) included six-foot-long eurypterids such as Pterygotus anglicus. Surely, a major reason for today's insects being small is that their size suits the remaining environmental niches now available for such versatile creatures.
L. Clarke, Uxbridge, Middlesex.

□ MUCH OF John Stanley's exposition is incorrect. Insects lose little water when they moult and (by his own dimensional argument) it is the smallest which are then most at risk through desiccation. Respiration is not limiting. Many insects inspire and expire not unlike ourselves, while some can pump air in at the front and out at the rear end, which is even more efficient. Insect flight muscle respires at a higher rate than any other known tissue. It is ridiculous to select a particular insect like an aphid or butterfly and say that at elephant size it could not get enough sap or fly. One would not get a viable mouse, if one simply blew it up 30-fold. A beetle's mouth parts are far more efficient than those, for example, of a tortoise, while a bug a few feet long which injects enzymes into its prey and then sucks up the soup could be a formidable predator, protected by far better armour than any present-day carnivore. On a strength-for-weight basis, insect wing material is better than that of a bird, and on simple engineering principles, a tube, which is the basis of the insect skeleton, is a more efficient structural member than a solid rod like a bone: it would be better than an elephant's leg at elephant size. And since the insect absorbs most of its skin-skeleton before moulting and re-uses it towards the next one, it is also a very economical system. By brain transplants, we have successfully made immature insects grow to abnormally large size, including examples of those many insects in which the wings grow appreciably during the larval stage; true, if one makes a winged adult grow and moult by such techniques its wings get in a frightful mess, but wingless adults like stick insects

naturally go on growing as adults, and the termite queen grows to an emormous size while adult. The only physical reason we can suggest why the terrestrial insect may be limited in size is that when it moults, it must go through a brief stage when it inflates its gut with air to expand the new skeleton before making it rigid. Could it produce sufficient internal pressure to do so if it were very large? If it immersed itself in water at this stage there would be no problem: crabs and lobsters manage this very well by swallowing water. There are of course a multitude of biological reasons why today's insects are not bigger, the most obvious of which is that they are doing very nicely at their present sizes and there's nothing to be gained by being bigger. But when they inherit the earth, as they undoubtedly will, I for one would not put it beyond them to produce some monsters.
(Sir) James Beament, FRS, Queen's College, Cambridge.

☐ I WAS taught that the limiting factor for insect growth was respiratory, but I would not contradict Sir James Beament unless his own argument was flawed. He suggests that the moulting insect inflates its gut with air to stretch the new exoskeleton, thus limiting the insect's size because the larger the gut, the more effort is required to inflate it. This is not so, as any anaesthetist will tell you. The pressure within an inflated elastic container is related *directly* to the tension in the wall of the container and *inversely* to the radius. This is Laplace's Law and is familiar to anaesthetists because it is important to respiratory physiology. The obvious result is that as an inflated container grows bigger, the pressure required to inflate it becomes *smaller* to the limit of the elasticity of the container. Anyone blowing up a balloon experiences this: the extreme effort to start, followed by an easy inflation. The balloon becomes more difficult to inflate beyond a certain point, but only because it has reached the limit of its elasticity. Other phyla have evolved creatures of all sizes at some time in history, but not insects. Sir James's gut-inflating insects would have it easier as they grew bigger, assuming that their gut grew with them, so there must be some other factor which prevents them growing.
John R. Davies, FFARCS (Consultant Anaesthetist), Lancaster.

☐ JOHN DAVIES is of course correct that the pressure drops as you inflate a balloon, and likewise inside an insect each time it blows

itself up when it moults. The factor Mr Davies has overlooked is that an insect moults many times and the walls of its 'balloon', i.e. its external skeleton, must be thicker every time. Indeed, suppose by moulting a few times it doubles in length, it becomes eight times heavier; its skeleton must then be about four times as thick to support this weight after it has inflated itself. So the pressure needed to start inflating the skeleton at each moult goes up steeply with size. The same argument defeats the saying: 'If a flea was as big as an elephant it could jump over the Houses of Parliament', because weight increases as the cube of length, whereas muscle force only as the square.
(Sir) James Beaument, FRS, Queen's College, Cambridge

QUESTION: Why is New York known as the Big Apple?

□ THE Big Apple was a bar on 42nd Street in New York which was much used by jazz musicians in the Twenties. When musicians bumped into each other while touring in the States they would always arrange to meet up again in the Big Apple, and in time this became synonymous with New York City.
Sharon Simpson, London W14.

□ THE city of New York for many years has had a large Spanish-speaking population. It is said that one member of this population saw the city (Manhattan in particular) as one large city block – '*una manzana grande*'; in Spanish *manzana* also means 'apple'.
Rick Holland, Cheadle Hulme, Cheshire.

□ THE explanation that I once heard is that in the 1920s and 1930s, jazz musicians in America referred to engagements in large towns and cites as 'a bite of the apple'. The largest city and most prestigious venue was New York – hence the Big Apple.
Arthur Hasler, London N22.

□ TO THE early Protestant settlers in rural America, urban New York, with its confidence men and painted ladies, was seen as a den of sin and temptation which threatened their new Garden of Eden. Hence 'The Big Apple'.
Simon Bendle, Upminster, Essex.

□ THE Big Apple was one of the many dances which proliferated during the 1920s and 1930s. It first appeared in New York about 1935.
Munroe Hall, Bury, Lancs.

□ AS A born and bred New Yorker, I never heard New York City referred to as the Big Apple before the mid-70s. At that time, New York City was bankrupt. Businesses were moving out and tourism was plummeting. It was in the course of the expensive publicity campaign designed to improve the city's image that the phrase first came into common use. Why the 'Big Apple'? Well, New York (the state) was at the time the country's biggest producer of the fruit. Patrons of supermarkets all over America were familiar with 'New York Apples'. Thus the slogan 'New York City – the Big Apple' was developed to sell the city to middle America. New Yorkers, of course, never use the phrase.
Maureen Basedow, W. Germany.

QUESTION: Which Roman numerals for 1990 are correct – MXM, MCMXC, MDCCCCXC or MCMLXXXX or some permutation?

□ BECAUSE of the way Roman numerals are built up, there is no set way of representing a certain number. As a 'rule of thumb', you shouldn't use more than three of the same together. For example XXX is fine to represent 30, but XXXX is not used for 40 (XL would be better here). This is because of the 'ten before' system in Roman numerals. By putting a lower value numeral before a higher value numeral, we are effectively saying 'this many before'. For example IX means one before ten, which is 9. So, in this case MCMLXXXX wouldn't be used. Also, MDCCCCXC wouldn't be used. In fact this hasn't been used since the 1800s. This, of course, leaves MXM and MCMXC. It doesn't really matter which one you choose, but 'ten before a thousand' isn't usually used. So, I would use MCMXC. But this is only my opinion!
Dean Garraghty, Doncaster.

□ ROBY'S *Latin Grammar for Schools*, Chapter X, is probably as good a guide as any to classical (Augustan) usage, and he gives some forms like IIC for 98 which are entirely out of use now.

My judgement of usage over the last century or so is that the 'subtractive' forms like IV should only be used with one symbol preceding another of value not more than ten times as great; and they are then favoured but not essential. This would allow CM for 900 but not XM for 990. So I would use MCMXC for preference, but regard MDCCCCLXXXX as quite acceptable if I wanted to fill up more space (which is why clockmakers prefer IIII to IV in general). MDCCCCXC has some classical basis, as Roby gives only DCCCC and not CM, but MCMLXXXX would be a little eccentric.
George Toulmin, Cheltenham, Glos.

QUESTION: Why, precisely, 78, 45, 33 and 16 rpm?

☐ THE choice of 78 rpm for turntable speeds (or occasionally 80 rpm and other variants, indicated on the label) was an early compromise between a faster speed – of say 100 rpm – which gave superior sound quality (but with a correspondingly shorter playing time) and an equally randomly chosen slower speed of 40 rpm. Early hand-cranked machines were most comfortably operated at a speed of around 80 turns per minute. With the introduction of electrically-powered machines, a motor designed to run at 3,600 revolutions per minute and utilising a 46:1 gear ratio gave a speed of 78.26 – close enough to the old randomly chosen speeds of between 75 and 85 rpm. The choice between 33⅓ and 45 was the result of a battle between rivals RCA and Columbia (CBS) to develop a micro-groove, longer playing record. Unwilling to co-operate, they developed their own separate systems. (Remember cassettes versus cartridges; four quadrophonic sound systems; Betamax versus VHS; Sky versus BSB?) By the mid-Fifties, most major companies were offering both – the 45 for popular repertoire and the 33⅓ for classical music. At half the latter's speed, the 16⅔ was reserved for the spoken world only, and died an early death.
Malcolm Jones, Wimbledon, London SW19.

☐ THESE numbers are not multiples of each other. Therefore their harmonic frequencies do not coincide. Each doubling of frequency halves the amplitude in their electronic waveform so the resonances do not interfere until 16 times 78, for example. By which time the

energy levels are so small it hardly matters anyway. Quite useful in things like gramophone records, vehicle body shells, precision oscillators and whatnot.
Lyndon Elias (Eng. Tech., AMIElecIE), Didcot, Oxon.

QUESTION: If trapped in a plummeting lift, what is the best position to assume to minimise injury?

☐ THE safest position is one where the legs are slightly bent, rather than braced. Survival depends on the length of drop, of course, but at least this position ensures that the thigh bones are not driven upwards into the abdominal cavity. Jumping upwards to reduce damage is not recommended, for three reasons. First, it is very difficult to time, and could worsen the situation if you land on the floor of the lift in an uncontrolled way. Second, by the time you have thought about this tactic you will already have impacted. Third, if you have time to think about this, and act on it, you have already fallen too far to survive. As a survivor of a drop in an ancient goods lift back in 1962 (three-and-a-half floors with a load of two tons of chewing gum) I have to warn your readers that all is not yet over with the first impact. Close inspection of the bottom of lift shafts reveals a series of springs designed to absorb energy. This energy has to be expressed in some way, and in this case it has the effect of propelling the lift back up the shaft. You will return up the shaft with a slightly reduced velocity to that with which you descended only a few seconds ago. At the top of your rise you will experience an instant *déjà vu* as you descend again. After approximately five repetitions of this experience you will come to rest. Thus you will have plenty of time to practise any position which comes to mind, consider the nature of human existence, or just let blind terror take over. After this you can consider the next problem: how to get out of the wreckage. I am happy to say that I emerged uninjured but shaken. Others have not been so lucky.
Stephen Lutman, Faversham, Kent.

☐ ANY position you adopt depends on the early recognition that the lift is in free fall. For this reason you should always carry a set of bathroom scales which you can stand on in the lift. You should of course ignore the initial drop in weight as the lift

begins a normal descent, but you should then watch avidly in case the reading approaches zero for more than a second. Having established that all is not well, your safest position is on top of the other occupants of the lift. One should therefore never travel in a lift less than half full, and if the choice exists one should choose fellow passengers who are overweight. This not only offers the greatest cushion on impact but generally they are less mobile when fighting for position.
Peter Jackson, Prees, Shropshire.

QUESTION: There are green insects, green reptiles and green birds, but no green mammals. Why?

□ THERE are in fact green mammals: the two-toed sloth and three-toed sloth (*Choloepus* and *Bradypus*). However, these are not truly green, but have specially adapted grooves in the hairs of their fur to which cling a blue-green algae (*cyanophyta*). The algae give the overall appearance of green fur. As students of behavioural ecology, we cannot envisage an adaptive reason for the lack of green mammals. We would like to suggest a physiological constraint on the pigmentation of mammalian hair.
Philip Bateman, Fiona Clarke and Emma Creighton, the Open University, Milton Keynes.

□ THE green coloration of reptiles and birds is a mixture of yellow and blue. The yellow is a pigment, while the blue is a refraction effect called Tyndall blue, produced by transparent particles dispersed in a transparent medium with a different refractive index. Tyndall blue can and does appear in eyes, scales, feathers, and skin, where there are transparent substances of uniform texture, in which minute air bubbles or other transparent particles may occur. It cannot appear in hair which is never uniform in texture but always consists of stringy bundles. We can imagine mammals with green skin, made by adding a yellow pigment to the Tyndall blue of a mandrill's cheeks, but it is difficult to imagine a selective advantage for them. Green is a camouflage colour, not a signal colour. To be useful to a mammal, it needs to be in the hair.
Donald Rooum, London SW2.

□ THERE is another way in which mammals can be green, besides the Tyndall effect. A mixture of black and yellow gives a dull green colour, which might make a better camouflage than the brighter greens produced by the blue-yellow mix. We cannot think of many species of mammals which are green because they mix yellow and black but some squirrel monkeys have an olive-green appearance by having black tips to yellowish hairs.

Peter Cotgreave, Arne Mooers and Andy Purvis, Department of Zoology, University of Oxford.

QUESTION: Who invented traffic lights and where were the first ones situated?

□ THE first traffic signal was invented by J. P. Knight, a railway signalling engineer. It was installed outside the Houses of Parliament in 1868 and looked like any railway signal of the time, with waving semaphore arms and red-green lamps, operated by gas, for night use. Unfortunately it exploded, killing a policeman. The accident discouraged further development until the era of the internal combustion engine. Modern traffic lights are an American invention. Red-green systems were installed in Cleveland in 1914. Three-colour signals, operated manually from a tower in the middle of the street, were installed in New York in 1918. The first lights of this type to appear in Britain were in London, on the junction between St James's Street and Piccadilly, in 1925. They were operated manually by policemen using switches. Automatic signals, working on a time interval, were installed in Wolverhampton, in 1926. The first vehicle-actuated signals in Britain occurred on the junction between Gracechurch Street and Cornhill in the City in 1932. By some strange quirk, these were also destroyed by a gas explosion. Standardised red-amber-green signals are now universally adopted. The book *Eureka* (ed. Edward de Bono, Thames & Hudson, 1979) says: 'Boring standardisation has replaced such eccentric specimens as the elegant gilded columns of Fifth Avenue, each surmounted by a statuette, and the traffic lights of Los Angeles which, not content with changing mutely, would ring bells and wave semaphore arms to awake the slumbering motorists of the 1930s.'

Andrew McLachlan, Porthcawl, Mid-Glamorgan.

QUESTION: Whatever became of the Flat Earth Society?

□ MY MATHS teacher once told my class that he was the last remaining member of the Flat Earth Society, after a successful voyage by all the other members to find the edge of the earth.
Timothy Dale, Byker, Tyneside.

□ THERE ARE a few Flat Earth societies still operating in various parts of the world, for example in California and in India, but the original Flat Earth Society launched here in England effectively ceased to function in the mid-Seventies, after the death of Sam Shenton, its long-time mainspring and advocate. There are still Flat Earth believers in this country, but to the best of my knowledge they are without an organisation to help them publicise their beliefs. Through the good offices of Ellis Hillman, a councillor of the defunct Greater London Council, the Science Fiction Foundation obtained from Mrs Shenton her late husband's literary effects. The collection is available for viewing and research to any bona fide inquirer. Applications to view the collection should be made in term time to Mr Andy Sawyer, The Librarian and Administrator of the Science Fiction Foundation Collection, Department of Special Collections and Archives, Sydney Jones Library, University of Liverpool, PO Box 123, Liverpool L69 3DA.
Charles Barren, Past-Chairman, The Science Fiction Foundation, Gravesend, Kent.

□ FOLLOWING the death of Mr Shenton in 1962, Patrick Moore, the astronomer, strongly argued against dissolving the society. It is now essentially a society for challenging 'scientific orthodoxy' in the style of its late Victorian and Edwardian predecessors, the Zatetic Society and the London Dialectical Society. Although the society is subterranean and somewhat elusive, it has managed to deliver lectures at Oxford Polytechnic, Portsmouth Polytechnic and Liverpool University. Perhaps its most notable success was its intervention at the Oxford University Scientific Society where a motion that 'This house believes that the earth is flat' was carried unanimously.
Ellis Hillman, Hendon, London NW4.

☐ THE Flat Earth Society lives on, growing in influence and eccentricity since its change of name. It is now known as the Adam Smith Institute.
John Nicholls, Cranfield, Beds.

QUESTION: Why are 'square' biscuit tins not actually square? The lids only fit one way round.

☐ THIS is to enable the empty tins to be packed more efficiently when being transported to the bakery. If the tins were square, they would have to be packed separately, one on top of the other. As each tin would be empty, this would mean that the lorry was carrying more empty space than tins. Because they are slightly oblong, it is possible to stand two tins on their short edge inside another tin and then use a fourth tin as a lid, which means you can now carry four tins in the space that would previously only hold two. Therefore the number of lorries needed to deliver a consignment of tins is instantly halved. Clever!
Chris Quinn, Huyton, Merseyside.

QUESTION: Apparently the 'HP' in HP Sauce stands for the 'Houses of Parliament'. But why?

☐ IN the late 1890s Samson Moore was a prosperous vinegar brewer. His ambition was to manufacture a sauce that would become a household name. When he visited Mr F. G. Garton of Nottingham trying to recover a business debt he discovered that he was brewing a home-made sauce that 'smelled uncommonly good'. Attached to the basket cart was a board with the sign 'Garton's HP Sauce'. When asked for an explanation of the letters HP Mr Garton replied he had heard a faint rumour that a bottle of his sauce had been seen in a restaurant at the Houses of Parliament. Within minutes Mr Garton's debt had been cancelled and he was paid £150 for the name and the recipe. Further information available in *The True Story of HP Sauce* by Dinsdale Landen and Jennifer Daniel.
Alan W. Brown, Edinburgh.

QUESTION: If Guy Fawkes had lit the gunpowder would it really have killed King and Parliament, or just given them a bit of a fright?

□ THE short answer is that the King and those with him would probably have been killed. Although superseded by more powerful explosives, black gunpowder was, by the time of the plot, sufficiently evolved to be a very dangerous commodity indeed. Ignited *en masse*, in a cellar, it would lack the shattering effect of modern high explosives but it would certainly have caused extensive demolition, probably accompanied by fire. Black gunpowder is still a very popular explosive in quarries in various parts of the world.
(Dr) M. Rasburn (MRSC, C. Chem.), N. Whittington, Chesterfield, Derbys.

QUESTION: Why are there 60 seconds in a minute, 60 minutes in an hour and 24 hours in a day? Who decided on these time divisions?

□ THE DIVISION of the hour into 60 minutes and of the minute into 60 seconds comes from the Babylonians who used a sexagesimal (counting in 60s) system for mathematics and astronomy. They derived their number system from the Sumerians who were using it as early as 3500 BC. The use of 12 subdivisions for day and night, with 60 for hours and minutes, turns out to be much more useful than (say) 10 and 100 if you want to avoid having to use complicated notations for parts of a day. Twelve is divisible by two, three, four, six and 12 itself – whereas 10 has only three divisers, i.e. whole numbers that divide it a whole number of times. Sixty has 12 divisers and because 60 = 5 × 12 it combines the advantages of both 10 and 12. In fact both 12 and 60 share the property that they have more divisers than any number smaller than themselves. This doesn't, of course, explain how this system spread throughout the world.
Phil Molyneux, London W2.

QUESTION: What is the basic definition of treason? Is it

correct that capital punishment remains on the statute book for such an offence?

☐ THE basic definition of high treason is set down in the Treason Act 1351, which declares that it is committed when a person 'doth compass or imagine the death of our lord the King, or our lady his Queen, or of their eldest son and heir'. The act also makes it a treason to 'violate' the King's companion, eldest daughter unmarried, or the wife of the King's eldest son and heir; or to 'levy war' against the King, or to be adherent to the King's enemies; or if a person 'slea (*sic*) the chancellor, treasurer, or the King's justices'. Later acts have added to this definition, particularly the Treason Act 1795, which makes it treason to plot to kill, wound, harm or imprison 'the person of our sovereign lord the King'. For 'King' we may also read 'Queen' as appropriate. Only a person who owes a duty of allegiance to the Crown may commit treason. Generally, there must be evidence of an 'overt act' to prove the offence. The penalty for high treason is death. The death penalty also attaches to 'piracy with violence', an offence under the Piracy Act 1837. Reference: Archbold: *Criminal Pleading, Evidence and Practice*, 43rd edition.
P. J. Geering, Crown Prosecution Service Headquarters, London SW1.

QUESTION: Why do we have a Royal Navy and Royal Air Force but not a Royal Army?

☐ THE REASON for the British Army not having the prefix 'Royal' is because only certain regiments and corps are called 'Royal'. The prefix Royal before the title of a unit is considered an award in much the same way as a battle honour. The regiments with this prefix are entitled to wear the coveted blue facings on collar and cuffs on ceremonial scarlet tunics. There have been some notable exceptions, such as the East Kent Regiment (The Buffs) who refused the distinction as it would mean losing their famous buff facings.
M. Ochiltree, Benfleet, Essex.

☐ UNLIKE the Army, the Navy has always been a single, national

organisation. To defend his realm, Alfred the Great founded the English navy as a large but single unit. For his land forces, he relied on a number of armies supplied by the shires. Thus, although not titled as such, the navy was truly 'Royal'. This pattern continued for centuries. The nobles had their own armies which were expected to rally round the sovereign in times of crisis. Indeed, the term 'The Army' did not come into use until the middle of the 17th century, by which time the Royal Navy had been established on a permanent basis for many years.
John Mack, London SE8.

QUESTION: What is the meaning of life?

☐ IN Douglas Adams's book, *The Hitch-hiker's Guide to the Galaxy*, we are informed that the computer, Deep Thought, ponders over a period of 7½ million years the question of the meaning of Life, the Universe and Everything. It is widely understood that this machine calculated the total answer to these three separate concepts as 42. Thus dividing 42 by three, it can be deduced that the meaning of life alone is 14. This, however, can only be assumed if the ratio of Life to both the Universe and Everything is 1: 1: 1.
Khairoun Abji, Luton, Beds.

☐ WHAT we do know with certainty is that we were not once, are now, and will not be again.
Brian Mendes, Bromley, Kent.

☐ LIFE is a sexually transmitted condition with a 100 per cent mortality rate.
P. Mellor, Centre for Software Reliability, City University, London EC1.

☐ LIFE is not a linguistic item and hence has no meaning. The question makes as much sense as 'What is the meaning of lumbago?'
Graham Bryant, Nottingham.

□ LIFE is an acronym invented by Mr Kenneth Baker: Let In Free Enterprise.
(Dr) P. V. Youle, New Milton, Hants.

□ MY OLD pal Plotinus has it thus: 'If a man were to enquire of Nature the reason of her creative activity, and she were willing to give ear and answer, she would say, "Ask not, but understand in silence, even as I am silent and am not wont to speak".'
N. J. Crofton-Sleigh, Norwich.

□ THE *Concise Oxford Dictionary* states that life is a 'state of functional activity and continued change peculiar to organised matter and especially to the portion of it constituting an animal or plant before death.' God knows (*sic*).
Jeff Thirburn, Nuneaton, Warwickshire.

□ LIFE has no meaning related to an external frame of reference, only the meaning that you decide to give it. It follows that any such meaning given is as valid as any other for you, and any change is also up to you. Have fun being Cesare Borgia on Wednesdays and St Francis on Thursdays.
Brian Cattermole, Stevington, Beds.

□ BEFORE directing the questioner to the nearest dictionary or his local priest I would strongly advise that this is a question not to be asked, unless rhetorically. History shows that individuals who asked this of themselves or others are prone to insanity, alcoholism or other addictions, even visions of religious ecstasy: none of these help in the least with an answer, only offering a temporary palliative for the passing of life while it is being experienced, or in providing hope for the hopeless. Matters such as destiny, happiness and other connected issues only complicate the question and should not be dragged on to the stage of reasoning. The greatest minds that have ever lived have not come near to answering this question; choose what eschatology you will for now. The chances are that whichever one you adhere to, we have all got it wrong (if only fundamentalists knew as much). This is a great mystery and long may it remain so. There is something a little dull about the prospect of knowing everything and our humble brains are not wired for that prospect. Life is for living, surely.
James A. Oliver, London WC2.

□ ACCORDING to a BBC2 *Horizon* programme (not screened on April 1) the meaning of life may have something to do with the notion that the most important living entity on this planet, the Earth itself, may regulate various life forms within its confines in order to ensure its own survival. Thus, for example, although the sun is now very much hotter than it was at the dawn of life, the proportion of oxygen in the atmosphere has remained more or less constant at 21 per cent, any greater or lesser amount being catastrophic. This suggests some kind of self-regulating mechanism which may be provided by the gases, particularly from manure, of all living things. That would also explain various epidemics and natural disasters as Mother Earth controls the number of living creatures and thus the level and mixture of atmospheric gases. What the meaning of life is for Planet Earth is another matter.
D. Fisher, Maidenhead, Berks.

QUESTION: Why is an ice-cream cornet with chocolate flake known as a '99'?

□ IN 1930/31 my grandparents, William Henry and Laura Michael, took over a sweetshop at 99 London Road, Stockton Heath, Warrington. They stayed there until 1935. They started to make their own ice-cream, and I can remember an electric motor bolted to the red tiles on the floor and an ice chest in the yard. They served wafers and cornets, and scoops of ice-cream in customers' cups and glasses. Then they started to serve cornets with a Cadbury's Milk Flake pushed down into the ice-cream in the cornet, and I believe that was the origin of the 99-er. The fresh milk for the ice-cream was supplied by Claude Hughes of Grappenhall Road, Stockton Heath, in milk churns carried by horse and trap. Just before Claude died in 1969/70, I lent him a small album of photographs showing him delivering to the shop, and I never got them back.
Enid Spilsbury (née Michael), Stockton Heath, Warrington.

□ THE designation of 99 applies specifically to Cadbury's Chocolate Flake and its origins go back to the 1920s when Cadbury sales managers were actively co-operating with Italian ice-cream manufacturers in the North-East and Scotland to enhance their products.

Cadbury's Flake was first included in ice-cream sandwich wafers. It needed to be specially produced to the appropriate size. Later the cornet with the flake placed temptingly on top became the typical presentation. There are alternative explanations for the term '99' which run in company folklore: (1) In the days of the monarchy in Italy the king had a specially chosen guard consisting of 99 men, and subsequently anything really special or first class was known as '99'. (2) The name originated from the game housey-housey (now called bingo). The caller would refer to certain numbers with a form of slang. 'Clickety click' was 66 and 'top of the house' was 99.
R. B. Shaw, Cadbury Ltd, Bournville, Birmingham.

QUESTION: What are the true capabilities of TV detector vans?

□ It is easy to detect the magnetic field radiated from the deflection coils of the picture tube at a frequency of around 15kHz. With sensitive instruments it is possible to detect emissions from the set, and from its aerial, due to the local oscillator used to demodulate the incoming signal. In this way it is possible to distinguish the TV channel being watched and to distinguish TV channels from a video recorder, or computer equipment. However the true capability of the vans lies in their ability to 'remind' you to get a licence. The simplest method of detecting an unlicensed TV is to listen at the front window. It is also possible to detect local oscillator radiation from a radio. This had been used by MI5 (see, for example, *Spycatcher*) to detect when a radio receiver is tuned to a particular station. The radiation from the VDU and keyboard of a computer can be picked up on a short wave radio and decoded to display the data from the computer screen. All these emissions can be screened against, but the cost of effective screening, including metal shields and aerial filters, is probably more than that of a licence.
David Gibson, Leeds.

□ The detector vans operated by the TV licensing arm of the Post Office can pinpoint a set in use at a range of up to 35 metres. They can determine the position of a set to within two feet and the programme being watched. To make evasion even

more difficult, TV Licensing has brought into use hand-held detectors which can penetrate areas such as blocks of flats and pedestrian housing estates where detector vans are less convenient to operate.
Brian Hickman, Public Relations Department, The Post Office, London EC1.

☐ I CHALLENGE any reader to report having been caught by a detector van. The whole idea is a monstrous hoax perpetrated by propagandists such as Mr Hickman. The authorities identify licence-dodgers in much more mundane ways: when you buy or rent a TV, that fact is reported. Records are compared. They write to you and threaten you. *In extremis* they knock on your door.
R. M. Stewart, Caterham, Surrey.

☐ I CAN confirm what Mr Stewart says. Approximately annually I get either a form or a visit from the TV Licensing Authority to inquire why they have no record of a TV licence at my address. I then patiently explain approximately annually that it might be connected with the fact that I am one of that eccentric 1 per cent of the population who refuse to have a television.
Terry Richter, Fareham, Hants.

QUESTION: On several items of post I have received from large organisations the number 15302 appears with the address. What does this signify?

☐ THE number is a special Royal Mail code which allows organisations making large mailings to get discounts on their postage costs. In return for the discount they have to do a lot of the Royal Mail's usual work; they have to sort their mail in advance in a complex scheme called Mailsort/Presstream.
Peter Baum, London N8.

☐ THE UK's 1.5 million postcodes have been summarised for computer sorting using some 1,600 new codes. The questioner gives his number as 15302. The first three digits (153) identify this as Suffolk, and the last two (02) tell the computer it is CB9 (Haverhill). One quarter of all UK mail is now sorted by businesses in this way. Not all print the number; some do, for

visual checking before posting. The system saves money for the sender and improves the accuracy and speed of delivery.
Graham Hughes, Head of Marketing, Royal Mail Oxford (Mailsort code 13501).

QUESTION: Why does the tax year not run from January 1 to December 31?

□ THE civil calendar running from January 1 to December 31 is still a new-fangled thing in the eyes of English tax law. Up to the middle of the 18th century, the year for legal, accounting, and tax purposes had always begun in spring, on Lady Day, March 25 (still in occasional use as one of the traditional 'quarter days' for collection of rents and dues). The English calendar used to be based on the old Julian calendar, invented in ancient Rome. It had been getting more and more badly out of step with the seasons as the centuries wore on. In the rest of Europe, reform of the calendar to the current model had been brought in from 1582 onwards. Nearly two centuries later, a British government finally decided to bring our calendar into line with the rest of Europe. By then there was a confusion of incompatible calendars and dates between Britain and the Continent, always 11 days apart (and for part of each year labelled with a different year number). In 1751, the Calendar Act set the big changeovers for British harmonisation in the following year, and recognised officially for the first time in England that the year begins with January 1. So 1751 ended early on December 31, and January 1 became New Year 1752. Later in 1752, the calendar was made to jump directly from September 2 to 14, to bring the dates of the month, as well as the year-numbering, into line with the Continent. This was the occasion of the famous cry 'Give us back our 11 days!' Those changes were too revolutionary for the deeply conservative tax accountants of the 1750s. They went on counting a full year from Lady Day of 1751 to Lady Day of 1752 as they always had done, and then again to 1753. But this time, because of the 11 days that had been cut out of the previous September's calendar, the next full year ended, not on March 24 as it always had done, but on April 5, 1753, by the new calendar. And we have simply carried on with the anniversary of this date ever since. To be fair to the tax accountants, one result and maybe an aim of their conservatism was

that people were not charged a full year's taxes for a year which had been shortened by 11 days. Perhaps in this way the people really were given back their 11 days. Or perhaps the effort of calculating taxes in reduced proportion for a short year was just too much for all concerned and maybe we are still dealing with the results of a decision that it was not cost effective.
Terry Sandcliffe, London SW19.

□ ONE minor correction to Mr Sandcliffe's answer. If the adjustment was to compensate for the loss of 11 days the end of the tax year would have shifted from March 24 to April 4. In fact the passage of the Calendar Act meant that the period January 1–March 24, 1752 (which would have included February 29) was wiped out of existence. The financial year to March 24, 1752 (old style) would thus have had 366 days. The Government, not wishing to encounter a further demonstration on the issue, decided to keep the 366-day year by adding on the extra day, hence the year end of April 5.
Mitchell Sandler, London N17.

QUESTION: Do elephants really have such good memories?

□ THE ORIGIN of the belief that elephants have long memories comes from the works of 'Saki' (H. H. Munro), 1870–1916. In his book, *Reginald On Besetting Sins* (1910), he wrote: 'Women and elephants never forget an injury.' Readers will be able to judge for themselves whether this is likely to be true of elephants from their personal knowledge as to whether it is true about women.
A. J. G. Glossop, Pwllheli, Gwynedd.

□ THE BELIEF that elephants have good memories is older than Saki's epigram; in fact it has an ancient lineage. Plutarch (1st century AD) repeats a story of Hagnon of Tarsus (2nd century BC) about an elephant whose keeper daily defrauded it of half its provender. One day, however, as the owner looked on, the servant poured out the full measure of grain. The clever Nelly, seeing this, divided the grain into two heaps, thereby exposing the cheat. The belief is also common in stories from Mughal India, while Edward Topsell in *The Historie of Foure-Footed Beasts* (1607) wrote: 'when they are hurt by any man, they seldom

forget a revenge.' Elephants, like Androcles' lion, are also said to remember acts of kindness; although, sadly, these are not so many as injuries.
Stuart McLaren, Norwich, Norfolk.

□ COLONEL W. Williams, known as 'Elephant Bill', once gave a talk in Imphal in the forward area of the Burma Front to a large audience of members of the 14th Army. One of his stories was of an elephant with a huge abscess on his back, which Bill had to lance with a Burmese *Dah*. Each evening the wound was washed and dressed by Bill at sundown. When the wound healed, the 'patient' went to work in a different area for some years. By chance this animal and Bill came together again and the elephant came to his bungalow at sundown and knelt down to show the scar (or get treatment). He certainly remembered the place and the man.
Ken Llewellyn (ex-23rd Army Air Support Control), Cardiff.

QUESTION: What do the pyramid and the eye represent on the American $1 note?

□ THE DEVICE on the note is the reverse side of the Great Seal of the United States. The seal was adopted by Congress on 20 June 1782. Only the obverse was ever cut and put to use, although the design of the reverse still exists in theory. The symbols on both sides emerged after a long period of discussion, as analysed very ably in *The Eagle and the Shield* by Richard Patterson and Richardson Dougall (Department of State, Washington, 1976). The symbols on the reverse are an unfinished pyramid of 13 courses, an eye representing Providence, the date 1776 in Roman numerals and the mottoes: '*Annuit Coeptis*' and '*Novus Ordo Seclorum*'. The first is a phrase from Virgil and can be said to mean 'He favours our undertakings' – the 'he' being the deity represented by the eye. The second means 'A new order of the ages' and is also from Virgil. There is no doubt that the eye and the pyramid are Masonic in origin, and it seems likely that Francis Hopkinson, a Mason, was responsible for bringing these elements into the national emblems. The reverse of the seal was incorporated into the dollar bill by an act of President Roosevelt, dated 2 July 1935.
William G. Crampton, Director, The Flag Institute, Chester.

□ THE eye (or deity), in looking down on the pyramid, can see all of its sides equally (excluding the base) and as such is a representation of democracy. At any other corner, the eye could only see two of its faces.
David Shakespeare, London SW8.

□ IN KURT VONNEGUT's book, *Breakfast of Champions*, the author writes: 'If they [the Americans] studied their paper money for clues as to what their country was all about, they found, among a lot of other Baroque trash, a picture of a truncated pyramid with a radiant eye on top of it. Not even the President of the United States knew what it was all about. It was as though the country were trying to say to its citizens, "IN NONSENSE IS STRENGTH".'
Daniel Jones, Northants.

□ ROBERT ANTON WILSON and Robert Shea, in their paranoid conspiracy novel, *Illuminatus*, quote the story that the Great Seal was given to Benjamin Franklin by a masked stranger who appeared in Franklin's garden one evening. American friends tell me this story is well known. (In fact, when I was at college, a fellow student checked every single reference from *Illuminatus* in the university library, and found them all to be genuine.) The masonic origin of the symbol is hardly surprising, given the connection between freemasonry and Liberal politics in the 18th century.
Daniel Jacobs, London NW4.

QUESTION: Can Aids be transmitted by mosquitoes, in the same way that they infect people with malaria in tropical countries?

□ THE QUESTION has been carefully considered by an expert panel and their conclusions, entitled *Do Insects Transmit Aids?*, published by the Office of Technology Assessment of the United States Congress (1987). Theoretically there are two ways in which biting insects or acarines might transmit HIV infections: by biological transmission or by mechanical transmission. Biological transmission is the kind of cycle known for malaria parasites and numerous truly insect-transmitted viruses (arboviruses), e.g.

yellow fever virus. Whereas yellow fever virus grows in and can be transmitted by mosquitoes in the laboratory and grows in mosquito tissue cultures, experiments have failed to show any evidence that HIV can grow in various insects or insect or tick cell cultures. Certain viruses, e.g. Rift Valley Fever virus, can be mechanically transmitted without replication in the mosquito, i.e. when a feeding mosquito is disturbed, virus adhering to the mouthparts is carried to another person or animal on which the bloodmeal is completed. However, unlike Rift Valley Fever virus, the concentration of HIV in the blood is very low and calculations show an extremely small chance of mechanical transmission of an infectious dose. In Africa, where HIV infection and biting insects are very common, infection is virtually only seen in sexually active adults and in babies of infected women but rarely in children, whereas malaria and arbovirus infections are common in children. Thus there seems little possibility of insect transmission as a significant factor in the spread of Aids.
(Drs) Colin Leake and Christopher Curtis, School of Hygiene and Tropical Medicine, London WC1.

□ IF BLOOD-sucking insects did inject the blood obtained from one person into another, they might transmit Aids and some other diseases. Fortunately for man they don't. If they inject anything when they bite it is a salivary secretion, usually through a separate channel in the mouthparts to the one taking in the blood. The saliva contains an anti-clotting agent to prevent blocking the tube through which the blood is obtained, and it is this secretion which causes some people to react after the bite. A mosquito obtains the malarial parasite in infected blood but inside the insect the parasite changes its form and must get into the mosquito's salivary glands to be injected into another person. There is no evidence that the Aids virus can get into the salivary glands. The situation appears to be similar for most of the piercing blood-suckers such as fleas, lice, bedbugs and ticks, and it is not thought that Aids (or hepatitis B) could be transmitted by their bite.
(Sir) James Beament, Queens' College, Cambridge.

QUESTION: Can anybody complete the long-forgotten Cockney alphabet (A for 'orses, G for police, etc.) that I learned as a boy?

□ THE COCKNEY alphabet is essentially a set of oral puns which lose most of their wit in print. Far from being long-forgotten, it is still evolving in the oral tradition.
P. Stephenson, Buxton, Derbyshire.

□ ERIC Partridge's 1961 book, *Comic Alphabets*, documents many versions, which he dates back to bored signallers in the 1914–18 war playing about with their 'signalese' phonetic alphabet.
Graham Gooday, Aberdeen.

□ **A** for 'orses; cadopear; ism; Gardner. **B** for lamb; brooke; strength; honey. **C** for th' Highlanders; looking; yourself; ships. **D** for dumb; ential; rent; salmon; mation; Just Men. **E** for brick; Adam; so careful; Bartok; lin Waugh. **F** for vescent; yours; calf; so nice. **G** for Indian; police; goodness sake. **H** for himself; retirement; teen. **I** for Novello; the engine; luting. **J** for oranges. **K** for tea; restaurant; teria; nuts; ances. **L** for leather; goblin; fairy. **M** for sis; size; ever blowing bubbles. **N** for lope; mation; a stretch, duration etc.; a penny; cement; Pasha. **O** for the wings of a dove; the rainbow; coat; my dead body; sexed; joyed. **P** for ration. **Q** for a bus; a song; billiards; everything. **R** for mo; bitter; Askey; English; ritis. **S** for you. **T** for two; aching; golf. **U** for me; instance; Fox; ia; nerve. **V** for France; voce; hospital; De Gaulle; the difference. **W** for a quid; quits. **X** for breakfast. **Y** for mistress; sake me; get me; husband. **Z** for breezes; 'e to do it, maister.
Peter Stewart, Epsom, Surrey.

QUESTION: *The Book of Revelation* (ch. 13 v 18) says that the mark of the beast is six hundred and sixty-six. What sort of mark would that be? In Roman numerals the number is DCLXVI.

□ 'LET HIM who has wisdom count the number of the beast, for the number of the beast is the number of a man.' In Greek (in which the *Book of Revelation* was written) and also in Hebrew, there were originally no numerals so individual letters were used to symbolise them. Alpha and aleph stood for one, beta and beth for two, etc. When 10 was reached (iota and iod) the numbers then proceeded in decades, kappa and caph for 20, etc., and similarly

when the tens were exhausted letters stood in for 100, 200, etc. One of the intriguing effects of this system is that every word has a numerical equivalent which can be obtained by adding together the values of its letters. Since the number of the beast is the number of a man, it is logical that the number 666 stands for some individual. The most plausible candidate seems to be the Roman Emperor, Nero, since when his name is written as Neron Caesar in Hebrew the characters make up the magic total. (There are other clues in the text to support this identification and Nero's persecution of Christians after the fire of Rome would also be likely to make him and the Antichrist one and the same person in early Christian eyes.) There is no biblical foundation to suggest that the mark of the beast (placed on his follower's foreheads) is actually the number 666. This is simply an idea that was popularised by the horror film, *The Omen*. Since it is written 'that no man could buy and sell except that he had the mark of the beast upon him' many fundamentalist Christians in the United States look with suspicion on the security holograms of their credit cards. (And who's to say they're so very far from wrong, eh?)
W. A. Saunders, London.

□ THE picture described is of two beasts – the first (ch. 13 vv 1–10) out of the sea (i.e. foreign, the Roman imperial power): the second (ch. 13 vv 11–18) out of the land (i.e. indigenous, the local ruling Asian council). The graphic imagery is the language of Jewish apocalyptic, in this case deliberately borrowing from the beasts of *Daniel* ch. 7 v 3f. The Emperor Domitian had recently declared that he was to be known as Dominus et Deus ('ruler and God') hence the beast having a blasphemous name (Revelation ch. 13 v 3). The strange comment about the fatal wound to one head of the beast (ch. 13 v 3) refers to the suicide of Nero. The second beast (i.e. the Asian Council) derived its authority from Rome . . . There is also a possible reference to the inscriptions on Domitian's coins, which were in Latin 'Imperator Caesar Domitianus Augustus Autokrator Kaisar Dometianos Sebastos Germanikos', which, if abbreviated to 'A KAI DOMET SEB GE', would add up to 666. So the reference to the mark of the beast is probably a reference to the persecution of Christians by Domitian at the end of the 1st century AD: either they denied Christ and gave their loyalty to the Emperor (false '*dominus et deus*') or they faced death. There have been numerous attempts over the centuries to find a current

'Antichrist'. Some have even tried to make it fit Henry Kissinger or the EEC. Any ideas on new candidates?
(Rev.) Anthony E. Buglass, Amble, Northumberland.

□ THE contributions so far on this topic remind me of an explanation that was current during the last war. This sought to prove that Adolf Hitler was indeed the Beast. The proof required the number 100 to be given to the first letter of the alphabet, 101 to B, 102 to C, and so on, finishing with 125 for Z. By simply totalling the numbers appropriate to the letters of Adolf's surname, lo and behold, we finish with 666. Ingenious, if nothing else.
George Harrison, Stretford, Manchester.

□ I AM much amused by the deep theorising over this. The answer is simple. The Jews believed the number seven to be the number of perfection, since God created the world in seven days. This is why the dates of Jewish festivals reflect a pattern of seven. The idea was carried over into early Christian belief and is much used in *Revelation*, e.g. seven churches, seven bowls, seven seals. To say, then, that the mark of the beast is 666 declares that it has failed to reach perfection and, although powerful, is not God.
(Miss) H. Fitch, Theydon Bois, Essex.

QUESTION: Where, when and by whom were semi-detached houses first built?

□ I DO NOT know where the first semi-detached house was built but I have it on reliable authority that the second one was built just next door to the first.
George James, Shepperton, Middx.

□ THE origin of the semi-detached house, at least in London, is explained in *The Book of London*, which I edited for Weidenfeld last year. The Georgian terrace held sway until the last decade of the 18th century, when inflationary pressures pushed up building costs and left some terraces uncompleted, similar to the problems today in Docklands. Building houses in self-contained pairs meant that it was easier to stop when the money ran out. The architect and developer, Michael Searles, is credited with London's earliest semis, built in Kennington Park Road in the early 1790s. He

followed these with a development in Greenwich and the Paragon in Blackheath. Then, as now, south London was at the cutting edge of innovation.
Michael Leapman, London SW8.

□ MICHAEL LEAPMAN is nearly there – but not quite. Architect Michael Searles (a Greenwich man) may well have been inspired by the pair of houses built in Blackheath in 1776 by Thoman Gayfere and John Groves, both of Westminster. The houses, which stand today on the west edge of the Heath and are known as Lydia and Sherwell, are, by legend, the first semi-detached houses certainly in London. That is, if you take the meaning of semi-detached to be two houses consciously designed to look from a distance like one. Pevsner/Cherry in their book, *London 2: South*, give the Gayfere/Groves houses the accolade. It is a credit which we at the Blackheath Society will stoutly defend. Searles's first semis followed about 30 years later. But if it is the terrace form in question then Searles is your man.
Neil Rhind for The Blackheath Society, London SE5.

□ SORRY Blackheath! Richard Gillow of Lancaster (1734–1811) was designing 'semis' or pairs of houses in that town as early as 1758/9, in Moor Lane. The earliest identifiable surviving pair is that built in 1760 at Fleet Bridge (now facing the bus station and partly demolished) for Captain Henry Fell. These are very similar to a pair in St Leonardsgate which may be the buildings designed by Gillow in 1765/6 for Edward Salisbury. Captain Fell occupied one of his houses himself but the others were built to be let. Gillow obtained estimates of £110 for building William Braithwaite's houses in Moor Lane in 1759 and reckoned they would let for £4 per annum each. *Pace* Pevsner, no legend here: the evidence is in the Gillow archives in Westminster Public Library. Richard Gillow was the son of the founder of the cabinet-making dynasty, and seems to have studied architecture in London. From 1757 to the 1770s he provided designs for numerous public and private buildings in the Lancaster area. The architectural work of Richard Gillow was the subject of my dissertation at Cambridge in 1982. I used the Gillow archives to establish beyond doubt that Richard Gillow designed a considerable number of buildings in this period.
P. A. Harrison, London SW16.

☐ SORRY, Blackheath! Sorry, Richard Gillow of Lancaster. What must surely be counted as the first pair of semi-detached houses, nos 808–810 Tottenham High Road, London N17, date from 1715–1725 – thus predating Gillow's work by something like 50 years. This pair of houses makes a noble and remarkably balanced visual ensemble still, despite later shopfronts. For an illustration see Dan Cruickshank and Peter Wyld's fascinating *London: the Art of Georgian Building*.
Philip Maher, Marston, Oxford.

☐ IT WAS always my belief that the semi-detached dwelling originated in the ancient Inca civilisation of South America. This novel idea greatly impressed the Spanish *Conquistadores*, who brought the concept to Europe in the 16th century, and gave it the name '*Casa Doble*'.
Vaughan R. Hully, Warley, W. Midlands.

☐ SUMMERSON's *Georgian London* states that the Eyre Estate in St John's Wood 'was the first part of London, and indeed of any other town, to abandon the terrace house for the semi-detached villa – a revolution of striking significance and far-reaching effect.' One reason why the semi-detached house was so frequently built between the wars was that motor buses could still operate profitably in new, less densely developed suburbs where passenger loadings would have been too low to justify building new tramways and railways. Another reason was that Town and Country Planning zoning introduced in new suburbs from 1909 onwards provided for different residential areas to be developed at varying densities, usually between four and 12 houses per acre. Plots in the middle zones were too small for detached houses but too large for terraces and therefore most suitable for semi-detached houses. The archetypal outer London semi may appear more prevalent than it really is because some developers erected semi-detached houses on the principal main road frontages but built terraces in the hinterland.
John Tarling, London SW15.

☐ THE semi-detached houses identified by your correspondents are all far too modern. Here in Cornwall we have a pair of semis dating from the Roman occupation of Britain, in the 2nd and 3rd centuries AD. The stone-walled village of Chysauster near

Penzance had the remains of a house which clearly takes the form of two semi-detached dwellings.
D. Stewart, Helston, Cornwall.

□ I THINK Warwick can go one better than Blackheath, Lancaster and Tottenham in that it can boast a pair of semi-detached houses which date from the late 1690s. The impressive building, which stands near the site of the old Northgate into the town, looks like one house, but is in fact two, divided by a central carriageway.
Amanda Clarke, Warwick.

□ IF A semi-detached house is one which was designed as a symmetrically arranged pair there are several surviving examples in Coventry, dating back at least to the 14th century. Nos 169–170 Spon Street, Coventry, which was repaired under the supervision of the architect F. W. B. Charles in 1969–70 for the City of Coventry under the Spon Street Townscape scheme, is a good example of 14th-century date. Further along Spon Street is a 16th-century three-storey pair of town houses from 8–10 Much Park Street which was dismantled and reconstructed by Mr Charles on its present site in 1971–74. Both these examples had houses built up against them, as the street frontage filled up, and we feel sure that there must be many earlier examples which have become absorbed within later terraced development along urban streets. On the principle of originally detached, subsequently attached, we would be interested in hearing how common this type of 'semi' was in medieval towns.
George Demidowicz, Conservation Officer, City of Coventry.

QUESTION: If I were to travel a complete circuit of the M25 how many miles would I save by driving anti-clockwise as opposed to clockwise?

□ THE distance saved is not dependent on the length of the circuit but only on the width of the separation between the two carriageways. In fact it is 2π times the average separation. The answer depends on which lane the driver uses. In the inside lane, supposing each lane is 3 metres wide and the central reservation is 6 metres across, the distance saving is $2\pi \times ((5 \times 3) + 6) = 142$ metres. Observation shows, though, that in practice no one uses

the inside lane on the M25. More probably, the journeys will be made in the two 'fast' lanes, which are separated by just 9 metres. This means a saving of $2\pi \times 9$, or only 57 metres out of a circuit length of roughly 200 kilometres.
Peter Telford, Redhill, Surrey.

□ PETER TELFORD is much mistaken. His formula would only apply if the route round the M25 formed a perfect circle, which it does not. Part of this motorway may be in circular form but there will be straight sections. Assuming that these were to turn off at right angles the distance saved would be eight times the separation, as opposed to 6.28 times the separation for the circle. So the factors will change constantly, depending on the radius of the road at any given point. Theoretically it is almost impossible to calculate the exact mileage saved, and the only practical way is to drive round both routes and take the difference in distances. However, I can assure you that the distance saved would be a very small fraction of the actual distance travelled.
Christiaan Jonkers, Stourbridge, W. Midlands.

□ I MUST defend Peter Telford and challenge Christiaan Jonkers. The distance saved is indeed twice π times the average separation, and can be proved mathematically to be so. Further, the circuit does not have to be a circle, or anything like one. All that is needed is that the curve followed by the motorway be sufficiently smooth (that is, that the curves have large radius compared to the turning circle of the car), and motorways with sharp corners are not too popular with the Department of Transport. Whether or not there are straight sections is a complete red herring. Actually, there is just one thing that might disturb the calculations. They do assume that the motorway is flat (planar). But I doubt that the ups and downs affect the final answer all that much, since again they are never too drastic.
(Dr) Peter McMullen, Dept of Mathematics, University College, London.

□ MUCH as I dislike disagreeing with a colleague, I feel that I must do so. Dr McMullen ignores an important factor. A simple consequence of Pythagoras's Theorem is that overtaking manoeuvres usually result in drivers travelling further. Due to this, there can be considerable variability in the total distance travelled

between successive circuits of a ring road, even for journeys made in the same direction. Although pure mathematics could be used to estimate the effects this would have on journeys around the M25, perhaps someone should experiment.
(Dr) Stephen Gallivan, Dept of Statistical Research, University College, London WC1.

☐ IF WE allow the earth to be a perfect sphere then the quantity twice π times the carriageway separation is too much. A correction equal to four times π times the area of London (i.e. enclosed by the M25) divided by the area of the earth must be subtracted.
Jonathan Fine, Huntingdon, Cambs.

☐ YOU cannot travel a complete circuit of the M25. The motorway gives way to the A282 at the approaches to the Dartford Tunnel.
T. J. Allen, Hindhead, Surrey.

☐ A FRIEND and I decided to experiment. We first calibrated our milometers to make certain they read the same distance for a stretch of road, and then I drove clockwise and my friend anti-clockwise on the M25. Our starting and finishing point was the South Mimms service station. The result was surprising: clockwise 120.30 miles, anti-clockwise 120.80 miles. We agreed that we would stay in the slow lane as far as possible, only moving to the middle lane when appropriate. Neither of us used the outer, fast lane. However, the discrepancy of 0.5 miles seems to have occurred because of a diversion on the anti-clockwise circuit, immediately south of the Dartford Tunnel. So, at the moment, it is a shorter journey to take the clockwise carriageway, especially if travelling to Kent or Essex.
Penelope Edwards, East Finchley, London N2.

☐ I FEAR that Penelope Edwards and her friend have wasted both time and money in driving round the M25. A car's odometer only measures to the nearest 0.1 mile and, even if you can estimate distances by the partial change of the numbers, it cannot be better than 0.05 miles. Calibrating the odometers of the two cars against one another will not help because of this basic inaccuracy in the odometer's mechanism. If the distance over which they drove to calibrate them was 10 miles, then their calibration will be accurate to 0.05 miles in 10 miles, equivalent to 0.6 miles over the complete

120-mile trip; greater than the difference they found. Even if they had used the same car for the two trips, removing the need for calibration, it is unlikely that the result would be any more reliable, since the same trip made in the same car will not necessarily give the same measured distance every time. The basic problem is one that affects every scientist or engineer carrying out a measurement; the equipment must be able to measure smaller than the quantity being measured. Otherwise, it's like using a tape measure to find the diameter of a human hair.
Dudley Turner, Westerham, Kent.

QUESTION: Who was 'nosey' Parker?

☐ THE first supplement to the *Oxford English Dictionary* credits Compton Mackenzie with the earliest use of the expression in his 1912 novel, *Carnival*: 'I saw you go off with a fellah.' 'What of it, Mr Nosey Parker?' This was only two years after the earliest cited example of 'nosey' in the sense of 'inquisitive, curious', as used by H. G. Wells in *The History Of Mr Polly*. So the expression seems to have derived from early 20th century slang. However, I well remember as a lad an illustrated and informative item in a magazine which said that the original Nosey Parker was Matthew Parker, Elizabeth I's first Archbishop of Canterbury. I can find no confirmation of this in the hagiographic entry on him in the *Dictionary Of National Biography* or any other reference work I have been able to consult. The *OED* would have us believe that 'nosey' could not have been used in any sense as early as the 16th century: (1) 'One who has a large nose' is apparently not known before 1788; (2) 'Evil smelling', 1836; (3) 'Fragrant', 1892; (4) 'Sensitive to bad smells', 1894.
(Dr) Richard Dutton, Dept of English, Lancaster University.

☐ MATTHEW PARKER, who was Archbishop of Canterbury (1559–75), had rather a reputation for prying into the affairs of others. He therefore acquired the nickname 'Nosey Parker'.
William H. Watts, Leighton Buzzard, Beds.

QUESTION: What happened to the *Mary Celeste* after she was found abandoned?

☐ SHE was eventually taken back to New York and sold. The new owner sent her to Montevideo with a cargo of lumber. This appears to have been a pretty disastrous voyage: the ship lost some of her cargo and rigging in a storm on the way out and most of her living cargo of horses and mules (and the skipper!) on the return trip. Thereafter, she changed hands frequently, continuing to ply the American coastline and suffering a series of further mishaps. In 1884, she was acquired by one Gilman C. Parker, who, together with co-conspirators, decided to attempt finally to make some profit from the jinxed vessel. She was loaded with a cargo of junk registered as high-class merchandise and insured for $27,000, deliberately grounded on a coral reef in the Haitian Gulf of Gonave and set on fire, after the cargo and crew had been brought ashore. A claim was duly filed but the suspicious insurance companies sent investigators to question the crew. Parker and three of his partners were subsequently tried in Boston on a charge of barratry but freed because of a hung jury, though they never collected their insurance money. Eight months later, Parker died in disrepute and poverty; one of his associates was sent to a lunatic asylum and another committed suicide. The jinx pursued the *Mary Celeste* to the very end. For more details see John Godwin's book, *This Baffling World* (Bantam, 1973).
Philip J. Evison, London SW15.

QUESTION: Has anyone really had to wash up in a restaurant because they couldn't pay the bill? What are the origins of this idea?

☐ IN Bo Widderberg's excellent and apparently historical film, *Joe Hill*, about the American labour leader, he is shown ordering and eating a large meal in a non-union hotel, and then refusing to pay, hoping to be sent to the kitchen where he can organise the staff. It works!
(Dr) N. Palmer, Basel, Switzerland.

☐ SOME TIME in the late Fifties, a group of us were going to meet in north-west Scotland. One of the crowd turned up late because she had been hitch-hiking up on her own (you could do that safely then!) and had stopped off at an hotel for a meal. At the end of the meal she told the waiter that she had no money. 'So I suppose I

will have to wash up instead,' she said smiling sweetly, hoping to get away with it. Not a bit of it – the management whisked her off to the kitchens and she spent two days washing up before getting away.
(Miss) E. Innes, Manchester 20.

□ THOMAS HARDY'S *The Mayor of Casterbridge* is set in the 1840s, and Hardy looked back as far as the 1820s. In chapter seven Elizabeth-Jane tells her mother, 'We must pay our way even before we must be respectable', when the two are discussing how to find accommodation in Casterbridge. Elizabeth-Jane's solution is to approach the landlady of the Three Mariners Inn, 'As you seem busy here tonight, and mother's not well off, might I take out part of our accommodation by helping?' The narrator remarks: 'Such arrangements as the one Elizabeth proposed were not uncommon in country villages; but, though Casterbridge was old-fashioned, the custom was well-nigh obsolete here.' The notion of having to wash up if unable to pay the bill may arise from the custom Hardy knew of, although Elizabeth-Jane's practical approach to the landlady has an integrity which seems a world away from today's infra dig scenario in which the American Express card seems to have been mislaid.
Ruth Horton, King's Langley, Herts.

QUESTION: Who actually owns Buckingham Palace? It was purchased by King George III in 1761 and passed to his son, George IV. But I have been told that the wills of George III and George IV have never been settled.

□ UNDER the Land Registration Act 1988, anyone is entitled to find out the ownership of registered land in England and Wales. Of some 22 million properties and plots of land in England and Wales, more than 13 million are registered – although the remaining nine million are not. Assuming that Buckingham Palace is registered, then you can find out the identity of the freeholder for a fee of £10. A free leaflet on the procedure is available from HM Land Registry, Lincoln's Inn Fields, London WC2A 3PH.
David Northmore (author, The Freedom Of Information Handbook*), London W1.*

☐ I DOUBT very much that the Land Register will answer the question. While land in Central London has 'dealing' with the land within the meaning of the various Land Registration Acts, by and large, this means that there has to have been a sale of the land, for a transmission on death effective by an 'assent' does not need to be registered. I suspect that the title to Buckingham Palace is not registered, for it has apparently been in the ownership of the same family for nearly 230 years. This is always assuming that the family has not sold the palace, say, to the Property Services Agency or one of its predecessors in recent years. For this reason, the register is unlikely to reveal the ownership of property belonging to old landed families generally.
Thomas C. Sutton & Co, Solicitors, Bishop Auckland, Co Durham.

QUESTION: What is the miracle ingredient which makes contact lens cleaning fluid so expensive (£3 for 30ml = £57 per pint = £455 per gallon)? Is there an effective alternative?

☐ PERHAPS it's a heavy dilution of the miracle ingredient in Elizabeth Arden's Millennium Night Cream which retails at £47.50 for 50ml (= £539.60 per pint = £4,316.80 per gallon).
A. Mundy, Chingford, Essex.

☐ AND why is it sold in bottles containing enough to clean two lenses daily for three months with the instruction 'Dispose of unused contents within 28 days of opening'? I don't have six eyes.
Robert Hort, Bridgwater, Somerset.

☐ I HAVE worn hard lenses for 23 years, the last two pairs for seven years each, and was complimented each time I changed them on their relatively unscratched condition. My method? To soak: tap water. To clean: spit. And the golden rule: never polish.
Averill M. Laing, Ashtead, Surrey.

☐ A LITTLE Johnson's Baby Shampoo keeps my gas-permeable lenses shiny.
Lucia Costanzo, Brockley, London SE4.

□ FAIRY LIQUID works well as a cleaner of grease from contact lenses (hard) and plain water for everyday. These tips were given to me at an optician's. I have used them successfully for years, thus saving pounds. Also, I occasionally use a sterilising tablet (about six a year).
(Ms) B. Hutchinson, Caine, Wilts.

□ I CANNOT explain why the fluids are so expensive; perhaps it is connected with the fact that most solutions are produced by two manufacturers. Fairy Liquid and baby shampoo may work well with obsolete hard lenses but may not be as compatible with the newest gas-permeable lens materials and certainly are not compatible with soft lenses. It is positively dangerous to use spit to clean contact lenses as many potentially sight-threatening micro-organisms inhabit the mouth. The purpose of soaking the lenses overnight is two-fold: (1) disinfection and (2) to keep the lens surface in a state in which it is easily wetted with tears. Tap water may meet requirement (2) but it certainly does not perform duty (1). Like spit, tap water contains many micro-organisms, some of which can cause corneal ulcers which are not only excruciatingly painful but also sight-threatening.
A. J. Elder Smith, MSc, MBCO, DCLP, Harrogate.

□ THE 'miracle ingredient' is sterility. Contact lens solutions are supplied sterile, in sterile containers, and are governed by the Medicines Act. These products all require a 'product licence' before they can be sold in the UK. Product licences take up to six years to develop and require continuing safety tests after the licence is granted. Licensing takes time and money. The Department of Health Medicines Control Agency licence fees rose from £8,000 for a Section 104 licence in November 1989 to £13,600 in February 1990. A forecast has been given for a further rise to £20,000 from 1 December 1990 and further, as yet unspecified, increases from 1 April 1991. These government-imposed costs cannot be absorbed by the manufacturers alone.
Elizabeth Smith, Association of Contact Lens Manufacturers Ltd, Camberley, Surrey.

QUESTION: Why does Mickey Mouse wear gloves? Are there any films in which he isn't wearing them?

☐ Walt Disney was pushed into creating Mickey Mouse by the fact that he had just lost the rights to an earlier character, Oswald the Lucky Rabbit. Apart from the ears and tail the early Mickey is remarkably similar to Oswald and, like him, had no shoes and no gloves. In *Plane Crazy*, made as a silent film in 1928 and released later with sound, Mickey is barefooted and barehanded. *Gallopin' Gaucho* (again silent, 1928) sees Mickey in shoes for the first time and he kept them on for *Steamboat Willie.* The gloves came, I think, with either *The Barn Dance* (1928) or *The Opry House* (1929). As for the gloves, here's an explanation from Walt himself: 'We didn't want him to have mouse hands, because he was supposed to be more human. So we gave him gloves. Five fingers looked like too much on such a little figure, so we took one away. That was just one less finger to animate.' A very down-to-earth approach. And if you put gloves on a cartoon character, you don't have to animate all those wrinkles and lines. Incidentally, there's a similar evolutionary path that can be traced to the emergence of Bugs Bunny's gloves in *A Wild Hare*, Tex Avery's 1940 cartoon that gave us the classic phrase, 'What's Up Doc?'
Rolf Harris, Rolf's Cartoon Club, HTV West, Bristol.

QUESTION: When did the first 'Disgusted of Tunbridge Wells' letter appear in a newspaper? Why was he/she disgusted?

☐ I seem to recall that this was used in letters of complaint by Jimmy Edwards in the old *Take It From Here* radio programme.
Rita Kiernan, Nailsea, Bristol.

☐ The expression might have something to do with Dr William Webber, who caused the 'Webber Riots' in the town in 1864. He complained to the Home Office about a drain – see my book, *Royal Tunbridge Wells: A Pictorial History* (Phillimore 1990).
Roger Farthing, Tunbridge Wells, Kent.

☐ The editor of the *Female Tatler*, which first appeared in July 1709, asked her readers to send her 'the ridiculous things that happen at Epsom, Tunbridge and the Bath'. In August she referred to a letter from a lady in Tunbridge – 'a place resorted to by Persons with a Design to be as ill-tempered and censorious

as they possibly can'. Among such persons, it appears, were Lady Carper and Mrs Undermine.
Helen Mead, Oxford.

QUESTION: Did Napoleon ever say 'Not tonight, Josephine'? If not, who did?

☐ ALTHOUGH it is impossible to be certain, it is highly likely that this was said at Fontainebleau on 24 October 1809. At the time Napoleon had decided to divorce Josephine to marry the Archduchess Maria Louisa of Austria. I cannot do better than quote from R. H. Horne's *History of Napoleon*, 1884 (vol. II): 'Napoleon had rested at Fontainebleau on his way to Paris from the campaign of Wagram. He was quickly joined by Josephine, who hastened from St Cloud, with her usual eagerness to welcome him. She perceived a certain restraint and embarrassment in his manner towards her, and found the doors of communication between their apartments entirely closed; these were the first intimations she received of the approach of an event which had long haunted her imagination.'
D. Wardley, Halesowen, W. Midlands.

QUESTION: Why does one never see baby pigeons?

☐ ANYONE who has seen a young pigeon, or squab to give it its correct name, will not wish to see another. They are extremely fat, fed as they are on rich milk; the beginnings of their feathers are so waxy that they not only feel almost slimy, but flakes of it cover their bodies to give the impression of incurable psoriasis. They are also extremely ugly, bearing an uncanny resemblance to a former ancestor of theirs, the dodo, as they sit squirming in their nests.
Mick Allen, Brighton.

☐ THIS year, despite great efforts to discourage them, pigeons decided to 'nest' on my balcony. We live on the 21st floor. Two eggs were laid in the drain hole – there was no nest. Both parents sat on the eggs and seemed to change over every four hours. Eventually the eggs hatched and to my amazement the chicks were bright yellow – quite pretty in fact. The parents cared for them

marvellously. For hours one would stand with outstretched wings to shade them from the sun while the other brought food. This wonderful display of parental devotion was maintained until the babies were as big as their parents and had the same appearance. When they flew away one could not distinguish the babies from the adults.
Eileen Brennan, London W10.

☐ I THINK the questioner may be talking about feral pigeons which, by the time they leave the nest at about five weeks old, are fully feathered and about two-thirds the size of their parents. They are easily distinguishable to the trained eye. Two points one may look out for in young pigeons are the lack of 'wattles' above the nose (which grow quite large on adult birds) and also the size of the 'cere' (white outer ring of the eye), which is also larger on adults.
T. W. Lynn, Chopwell, Newcastle-upon-Tyne.

QUESTION: Who tested the first parachute and did he live to tell the tale?

☐ DISREGARDING Chinese acrobats who, in order to entertain the emperor in the 16th century, were supposed to have jumped from various heights with umbrellas attached to themselves, and Fausto Veranzio of Venice who is supposed to have tested a crude form of parachute in 1616, it is generally accepted that Sebastian le Normand of Montpellier in France was the first person to test a parachute. This he did on Boxing Day in 1783, jumping from the tower of Montpellier Observatory, attached to a rigid parachute made of canvas and wicker-work. He landed safely. Balloonists developed and refined this form of rigid parachute and made numerous descents, with varying degrees of success, as part of the general entertainment associated with ballooning. The originator of the folded parachute, capable of being stored in a container and opening on descent, was Major Thomas Baldwin of the US who, in 1850, began successful demonstrations of his equipment, again by dropping from a balloon. However, the parachutes suffered from the limitation that they were attached to the balloon and were only opened by means of the parachutist dropping away, pulling the parachute from its container and, when fully extended, breaking

the cord attaching the parachute to the balloon. The reputed inventor of the self-contained manually opened parachute capable of being worn about a person's body was Leo Stevens of the US who, in 1908, is said to have demonstrated such a parachute, though it was not until the First World War that such parachutes became generally available.
Steve Day, Salisbury, Wilts.

QUESTION: During the 1915–17 appearances of the Virgin Mary at Fatima, Portugal, three messages were delivered concerning future world events. The contents of two of these have been disclosed. Is there any information about the contents of the third message?

□ THE final message, allegedly from the Virgin Mary, was sealed in an envelope with instructions that it was to be passed on to the Pope, who was to reveal its contents to the world in 1960. When the time came, Pope John XXIII decided, according to Alfredo Cardinal Ottaviani, that 'it was advisable to preserve the mystery'. The child to whom the message was entrusted, when pressed about its content, gave the enigmatic reply that it was 'good for some; for others, bad'. These two facts together are in themselves revealing, and only if it were subsequently revealed that the message was 'His Holiness the Pope will disobey the direct orders of the Virgin Mary' would I be at all impressed.
Dave Godin, Sheffield.

□ THE third, and last, message given by the Vision of the Virgin Mary at Fatima predicts that the oceans will inundate coastal regions throughout the world between 1994 and 1997. This is according to Whitley Streiber in his book *Transformation* (Arrow, London, 1989, pp 61–63). He says that another Fatima prediction, that God would give a sign in the heavens that a great war would start, occurred on 25 January 1938. This consisted of a spectacular auroral display over Europe which preceded and forewarned of the Second World War. Pope John XXIII was said to have opened the envelope containing the third secret of Fatima, in 1960. Some accounts say that the cardinals who attended this event left the room with looks of horror on their faces. In contrast, Cardinal Ottaviani was quoted as saying: 'I, who have had the grace and the gift to read the text of the secret – though I, too, am bound

by the secret – I can say that all that is rumoured about it is sheer fantasy.'
Nigel Watson, Wood Green, London.

QUESTION: Why is depression the 'blues'? Why is a coward 'yellow'? Why is one 'green' with envy?

□ ASSIGNING colours to moods is tied in with Eastern philosophies, and the idea that the body emanates an aura of light, made up of the colour spectrum. Some mystics are able to see or sense these auras as colours, and are able to measure strengths and deficiencies in the areas assigned to each colour. These areas, or *chakras*, are defined as follows: red indicating sexuality or reproduction (and the basic emotion, anger); orange for the digestive system and expresses physical energy; yellow for the solar plexus area; green for the heart; blue in the throat and shoulders; indigo in the forehead (where lies intuition and healing); and violet in the crown of the head (for appreciation and creativity). Colour therapy, meditation and yoga are some of the alternative ways of actively promoting good health by concentrating on certain *chakras*. To answer the specific questions, feeling 'blue' signifies a need to encourage the blue *chakra*. (Depression and the inability to communicate are symptoms of a malfunctioning thyroid gland which lies in the throat area.) 'Cowardice', fear or lack of purpose shows a need to energise the yellow centre; 'contemplating one's navel' or focusing the mind's eye on this area promotes a sense of self-worth. The 'green envy' might be explained as a lack of love and respect for others. When all the colours are strongly balanced, the person is said to possess a strong 'spectral' light, or has 'attained enlightenment'. The study of colours can provide an insight on everyday phenomena: how we choose to decorate ourselves and our surroundings, Van Gogh's paintings, even politics. Do 'blue Tories' lack joy and honest communication, is 'red Labour' motivated by anger, and are 'yellow Liberals' afflicted by a sense of purposelessness? The continued and appropriate use of colourful expressions is evidence founded, not on scientific knowledge, but on instinctive biophilic awareness.
S. Dudley, Sheffield, S. Yorks.

□ I CAME across the following in an 1856 edition of *Chamber's*

Journal (Saturday, 12 July 1856; no. 132): 'In an article in the *Journal of Psychological Medicine* on Baron Feuchtersleben's Principles of Medical Psychology showing how the mind is influenced by a mechanical calling, there is this curious sentence: Rosch and Esquirol confirm from observation that indigo-dyers become melancholy; and those who dye scarlet choleric. Their observation regarding indigo-dyers affords a strong confirmation of the statement of that arch-quack, Paracelsus, who declared blue to be injurious. This would seem to suggest that our phrase "the blue devils" may derive from a scientific fact.'
Adam Roberts, Southampton.

□ I BELIEVE there is scientific proof of an association of mood with colour among the higher primates. Some years ago I was involved in the rehabilitation of a group of infant chimpanzees which had been confiscated from illegal dealers. The young chimps were being held in rather dreary surroundings before being moved to a rehabilitation camp in the forest, and I devised a series of behavioural tests, as much to keep the chimps from being bored as to advance scientific knowledge. Among these tests was one on colour preferences: wooden blocks, painted in a variety of colours, were put in front of the young chimps, and their choices were noted. Initially, the results were what would be expected from human children: a preference for bright primary colours. But when results were correlated with other factors, some interesting results were forthcoming. We noted colour choices in relation to weather (dull, cool, rainy days/bright sunny days), hunger (before feeding time when the subjects were hungry/after feeding), and companionship (tests done by an individual separated from the group/together with the group). All the negative factors (poor weather/hunger/loneliness) elicited a shift towards colour choices in which blues, as well as grey, brown and black predominated. On the other hand, positive factors (sunny weather/good food/companionship) shifted the colour choices towards reds, yellows and bright green. It was interesting to note that during this period, one of the group died. She had been maltreated by the person from whom she was confiscated, and was the weakling of the group. On the day of her death, all the other chimps chose dull, subdued colours. It was also interesting that the male self-appointed leader of the group always sought, by pushing and elbowing, to grab the most favoured colour, but was often outwitted by the eldest female.

All surviving subjects of these tests have returned to their forest home and, so far as we can tell, have integrated with the wild.
V. A. Sackey, Accra, Ghana.

QUESTION: Ladies' clothing always buttons right over left, men's clothing left over right. How has this come about?

☐ 'LADIES' were once dressed by maidservants; it is easier for a right-handed person to button another's clothing right over left. Men normally dressed themselves, and the opposite method is easier. Why such a custom should have spread from those classes rich enough to employ maidservants to ordinary people is something I should like somebody else to answer.
Simon Berlemont, Norwich.

☐ IT MAY be easier for right-handed maidservants to button up their mistresses' clothing left over right, but it is also easier for a right-handed male to subsequently unbutton said clothing.
Jeremy Haworth, W. Norwood, London.

☐ THERE is a historical reason. A gentleman's sword was always worn on the left side, so that it could be drawn with the right hand. If a jacket buttoned right over left, the handle of the sword would be likely to catch in the jacket opening when drawn, so any serious swordsman would demand a tunic which buttoned left over right. As an indication of a masculine lifestyle, this tradition was then extended to other items of menswear.
Paul Keers (author of A Gentleman's Wardrobe*), London W1.*

☐ I ONCE read in a scientific journal that babies are most frequently fed from the left breast, and in this position they are most conveniently kept warm by covering with the right-hand flap of clothing. Hence its fastening over the left flap.
Fay Charters, Middleton-on-Sea, W. Sussex.

☐ UNTIL the courts rule otherwise on the grounds of sexual discrimination, tailors should continue to button men's clothing left over right. Mine says that men often need to unbutton or unzip in a hurry and the vast majority are right-handed.
Max Engel, Northampton.

QUESTION: What is the derivation of the term 'round robin'?

☐ AN EARLY use of the term was aboard 18th century ships. Conditions were often very bad, and crews were known to mutiny. Sometimes this would take the form of a petition to the captain asking for better treatment. The usual reaction of the captain was to look for the name at the top of the left-hand column, and hang him from the yard-arm. To get round this, the crew would instead sign a 'round robin' in the shape of a circle. This, however, did not help much, because the captain would then take reprisals against the man whose name was in the 12 o'clock position (known as the 'ringleader'). Apart from the obvious alliteration, I do not know why it should be called a 'robin'.
Keith Trobridge, Shipley, W. Yorks.

☐ AN EARLIER use of the term was as a blasphemous name for the sacrament, c. 1555: 'There were at Paules fixed railing bils against the Sacrament, terming it Jacke of ye boxe, the sacrament of the halter, round Robin, with lyke unseemely termes.' (Ridley, quoted in *Oxford English Dictionary*).
Frank Cummins, Warley, W. Midlands.

QUESTION: In the story of Goldilocks and the Three Bears, why is it that Daddy Bear's porridge was too hot, Mummy Bear's porridge was too cold and yet Baby Bear's was 'just right'? These observations appear to place the temperature of the smallest portion between that of the largest and middle-sized portions. Is there some simple explanation of the anomalous cooling rates of the three bowls?

☐ IGNORING for a moment the insulating properties of the Bear family's breakfast porcelain, let's apply Newton's law of cooling. Heat loss varies as temperature difference (which at the start is the same for all three) multiplied by surface area. Rate of cooling varies as rate of heat loss divided by volume. Suppose that Baby Bear had half as much porridge as his mother and one-third as much as his father. In most families, adults use the same set of dishes while babies have their own smaller dishes, usually prettily decorated (Baby Bear's may have had pictures of cuddly little

men on it). Mummy's shallow pool of porridge cools more quickly than Daddy's deeper portion; as long as the radius of the adult dish is between 1.45 and 1.8 times that of Baby's dish, Baby's porridge will cool at a rate part-way between that of his father and that of his mother. This is of course a simplified calculation. As different rates of cooling take effect, it becomes necessary to take temperature difference into account, involving the use of calculus. The insulating power of the dishes would also have to be allowed for, together with any difference in insulation between the two types of dish.
(Miss) C. A. Bryson, West Kirby, Merseyside.

□ WHEN considering the problem, one must surely examine the character of the porridge thief herself. Given that Goldilocks has trespassed on the property of the three bears, and stolen their porridge, would we be correct to take her testimony concerning temperatures of the porridge at face value? I contest that it is simply wilful whim that causes her to eat the porridge of Baby Bear and the temperature argument is a smokescreen to divert attention from her theft. Why are our sympathies aroused by Goldilocks when it is the three bears who suffer the trauma of coming back to find that their home has been invaded, that they have been robbed, and that the interloper is asleep in one of their beds?
Bruce Beattie, London EC1.

□ BEAR society is male dominated . . . the intended time of consumption was when Daddy Bear's porridge was just right, at which time Baby Bear's would have been too cold and Mummy Bear's would have congealed. It's just that Goldilocks got there early.
John Higgs, Stoneygate, Leicester.

□ THE questioner assumes that Mummy Bear had the middle-sized portion. The fact that her porridge was cooler than her child's suggests that this was not so. There are two probable reasons for Mummy Bear's small serving; both reflect badly on the state of equality in ursine society. Times were hard in the woods of fairytale land and porridge was often a rare commodity. If stocks were running low, it is all too likely that noble Mummy Bear would go without in order to fill the stomachs of her husband and child. Or, after pressure from the media and her partner, Mummy Bear

may have become depressed about her ample figure (7 ft tall, 22½ stone) and felt obliged to go on a diet.
M. Hewett, Connahs Quay, Clwyd.

□ NURSERY tales, like nursery rhymes, are hotbeds of cultural propaganda. Daddy Bear is a macho male – red-hot porridge, rock-hard bed. (You even see him on television, drinking beer with the lads.) Mummy Bear is a wimp. Bàby Bear, with whom readers are intended to identify, is superior to Mummy, doing its level best to emulate Daddy, and the little brat is always right.
(Prof.) Ian Stewart, Mathematics Institute, University of Warwick, Coventry.

QUESTION: Quite often I have my cotton socks 'blessed'. Can anyone tell me the origin of this saying?

□ GEORGE Edward Lynch Cotton became Bishop of Calcutta in 1858 and while there established schools for Eurasian children. A man of great sensitivity, he ordered crates full of socks for the children, to be worn during lessons. It was the rule of the Bishop to bless all goods which arrived at the schools. A zealous member of staff one day distributed socks before the blessing, so thereafter every time a shipment arrived a note was placed on them to the effect: 'Cotton's socks for blessing'. Cotton's socks soon became corrupted to cotton socks. When the Bishop was drowned in the Ganges on 6 October 1866, a despatch was sent to the Archbishop to ask: 'Who will bless his cotton socks?'
(Mrs) Jane M. Glossop, Pwllheli, Gwynedd.

QUESTION: Why 'piggy bank'? Why not lamb, cow or donkey bank?

□ THIS originates from about the 16th century. The pig is the only farm animal that is of value only when dead. Thus the 'bank', traditionally made out of china, was so designed that it had to be broken in order to be opened – symbolically 'killing the pig'. Other farm animals do not have to be killed before they are of use. For instance, the cow can be milked, the bull put to stud, eggs obtained from hens and so on.
R. Thomas, Bridgend, Mid-Glamorgan.

□ IT APPEARS that livestock farming is not R. Thomas's forte. Sows and boars produce progeny, like cows and bulls, ewes and rams. Like fattening pigs, fattening cattle and fattening lambs are also 'of value only when dead', to use Mr Thomas's unfortunate phrase, which is also, however, a far from accurate statement. Perhaps the answer is simpler: because it was only this little piggy that went to market?
John Nix, Emeritus Professor of Farm Business Management, Wye College, Ashford, Kent.

□ AT ONE time, people used to keep their money in pots made of a type of earthenware called pigge. These so-called 'pigge banks' were not at first made in the shape of pigs, but presumably some manufacturer thought it was funny to do so.
Peter Morris, Norwich.

□ THE PIG is an ancient symbol of wordly wealth throughout China and Southeast Asia. Pottery models of pigs were made as funerary offerings and were often stuffed with paper 'money' specially made for funerary purposes. The earliest example of a piggy-bank I have seen is a 12th–13th century Majapahit terracotta of a very chubby pig from Java. It is hollow with a thin slot in the top of its back. Similar piggy-banks were produced in Java and Sumatra between the 12th and 17th centuries. Since the earliest European example I have seen is an early Delft blue and white piggy bank dating from around 1610, I have always assumed that the Dutch imported the design from Indonesia.
Nigel Palmer, London SW15.

QUESTION: What is the origin of the crescent moon symbol seen throughout Islamic cultures?

□ ISLAM emerged in Arabia where travel along the desert trade routes was largely by night, and navigation depended upon the position of the moon and stars. The moon thus represents the guidance of God on the path through life. The new moon also represents the Muslim calendar, which has 12 months each of 29 or 30 days. So in Islam the lunar month and the calendar month coincide, and the new moon is eagerly awaited, especially at the

end of the month of Ramadan when its sighting means that the celebrations of 'Id al-Fitr can begin.
Linda and Phil Holmes, Cottingham, N. Humberside.

□ THE USE of the so-called crescent moon in many Islamic symbols cannot be related to the importance attached to the new moon in Islam. The moon depicted on many Islamic flags is the old moon, the reverse shape of the new moon, which is like a letter C backwards. Again 'crescent', implying 'increasing', is properly applicable only to the young moon: the old moon is diminishing in phase. Presumably the moon is depicted as a crescent in Islamic, and many other, contexts as that shape is unambiguously lunar.
A. A. Davis, London SW7.

□ ALTHOUGH the crescent is indeed a very widespread motif in Islamic iconography, it is not Islamic in origin nor exclusive to that religion. The emblem has been used in Christian art for many centuries in depictions of the Virgin Mary, for example. It is in fact one of the oldest icons in human history, having been known in graphic depictions since at least as early as the Babylonian period in Mesopotamia. The stele of Ur Namu, for example, dating from 2100 BC, includes the crescent moon to symbolise the god Sin, along with a star representing Shamash, the sun god. Later the moon became a female deity, typified by the goddess Artemis and her many counterparts, including Diana, who was celebrated as the moon-goddess in Roman times and depicted with a crescent on her brow. The device seems to have entered Islam via the Seljuk Turks who dominated Anatolia in the 12th century, and was widely used by their successors, the Ottoman Turks, who eventually became the principal Islamic nation, and whose Sultan held the title of Caliph until 1922. The story that the Ottomans adopted the crescent to symbolise their conquest of Constantinople must be dismissed as mere legend, since the device considerably predates 1453. In the late 19th century the Pan-Islamic movement sponsored by the Sultan Abdul Hamid II used the crescent and star on a green flag as part of its propaganda, and from this were derived the flags of Egypt and Pakistan and many other Islamic states.
William G. Crampton, Director of the Flag Institute, Chester.

□ A DETAILED answer will be found in the entry '*Hilal*',

Encyclopaedia of Islam (second edition, Brill, Leiden, 1960). Professor Richard Ettinghausen, writer of the entry, notes that the crescent moon (*hilal*) motif is featured with a five or six pointed star (the latter known as Solomon's shield in the Islamic world) on early Islamic coins circa AD 695, but it carried no distinct Islamic connotation. Some 500 years later, it appears in association with various astrological/astronomical symbols on 12th century Islamic metal-work, but when depicted in manuscript painting, held by a seated man, it is thought to represent the authority of a high court official: 'the sun [is] to the king and the moon [is] to the vizier . . .' Its use as a roof finial on Islamic buildings also dates from this medieval period but the motif still had no specific religious meaning as it decorated all types of architecture, secular as well as religious. In fact Ettinghausen argues that it was the European assumption that this was a religious and national emblem that led to several Muslim governments adopting it officially during the 19th century.
(Dr) Patricia Baker, Farnham, Surrey.

QUESTION: In chapter five of *English History 1914–45*, A. J. P. Taylor states: 'The passport was, of course, required by foreign governments. British citizens do not need a passport to leave this country in peacetime or to return to it.' Is this still the case?

□ YES, A. J. P. Taylor was right, one can leave the UK and return without a passport – although strictly speaking this does not apply if one is flying. Clause 42 of the Magna Carta states: 'Any freeman may travel abroad without let or hindrance of the King and return safe and secure by land and by water except in the time of war.' I know because several years ago our son found his passport was out of date late in the day before he was due to go on holiday with his girlfriend. The Public Records Office looked it up for me and explained that France, his destination, could refuse to let him in, but in July at the height of the holiday season the French authorities probably would not notice his passport was out of date. I was advised, however, that he should have on him the above Magna Carta clause, in case his exit from or re-entry to this country was queried with an out-of-date passport.
(Mrs) V. M. Crews, Beckenham, Kent.

☐ BRITISH citizens aren't citizens as such but only subjects of the Crown and we do need the permission of the Sovereign to leave the country – otherwise we might all leave to avoid unpleasant wars and taxes and the like. Rather than take up her time writing letters allowing her trusty and well-beloved Waynes and Traceys to spend their fortnights in Ibiza, the Queen provides these passport substitutes. If you don't want to carry one, you could petition the Queen for a leave-giving letter, which might make quite an impressive travel document.
Humphrey Evans, London N7.

☐ DEPARTURE from the UK, with some important exceptions, is not subject to control but entry is. Taylor's remark is technically truer now than it was then because at that time 'British Citizen' was a phrase which had no legal definition. British subjects, including Commonwealth citizens, had the right freely to enter and remain in the UK before the nationality legislation of the 1960s which sought to control certain categories of 'coloured' immigration. The phrase 'British Citizen' was adopted in 1981 to define those who have the right of abode in the UK and do not require leave to enter. With the exception of a number of Citizens of the UK and Colonies under the previous nationality acts, others require leave and can be refused entry or have conditions placed on their stay. This includes many people who have only one of the limited forms of British nationality and Commonwealth citizens who are still British subjects. For immigration purposes a passport is evidence of identity, nationality (or citizenship) and (in the case of the UK) the person's immigration status. It is these factors, not the passport itself, which determine a person's entitlement to enter the UK. So the possession of a passport is not essential. The right to enter without leave is dependent on a legal status: having the right of abode. Principle aside, it's important for all and essential for many with the right of abode to have a passport. Anyone arriving without a passport has to convince the immigration officer at the port of entry that she has the right of abode and if she is unsuccessful may be refused entry. Until recently, such a person was entitled to remain in the UK for the purpose of an appeal. Under the Immigration Act 1988, however, a person arriving without a passport which shows right of abode (as British Citizen or otherwise) can't remain in the UK while waiting for the appeal to be heard, and needs leave to come to the UK to be at the appeal.

But the non-passport holder may never get to that point. Under the Immigration (Carriers' Liability) Act 1987, carriers by sea or air are liable to pay on demand £1,000 for every passenger requiring leave who fails to produce a valid passport or other document establishing identity and nationality or citizenship, and a visa if applicable. Although this does not apply to those with the right of abode, the carrier may be unable to establish or unwilling to assume that a person without a passport has the right of abode. If so, you won't get on the boat or the plane.
C. R. Bradley, School of Law, Polytechnic of Central London.

☐ IN 1973 I travelled from Heathrow to the Netherlands without a passport. I had quite a job to persuade a UK emigration officer to let me out of the country but he let me go reluctantly after I asked him if he could quote an act of parliament requiring British citizens to have a passport (I was sure that there wasn't one). The Dutch appropriate official, a member of the police force, when told I had no passport, merely smiled and said, 'Welcome to the Netherlands'.
Herbert Layton, Gloucester.

☐ SOME years ago a French immigration officer, after studying for a few moments the passport my husband had handed him, remarked quite politely that it was difficult to believe he was only 10 years old. My preoccupied spouse had mistakenly taken not his own but our younger son's passport with him on this solo journey; embarrassed and dismayed, he began apologising and explaining, but had hardly begun before the officer stamped the passport and handed it back to him with a shrug – a Gallic shrug, no doubt.
Merivan Coles, London SW5.

QUESTION: Are scientists any closer to answering the question: which came first, the chicken or the egg?

☐ ASSUMING that the chicken evolved from two other birds which were not quite chickens, then these two latter birds must have produced, at some time in the past, an egg out of which came the first chicken.
Geoffrey Samuel, Lancaster.

□ We must remember that the chicken is an actual chicken whereas the egg is only a potential chicken. Philosophically speaking, actuality always precedes potentiality, so the chicken came first. Probably.
Kishor Alam, London N14.

□ Kishor Alam argues on the basis of actuality preceding potentiality that the chicken must come before the egg. But from the egg's point of view, a chicken is only a potential egg (just as human beings are simply the way genes manage to perpetuate themselves).
David Lewis, St Albans, Herts.

□ The chicken is, of course, *Archaeopteryx*, the oldest fossil bird. It comes from the Solnhofen Lithograhic Limestone, from the late Jurassic rocks of Bavaria (that is about 150 million years ago). Its skeleton is so like that of contemporary dinosaurs that it is generally agreed that its ancestors were in fact small, lightly built dinosaurs. The dinosaurs were reptiles, and in some cases are known to have laid eggs, therefore it is likely that the egg came first. However, most fossil reptile eggs date from the later Cretaceous period (144–65 million years ago) and are those of large dinosaurs – large and relatively strong eggs which have a better chance of preservation than smaller ones. The oldest find reported (from the Early Permian – about 270 million years ago – of Texas) is so poorly preserved that palaeontologists are uncertain about its true identity. It may be the remains of an inorganic nodule – a chemical growth within the sediment. The earliest reptile fossils come from even older rocks: the Early Carboniferous (350 million years ago) of Scotland. So it is probable that the earliest eggs date from this time – 200 million years before *Archaeopteryx*. The egg is no chicken!
(Dr) Denis Bates, Institute of Earth Studies, University College of Wales, Aberystwyth.

□ Readers may be interested in the rather tongue-in-cheek article by Walter N. Thurman and Mark E. Fisher: 'Chicken, Eggs, and Causality, or Which Came First?' (*American Journal of Agricultural Economics*, May 1988). The authors conducted so-called 'Granger causality tests' using annual data from the

US Department of Agriculture on egg production and chicken population covering the period 1930–1983. Such tests can be used to see if there is an asymmetry between the value of the information provided by past observations of the variables in predicting each other's current values. Using regression analysis one attempts to discover whether variations in a series Y (say chicken population) can be adequately explained by its own past values, or whether lagged values of a second variable X (say egg production) contribute significantly to the equation. A similar regression would be carried out reversing the role of the variables. If it can be shown that X is needed to help explain Y (after accounting for the influence of past values of Y) but that Y is not needed to explain movements in X, then one may conclude that X 'Granger-causes' Y (after Clive Granger who first proposed the procedure). Using this approach in what Thurman and Fisher called 'the most natural application of tests for Granger causality' they concluded that the egg came first. However, readers may feel that this result should be taken with a pinch of salt, especially when they hear that other applications of the test have given rise to such perverse findings as 'GNP "causes" sunspot activity!'
Guy Judge, Emsworth, Hants.

QUESTION: Is there any scientific explanation for the phenomenon known as 'speaking in tongues'?

□ RECENT research by a Montreal-based neurolinguist, Andre Roch Lecours, involved recording the 'xenoglossic' speech of a number of pentecostal charismatics and of a 'schizophasic' who believed he was the 'instrument of malevolent wills from Mars, where he once worked as a crooner'. It emerged that the phonetic elements of the 'alien' speech were virtually all to be found in the speakers' native language, with a smattering of sounds from languages of which they had a little passive knowledge. The 'alien language' also stuck pretty much to the other conventions of the native language's sound system, although often simplified in form. And though it appeared to include word- and sentence-like entities, such speech was marked by very simple transformational rules, considerable repetition, and an emphasis on rhythm and melody – as in more common monologue forms such as recitative prayer

or political propaganda. A French neuropsychologist has reported how an English woman, who claimed to be a conduit for 'Pharaonic Egyptian', in fact drew from the repertoire of English sounds and euphonic principles such as alliteration – which would require a degree of self-control. Lecours suggests that 'speaking in tongues' is a 'learned game – and a rather simple one at that', which is based on making fluent utterances but with the semantic component switched off. Lecours' study had also included two healthy nurses and a professional poet, who were able to respond to the request to try to speak in a language they did not know by producing much the same kind of material. Furthermore, although the charismatics and the schizophasic claimed to be the instrument of some stronger will, they all produced on demand for recording. Flubbadub.
G. P. Collis, Liverpool 18.

☐ A PAPERBACK, *The Psychology of Speaking in Tongues*, by John Kildahl, published in 1972, provides what is described as 'a scientific account' in simple terms.
(Rev.) Michael Westney, Slough.

QUESTION: Is it true that if you throw a pea off the Eiffel Tower it can kill someone below?

☐ ONLY if it's in a tin.
Jacqueline Dunn, Manchester.

☐ FOR a light object like a pea to cause injury, it would need to be travelling as fast as a slow bullet – say 40 metres per second. There are two reasons why this speed would not be achieved. First, a fresh or canned pea would break up in the air before it reached that speed because of the force of wind resistance. This is easily observed if a canned pea is blown from a pea-shooter: it often breaks apart shortly after leaving the muzzle even though its speed is much lower than 40 metres per second. Secondly, even a dried pea will continue to accelerate only so long as its weight (the downward force) exceeds the air resistance (the upward force). All falling objects reach a speed where these two forces are equal and no further acceleration will take place. This is called the

'terminal velocity' and it is determined by the weight of the object, its shape, its surface characteristics and the temperature of the air. If we assume that a dried pea is 7mm diameter, weighs 400mg and is of 'moderate' smoothness, then in still air its terminal velocity is likely to be about nine metres per second. Being dried, it will probably not break up. At this velocity, the pea would be felt on the top of the head with an impulse equivalent to a new 5p coin dropped from about 600 millimetres. No injury would result. However, a hard smooth sea-pebble of the same size could reach a terminal velocity of about 50 metres per second and could injure.
Vic Seddon, Teesside Polytechnic.

QUESTION: 'Tie a yellow ribbon round the old oak tree.' Why yellow?

☐ DURING the American Civil War, Union soldiers were given the nickname 'yellow legs' by their confederate counterparts. The name referred to the uniform, with obvious derisory overtones. Mothers, wives, sisters and daughters of Union soldiers took to wearing yellow flowers (roses in particular) as a rebuke to this slander and to show solidarity with their menfolk. The yellow ribbon is a direct descendant of this.
Thomas Boyce, Doha, Qatar.

☐ THOMAS BOYCE comes close, but is not exact. Yellow was the distinguishing colour of the US cavalry since its official formation in March 1833, the colour of the trouser stripe and also of NCOs' chevrons and of piping on shell jacket or cap. It was not restricted to the Civil War, and it did not apply to all Union soldiers: the Artillery wore red stripes and pipes, and the Infantry varied but never wore yellow. Mr Boyce mentions 'mothers, wives sisters and daughters', but omits the most important category who 'in her hair would wear a yellow ribbon; would wear it in the springtime, in the merry month of May . . .'
Gordon Medcalf, Reading, Berks.

☐ IT MAY be true that there is a link between yellow flowers and the Civil War, but there seems to have been no link

with yellow ribbons. According to an article in *The Express* (Berkeley, California), yellow ribbons were first used in January 1981, to welcome home the Americans held hostage in Iran. The inspiration was the song, 'Tie a Yellow Ribbon Round the Old Oak Tree', although that had been written in 1972 and is about a convict returning home from jail. Even more confusing is that Larry Brown, one of the writers, claimed the centrepiece of the story on which he based the song was a white kerchief. He changed this to 'yellow ribbon' to scan better. There had been previous songs about yellow ribbons, such as 'She Wore a Yellow Ribbon' (title for the 1949 John Ford movie), but these cannot be traced back to the real, rather than the Hollywood, Civil War.
Richard Ross, London N4.

☐ ABOUT a year before the song was inflicted upon us I saw a short drama on American television that began on an overnight coach crossing America. One of the passengers has just got out of jail, is on his way home and doesn't know if his wife wants him back, but he has asked her to show him a sign (the colour was yellow simply because it was their favourite). The next morning, as the coach nears his home, all the passengers stare eagerly out of the windows to see if the ribbon is there . . . and the last shot of the film is the ex-con standing on his front lawn, staring up at the tree, festooned with ribbons.
Adam Kimmel, London N7.

QUESTION: When did the expression 'Russian roulette' first come into use? Why Russian? Are there authenticated cases of it being played?

☐ RUSSIAN roulette may have its origins in *A Hero of Our Time* by Mikhail Lermontov (1814–1841) where he tells of a Lieutenant Vulich whose only passion was for cards, where he usually lost – and most of his money at that. When an argument arose about predestination, he maintained there was no such thing and backed his belief with a wager of 200 roubles. He was taken up on the bet whereupon he walked to a wall with weapons hanging on it and at random took one of the pistols. He poured powder into the

touch-pan and asked the pistol's owner – a major – if the pistol was loaded. The owner didn't remember. Vulich held the pistol to his head and pulled the trigger. It misfired. Some of the onlookers said it wasn't loaded. Vulich cocked the gun again, aimed at a cap hanging over the window and a bullet pierced its centre.
S. Kaufman, Ilford, Essex.

□ THERE is a wealth of fictional references, notably the 19th century Russian writer, Ossendowski, in his unforgettable *Man And Mystery In Asia.* But the most well-documented factual example is surely Graham Greene's experience of at least six episodes. One took place (summer 1924 – January 1925) while he was up at Oxford: 'I would walk out from Headington towards Elsfield . . . a sodden unfrequented country lane; the revolver would be whipped behind my back, the chamber twisted, the muzzle quickly inserted in my ear beneath the black winter trees, the trigger pulled . . .' Evidence was left behind in the form of free verse permanently on his desk 'so that if I lost the gamble, it would provide incontrovertible evidence of an accident, and my parents, I thought, would be less troubled by a fatal play-acting than a suicide.'
John Bray, Haywards Heath, W. Sussex.

QUESTION: Why are pirates invariably depicted with eye-patches and wooden legs? Was there a higher incidence of industrial injury in their line of work, or were they just clumsy?

□ THERE was a high rate of such industrial injuries in all sea-faring between the middle of the 17th century and the end of the Napoleonic wars (the period featured in Hollywood swashbucklers). It could hardly have been otherwise. The most common form of sea engagement during that period seems to have been the medium or close-range firing of cannon broadside on, at, or between vessels. On to and into those ships came smashing cannon balls, which, when they did not decapitate or otherwise kill outright, lopped off limbs, or at least smashed them so destructively the only known chance for survival was prompt amputation. Cannonades brought down heavy timber on and through decks – more crushing injuries, more amputations –

and turned the wood of a ship into cutting projectiles. If muskets were used at closer range, a heavy musket-ball was at least as likely to smash a limb (needing amputation) as to pierce it. And in hand-to-hand combat to secure a ship, the cutlass was common, because as a slashing weapon it could be used with the minimum of footwork, in tight conditions. More severing injuries, and also vertical cuts to the forehead and down through the eye-area. Although soldiers during the same era faced similar dangers, the concentration of fire on the relatively small, man-filled target of a ship must have meant sailors/pirates had a very high chance of mutilation. An even bigger one of death. And at sea it isn't easy to run away.
Ann MacDonald, Clapham, London.

□ THE main cause, surely, was the type of artillery in use. Eighteenth-century cannons were loaded with coarse black gunpowder, and fired by putting some of the powder in a hole at the back of the gun and lighting it with a slow match. Although most of the powder would blast forward, an appreciable proportion would vent out through the touch-hole. Anyone firing a cannon was therefore very likely to get a blast of burning powder in the face, with a grave risk of eye injury. A smooth-bored gun, firing a roughly rounded shot with poor quality powder from a moving ship, would only have an accurate range of a few yards. It was probably customary to fire a broadside practically at the point of contact. At that range a cannon-ball fired into the side of a wooden ship would scatter large jagged splinters of wood about the deck. Anyone receiving a wound in the body would probably die of gangrene within a few days. Gangrene could be prevented in a limb injury, however, by rapid removal of the limb (first partially anaesthetising the patient with rum or laudanum – a solution of opium and rum), tying up the cut arteries and cauterising the stump in hot tar. Anyone who survived the immediate traumatic effect of this treatment would probably escape gangrenous infection, but would have to make use of a prosthetic device such as a hook or wooden leg.
Martin Guha, London SE3.

□ ONCE you've got a shiny new hook for a hand you'll discover why an eye patch is needed when you attempt to rub your eye.
Bridget Savage, Bexley, Kent.

☐ SAILORS of the period who were injured were discharged. As their trade was the sea, their only recourse to earn a living was piracy. Their physical disabilities were an advantage if they instilled fear into their unfortunate victims: the more ruthless they appeared, the greater their chance of success.
F. E. Jones, Gt Sankey, Warrington.

QUESTION: If you cut a worm in two does it become two worms?

☐ NO, the two halves differ. The full-grown garden worm, *Lumbricus terrestris*, has a body made up of about 150 tiny rings, each with hair-like, rearward barbs that make it hard to pull the worm from its hole, or to swallow in reverse. The mouth and first 31 rings form the pointed front. Then comes a thickened region, rings 32 to 37, the *clitellum*, used in sex: worms may be hermaphrodite, but pairs join in mutual '69s' on damp nights. The rest of the body is uniform until it flattens out at the anus. Cut a worm in half (please don't), and the front usually grows a new, if shorter, tail end. For the old tail, shorn of vital organs, it's the end; but that's not the end of the tale. *Lumbricus* and the other two dozen species of British earthworms (1,500 worldwide) are sophisticated tillers of the soil. However, in pond and stream there swims a more primitive worm, black and half an inch long: the flatworm (*planaria*). Cut one in two: the head grows a tail, the tail a head. Cut one in three: even the middle grows both new head and tail. Each part become whole is thought to carry the memories of its earlier entity; so beware, if you open this can of worms they may seek revenge. And they're carnivorous.
Bill Allen, Oxshott, Surrey.

QUESTION: I once read a nonsense poem that removed the apparently negative prefixes of words like 'inept', 'inert' and 'uncouth' to make new words: 'ept', 'ert' and 'couth'. I've searched for the poem since, but no luck. Can anyone help?

☐ THE POEM to which I think the question refers is 'Gloss' by an American poet, David McCord, which runs:

I know a little man both ept and ert.
An intro? extro? No, he's just a vert.
Shevelled and couth and kempt, pecunious, ane.
His image trudes upon the ceptive brain.
When life turns sipid and the mind is traught,
The spirit soars as I would sist it ought.
Chalantly then, like any gainly goof,
My digent self is sertive, choate, loof.

I hope this is of sistance.
J. D. Trehearne, Ealing, London W5.

☐ THE POEM is probably:

I dreamt of a corrigible nocuous youth,
Gainly, gruntled and kempt;
A mayed and sidious fellow forsooth –
Ordinate, effable, shevelled, ept, couth;
A delible fellow I dreamt.

Quoted by Willard R. Espy in his book, *The Game of Words* (Bramhall House, New York).
C. Sherris, Billingham, Cleveland.

QUESTION: Despite many years' experience teaching English as a foreign language, I have never been able to answer the question 'What is the difference between jam and marmalade?' Can anyone help?

☐ THERE is no difference: marmalade is yellow jam. The marmalade has its origins in the Greek *mel* meaning honey, which passed into Latin as *melimelon*, and then to the Portuguese *marmalada* from the word *marmelo* meaning quince. This quince jam called *marmelada* is still very popular in Portugal and became *marmelade* in the French. Marmalade is a yellow jam and has passed into the English language as such, though oranges and lemons are now used in place of quince.
Kristine Byrne, Lagos, Portugal.

☐ To SAY that marmalade is yellow jam ignores the use of citrus fruit, particularly Seville oranges, surely essential to any definition of marmalade (ginger marmalade being the exception that proves the rule). This semantic difference between the words comes from their history. 'Marmalade' does derive from the Latin for quince via Portuguese; quince paste, or *marmelada*, was a luxury imported from Portugal to England in the 16th century. Over the following century 'marmalade' was applied to pastes made from sugar and many kinds of fruit: peaches, damsons, oranges and lemons, as well as quinces; some recipes used almonds. The pastes were stiff and cut in slices to eat from the fingers; softer pastes with a higher water content simply didn't keep. 'Jam' entered the English language in the 18th century, making an early appearance in Mrs Mary Eales' *Receipets* (1718). It may derive from an Arabic word meaning 'to pack together'. Improved hygiene led to the development of runnier marmalades, similar to jam as we know it today. By 1861, Mrs Beeton stated that 'Marmalades and jams differ little from each other: they are preserves of half liquid consistency made by boiling the pulp of fruits and sometimes the rinds with sugar', with the proviso that marmalades were made from firm fruits, such as pineapples or the rinds of oranges; jams were made from soft fruit. For reasons which are not entirely obvious, the name marmalade stuck to orange preserves, while the more downwardly mobile fruit spreads were lumped together as jam. No doubt the EC will soon settle the argument for once and all with a directive on the subject. A fuller discussion of the history of marmalade is provided by C. Anne Wilson in *A Book of Marmalade* (1985).
Laura Mason, York.

☐ I SUGGEST we haul ourselves out of the morass of etymology and remember that language is a tool for naming things. In which case, for 99.9 per cent of the British, marmalade is made of oranges (or more rarely other citrus fruits) while jam is made of any non-citrus fruit. The 0.1 per cent also mess with things like turnips and rhubarb – these concoctions are called jam too.
John Stagg, London NW11.

QUESTION: What is the origin of the word 'hijack'?

☐ IT ORIGINATES from the prohibition era in America. Supposedly a member of one gang would approach the driver of a rival gang's bootlegging truck with a smile and a disarming 'Hi, Jack!' before sticking the muzzle of a gat in the face of the poor unfortunate, and relieving him of both truck and its alcoholic cargo.
Tim Wood, Cardiff.

☐ THE word 'hijack' has its origins in pre-revolutionary France. Impoverished peasants attacked and robbed aristocrats travelling in coaches through the countryside. The word they employed for this practice was '*échaquer*', which, sharing a common root with '*éjecter*' in the Latin word '*eiacere*', meant primarily the physical removal of the aristocrat from his carriage and of his possessions from his person, but also, through its onomatopoeic second syllable, contained elements of the peasants' anger, expressed in the guttural spitting sound used to pronounce the word and also possibly the sound of a knife entering and twisting up through the aristocrat's intestines. Wider implications of the word were explored in the revolution of 1789. The word reached England by way of the many English bandits who worked alongside their French colleagues. The reason for this was similar in many ways to the situation today where unemployed Englishmen pick grapes in France. In the 18th century the pickings were simply richer in France. The aristocrats were vain and haughty and felt themselves to be untouchable. This made it a simple matter to relieve them of their considerable wealth. I do not know whether the word was misheard as '*é Jacques*' and thus translated by the English brigands as 'i Jack' or if the word was taken as heard and, due to the similarity in 18th century rural English pronunciation between the 'e' and 'i' sounds, has simply come to be written down as 'hijack' by adding the 'h' an educated person of that time would have assumed a peasant to have left off. The word '*échaquer*' disappeared from French usage after the revolution. Today, the French use the word '*détourner*' which, in its mildness, perhaps best sums up the civilising influence of the revolution. It also reflects the changing usage of the word 'hijack' which today refers almost exclusively to the taking over by force of an aeroplane or other vehicle by a group of terrorists who wish it to go to a different destination. Thus the French have a new word for a word which originated in their own language.
Peter Bowen, London SW12.

QUESTION: Why does the Queen face right on coins but left on postage stamps?

□ THE design of coins is determined by a tradition going back at least to the time of Charles II that the direction in which the head faces should alternate between the coinage of successive monarchs. The only exception to this has been the coinage of Edward VIII, who insisted on his likeness facing left. It is not clear whether this was an expression of rebellion against convention, or vanity, to show what he regarded as his better profile, containing his hair parting. Edward VIII abdicated before being crowned, and no new coinage was released into general circulation during his reign, although a few experimental pieces were produced. Some coins were issued in British colonies, but none with a likeness of the King, though an appropriate design (facing left) had been chosen. It was nevertheless determined that designs for the coinage of George VI, his successor, should be prepared as if that of Edward VIII had been produced and as if it had depicted him facing right, thus reinstating the original tradition. The coinage of Elizabeth II has been in accordance with tradition. Postage stamps are quite different. Ever since the first prepaid adhesive stamps were issued in 1840, all standard issues have shown the head of the reigning monarch in profile (except between 1953 and 1967, with a three-quarters view of Elizabeth II) and facing left. The direction appears to have been determined solely by the fact that the earliest were based upon a medal showing Victoria facing left: it is possible that the direction was selected to conform with the coinage then in circulation. The rule does not apply to commemorative issues: three such stamps were produced showing George VI and Queen Elizabeth; the couple are shown in full-face or in profile facing right. An early commemorative stamp of Elizabeth II also shows her full-face: commemorative issues since 1966 have usually shown a profile view based on the bust designed by Mary Gillick for the pre-decimal coinage. Regular issues have shown a crowned bust based upon a plaster cast by Arnold Machin, who also designed the decimal coinage. Since 1973, many have shown a profile silhouette of the Queen facing right. Certain postage stamps issued to commemorate royal weddings have not contained the Queen's head at all.
John Richardson, Department of Human Sciences, Brunel University.

QUESTION: Is this a question.

☐ NO, this is a demonstrative pronoun.
Bob Gingell, Coventry.

☐ STUDENT lore has it that this appeared on a University of London finals paper in philosophy in the 1950s, and that one attempted answer ran: 'If that is a question, this is an answer.' Legend records that the student in question failed, but would have passed had he sat his finals in Oxford, where there is a greater tolerance of smart alecks.
Paul Richards.

☐ NO, of course it isn't a question, because it doesn't have a question mark. But this grammatical lapse is compounded by a logical one. It isn't a question because although it conforms (with the addition of the question mark) to the way we normally formulate questions in our language, it contains a logical mistake. The similarly structured 'Is that a quintain?' is both perfectly structured and perfectly meaningful in an appropriate context. But 'Is this a question?' lacks any context in which it would be appropriate. It commits what is known by logicians as a 'type error' and is meaningless in the same way as the statement 'the average taxpayer died yesterday' is meaningless – and for similar reasons. The latter is nonsense because the sorts of things that can be done by 'the average taxpayer' do not include 'dying yesterday'. In our non-question, the 'this' refers circularly – and emptily – to itself. Compare 'Is that a question?' which is OK because the 'that' refers elsewhere. The sorts of things that a question can do may not include asking a question about itself. There are, inevitably, odd cases where questions can ask questions about elements, or aspects of themselves ('Does this question start with the word "does"?'). But logic sensibly draws a firm line at circular vacuity.
(Dr) William Johnston, Arnside, Cumbria.

☐ I ANSWER 'Yes', since to offer any answer at all is to concede that it is indeed a question. Objectors can offer only a silence after the four words are uttered: any response would confirm my view. Thus, I can receive no valid objection. 'Is this a question?' is framed in accordance with common English usage for questions

(when correctly punctuated), and has received at least one answer. And so, if it walks like a duck and it quacks like a duck . . . I rest my case.
Bill Allen, Montrose Gardens, Oxshott, Surrey.

☐ BOB GINGELL's error is to ignore the vital contribution that quotation marks make to meaning. Had the question been whether 'this' is a question (which it was not) then the correct answer would have been that 'this' is not a question but a demonstrative pronoun. Dr William Johnston's position is self-refuting: it provides an answer – albeit a false one – to what it denies is a question. Moreover, the details of his answer show that he understood very well the meaning of what he claims to be a meaningless non-question. If we are to banish otherwise perfectly well-formed sentences merely because they are self-referential, what are we to do with Shakespeare's 18th Sonnet? '. . . So long as men can breathe or eyes can see/So long lives this, and this gives life to thee.'
Moshé Machover, Reader in Mathematical Logic, Dept of History and Philosophy of Science, King's College, London.

☐ COMPARE Wittgenstein's 'This statement is false'.
Robin Howard, Haywards Heath, W. Sussex.

☐ THIS is not an answer. But I recommend the full and highly entertaining discussion in chapters one and two of *Metamagical Themas* by Douglas R. Hofstadter which includes the classic 'This sentence no verb'.
Lesz Lancucki, London SW12.

☐ ALL these cunning answers are actually irrelevant because Shakespeare told us that 'that is the question'.
Michael Wilson, Wigton, Cumbria.

☐ THIS sentence no verb. Who cares. This reader bored. Time to bring this subject to a.
Christopher Turner, Sevenoaks, Kent.

QUESTION: There is no zero in Roman numerals. Who invented zero, and when?

☐ THE ancient Greeks were aware of the concept of zero (as in 'We have no marbles'), but didn't think of it as a number. Aristotle had dismissed it because you couldn't divide by zero and get a down-to-earth result. The Romans never used their numerals for arithmetic, thus avoiding the need to keep a column empty with a zero symbol. Addition and subtraction were done instead on an abacus or counting frame. About 1,500 years ago in India a symbol was used to represent an abacus column with nothing in it. At first this was just a dot; later it became the '0' we know today. In the 8th century the great Arab mathematician, al-Khwarizmi, took it up and the Arabs eventually brought the zero to Europe. It wasn't warmly received; the Italians in particular were very suspicious of any change to their ancestors' system of numerals. In 1259 a law was passed forbidding bankers from using zero or any of the new Arab numerals in their accounts.
George Auckland and Martin Gorst, Away With Numbers, *BBC Television, London W5.*

☐ A MONK called Abelard, who kept the accounts for a monastery in the West Midlands, heard of the new system and went to Spain during the Moorish occupation. He converted to Islam and returned to his monastery after 20 years' study with the precious knowledge of nothing.
Dennis Salt, Horsham, W. Sussex.

☐ MORE information can be found in Chapter 7 of Professor Lancelot Hogben's book, *Mathematics for the Million.*
Leslie Farmelo, Shoreham-by-Sea, Sussex.

QUESTION: In a restaurant, when do you become legally liable to pay the bill? Is it when you place your order, when the food is served, or when it is eaten?

☐ YOU become liable as soon as the contract is 'substantially performed'. You could keep two teams of lawyers happy for hours discussing precisely when this moment happens if you were prepared to pay for the privilege. More useful questions to ask would be: what is the last instant at which you can withdraw

from the transaction without liability of any kind (answer: the instant before you order); and if you can be proved to have intended not to pay, what actions expose you to criminal liability (answer: just about anything, though the precise moment at which you develop this intent will determine whether the appropriate charge is obtaining property by deception, obtaining services by deception, evading liability by deception, or simply making off without payment).
Steve Hedley, Fellow in Law, Christ's College, Cambridge.

□ IT WOULD appear that you become liable to pay before any of these. I have had the misfortune to pay a bill for a meal not having ordered, been served, or actually having eaten it. As soon as you make a reservation to eat a meal (or presumably step into a restaurant to eat one) you implicitly make a legal contract.
Mark Bridle, Southampton.

□ THE question was discussed in a case in the Thirties, which I recall as Lockett *v* Charles. The guest at a restaurant meal was taken ill afterwards and sued the restaurant. This was before the 'snail in the ginger beer bottle' case (Donoghue *v* Stevenson), so everything turned on whether there was a contract, to which the Sale of Goods Act, 1893, applied between the guest and the restaurant. The High Court held that the contract was made when the orders were placed, and that where two people go to a restaurant and place orders, the implication is that each becomes liable to pay for the food ordered by himself. This may be rebutted where the host has booked the table and indicated he will be entertaining guests. But the principle seems to be established: the contract is made when the orders are given. However, contracts made by conduct are notoriously difficult to define. So far as I know, the courts have not yet decided at what point the contract is made when a person boards a bus.
John Paris, Abingdon, Oxfordshire.

QUESTION: There used to be a BBC television rock music programme called *The Old Grey Whistle Test*. What is the origin of this title?

□ IT DATES back to the days of Tin Pan Alley, when music publishing companies would literally employ songwriters, working in the building on a nine-to-five basis, turning out songs on a kind of 'hit factory' conveyor belt. The Brill Building in New York, where Neil Sedaka, Carole King, Gerry Goffin, Ellie Greenwich and many more writers provided the charts with so many stunning songs in the late 50s and early 60s, was possibly the definitive example. What they were looking for were songs with a catchy chorus that could be hummed or whistled after the first time of hearing. At the end of a working week, the songs deemed to be the strongest were played to an in-house gathering of the 'general public' – the peripheral staff employed as maybe cleaners or doormen around the building. These people were known by the nickname the 'Old Greys' at that time. If, after hearing a song only once or twice, they were able to hum or whistle along to the chorus, the song was deemed to have the greatest chance of making the charts because it passed 'The Old Grey Whistle Test'. The phrase became general currency in the music business at that time. As to its literal application on the programme . . . well, we broke the rules. Many of the bands we featured during the mid-70s would have been embarrassed to have achieved success in the singles market at that time. Alex Harvey and Captain Beefheart hardly turned out top 40 songs on a regular basis.
Bob Harris, BBC Radio 1 (presenter of The Old Grey Whistle Test, *1972–79).*

□ THE programme's founder, Mike Appleton, chose the title in an era when cumbersome and meaningless names (like Monty Python's Flying Circus and Sgt Pepper's Lonely Hearts Club Band) were all the rage.
*Trevor Dann (*Whistle Test *producer 1984–87), London W1.*

QUESTION: Why do flamingos stand on one leg?

□ THE legs and feet of these birds have a high surface-area-to-mass ratio. They are therefore susceptible to heat loss, particularly if the bird stands still for long periods with its feet and legs in water. Many water birds have thus evolved the habit of standing with one leg tucked up into the feathers of the lower body, reducing the potential heat loss by 50 per cent.
Ian White, Bolton, Lancs.

QUESTION: How can I weigh my head?

☐ FILL a water butt until water flows out of the overflow. Let the water settle and then immerse the head completely, keeping it submerged until the water level has settled, having first arranged some method of collecting the displaced water that will flow out of the overflow. The volume of water displaced should then be measured and the experiment repeated, this time immersing the whole body. Again the volume of displaced water should be recorded. The ratio of the first volume to the second, multiplied by total body weight, gives the proportion of body weight that is due to the head. This method assumes the human body has a uniform density and does not take into account the contribution of any pegs on the nose needed to prevent drowning.
(Dr) N. J. Mason, University of Oxford.

☐ DR MASON's method does not allow for the dense nature of the head, which contains much bone. A more accurate method is to float in the barrel, adjusting your lung volume to leave the head completely out of the water. While holding your breath, top up the barrel to the overflow and then submerge completely, collecting the displaced water, and measuring its volume. Climb out of the barrel, without further spillage, and then refill the barrel, measuring the volume needed. The floating volume of the body (the volume to keep the head up) can be calculated from the difference of the two volumes measured above. The weight of the head is the floating volume (in litres) less the body weight (in kilos).
J. B. Diamond, Hertford.

☐ J. B. DIAMOND's formula yields a head weight of zero, which cannot be right, even in J. B. Diamond's case.
M. J. Lloyd, London EC1.

☐ FIND a long board with pivotal centre mounting (e.g. a seesaw): weigh yourself unclothed, then lie on the board with the pivotal point coinciding with the base of the skull. Have someone place weights on the head end of the board up to a distance not exceeding the length from the pivot to the heels in the opposite direction. When the seesaw is balanced, deduct the sum of the added weights from your total body weight to obtain the weight of your head.
Jane Pepper, Canterbury.

☐ ENTERTAINING but wrong. If it worked, so would perpetual motion. An approximate answer would be got with the aid of muscle relaxant, a gravity meter, and a blow from Mike Tyson. But for a less dramatic method, take a seesaw, a ruler, and a large inanimate object. Balance flat on your back on the seesaw, then bend your head forward on to your chest. The seesaw will tilt: shuffle along to restore the balance. Measure the distance you have to shuffle and divide this by the amount by which you moved (the centre of) your head. This gives the weight of your head as a fraction of your whole body weight.
Peter Green, Department of Mathematics, University of Bristol.

☐ PETER GREEN gives a neat answer but I am left wondering what to do with the 'large inanimate object'. Here is an alternative solution that, again, assumes you can estimate the position of the centre of gravity of the head. Take a plank longer than your body and place it across two weighing scales that act as pivotal points. Lie along the plank with head to the left of the left pivot, and move the right pivot until it reads the same as the left one. (Each reading will equal half the combined weight of body and plank.) Saw off and weigh a length of plank to the right so that the shortened plank overhangs each pivot equally. The weight of the head is equal to the weight of this off-cut multiplied by the distance of the centre of gravity of the head from the left pivot and divided by the distance from the centre of the off-cut to the right pivot.
Rob Johnsey, Redditch, Worcs.

QUESTION: What is the origin of the expression 'sent to Coventry'?

☐ THERE are two explanations. In the medieval period Coventry was an important venue for monastic establishments: there were at least six within a five-mile radius of the city. In particular there was a silent order of Carthusian monks, one of only nine in Britain. They were granted land at Charterhouse, just off the London Road. If the London House had a monk among its brethren who found it difficult to adhere to the constraint of silence, the chatterbox was 'sent to Coventry'. There he would have his own small but detached cell, complete with workroom and garden, where silence would be a way of life rather than an imposition. The second, and

certainly more popular, theory concerns the Civil War and the Royalist Duke of Hamilton's Scottish soldiers, who were sent as 'prisoners of war' to the parliamentarian city of Coventry. They were held in the disused medieval Bablak Church (now the active Church of St John). As there was little chance of escape outside the city wall, they were allowed to walk around the town during the day. While the citizens did not treat them cruelly, they must have found their Scottish accents and different mode of dress more than a little strange, and preferred to give them a wide berth. This form of cold-shouldering thus led to the modern expression.
Lesley Pritchard, City Guide, Coventry.

QUESTION: Why is no food blue?

☐ THIS is not quite true: a limited number of edibles can be found in this hue. In the search for true blue foods it is important to discount impostors like blueberries, blue cheese and Blue Nun wine, which never live up to their names and are usually grey or purple. There is, however, a variety of American corn known as blue corn, which can be obtained in some shops in the form of tortilla chips which are not only convincingly blue but surprisingly delicious. For the most impressive edible deep blue colour you have to venture into the world of fresh wild fungi. When the flesh of many varieties of Boletus is broken or cut and exposed to the air the off-yellow flesh immediately turns a dark royal blue. Unfortunately this spectacular pigment is destroyed by cooking, so they would have to be served raw if you wanted to give the impression of having spilt ink over the salad. For some wonderful photographs of blue fungi see *Mushrooms*, by Roger Phillips.
Alasdair Friend, Edinburgh.

☐ ALASDAIR FRIEND cites 'blue corn' (maize) as an example of blue food. This is not so simple. The maize grain is pinkish in colour until it is treated with a preparation of wood ashes, which turns it blue. This is but one example of a large range of plant pigments of the anthocyanin family, which are pink when acid and blue when alkaline. Since most plant foods are mildly acidic when fresh, anthocyanin-coloured foods are very rarely seen in their blue form. To see this effect very simply, try adding sodium bicarbonate

(alkali) to chopped red cabbage, and then reversing the effect with vinegar or lemon juice (acid).
Erica Wheeler, London School of Hygiene and Tropical Medicine, University of London.

☐ THE answer given by Alasdair Friend neglects the fact that blue food is not normally attractive to humans. Fifteen years ago I spent a year at the Australian scientific base at Mawson, Antarctica. As the base was cut off for most of the year, the cook had to bake bread for about 30 people. He occasionally got fed up with baking every morning and he would add a few drops of blue dye to the dough. Although in all other respects the bread was exactly the same, hardly anyone could bring himself to eat it and the cook had a couple of mornings free from baking while the blue bread went stale. If anyone complained, he just said that the blue bread was perfectly edible, as indeed it was.
P. M. Davies, Newport, Gwent.

QUESTION: What is the origin of the mortar-board headgear worn by graduates?

☐ IN THE European universities of the 12th century it was customary to award the graduating scholar a special cap, which was known variously as a *pileus* or biretta. It appears originally to have been a plain round bonnet crowned with a small tuft, or apex, and was worn over a skull-cap or coif. Around the year 1500 it became fashionable to pinch the crown of the cap into four corners, allegedly to represent the sign of the cross (universities were ultimately under the authority of the Pope). This came to be known as the *pileus quadratus* ('square cap'), and was referred to in English as the cater-cap or corner-cap. In some instances the cap developed into a more rigid, formalised headgear. Among Catholic clerics it became the biretta, still worn today, and the fins on its crown recall the quartering on the original *pileus*. Meanwhile in England, by the end of the 17th century, in the academic world the same cap had been reduced to a square of pasteboard covered with black serge and attached to a rigid skull-cap. This was the forerunner of the modern mortar-board. The original soft, flat cap is still worn by many female graduates and by female members of numerous church choirs.
J. P. Fortune, London SW6.

QUESTION: In French it's '*impasse*'; in English it's 'cul-de-sac', which, if it means anything, means 'bag's bottom'. Can anyone explain?

□ CUL-DE-SAC, meaning 'dead-end road', was in use in France in the 18th century and you will find the expression in several novels of the period. My *Petit Robert* also quotes Victor Hugo using it in this context. Presumably, we picked it up in this country sometime after that, while the French moved on to the more modern *impasse* (which, of course, we use too, meaning 'deadlock'). Cul-de-sac, or 'bottom of the bag', is a wonderfully graphic expression for a dead end, something you go down and can't find the way out of.
Claire Watts, London.

□ I CANNOT explain cul-de-sac but I can quote a similar example of what I call a 'false Gallicism' which may shed some light on the matter. *Brassière*, authentic French for 'child's sleeved vest', is a false Gallicism for authentic French *soutien gorge*, meaning literally, 'throat support' (French female anatomy seems to differ from its English counterpart). As far as I know, there is no English word for *brassière*. Perhaps we could follow the German *Bustenhalter* ('bust-holder').
Joseph Witriol, FIL Translator, London N12.

QUESTION: Why is a pirate flag called the Jolly Roger?

□ THE Pembrokeshire pirate Bartholomew Roberts, known as Barti Dhu or Black Barti, had as his personal flag a skeleton on a black background. Other pirates liked the design and copied it. Barti wore a red coat and the French nicknamed him '*Le Joli Rouge*', which was corrupted into 'Jolly Roger' and came to mean the flag rather than the person. Barti was a rather strait-laced sort of pirate who banned drinking on board ship, insisted on early nights for the crew and never attacked on a Sunday. He was killed in an encounter with a Royal Navy ship in 1722, aged 40. Yours with a yo-ho-ho and a bottle of rum.
Diana Salmon, Llanfyrnach, Dyfed.

☐ Yo ho . . . er, hang on a bit. May I contradict Ms Salmon? The Jolly Roger, or Skull-and-Crossbones, was first used by a French pirate, Emmanuel Wynne, about 1700.
J. Claydon, Newmarket, Suffolk.

☐ Another possibility is that English pirates in the Indian Ocean began to refer to the red flag of the Tamil pirate Ali Raja by his name and 'Ally Roger' or 'Olly Roger' was later corrupted to Jolly Roger. The English word 'roger', meaning a vagabond rogue, may be another explanation. David Mitchell, in his book *Pirates*, discusses this question and seems to prefer a derivation from Old Roger – a synonym for the Devil.
Graham Hulme, Leicester.

QUESTION: It is a much quoted maxim that there are only seven stories in fiction and that all others are based on them. Is it true, and what might these seven stories be?

☐ If it is true, do you think someone should introduce Barbara Cartland to the other six?
Jim McNeil, Sheffield, S. Yorks.

☐ I'm not sure about plots for stories, but plots for plays is something my father, the Irish playwright Denis Johnston, had a lot to say about. Originally he thought there were seven, but then he realised there are in fact eight:
1. Cinderella – or unrecognised virtue at last recognised. It's the same story as the Tortoise and the Hare. Cinderella doesn't have to be a girl, nor does it even have to be a love story. What is essential is that the Good is despised, but is recognised in the end, something that we all want to believe.
2. Achilles – the Fatal Flaw that is the groundwork for practically all classical tragedy, although it can be made comedy too, as in the old standard Aldwych farce. Lennox Robinson's *The Whiteheaded Boy* is the Fatal Flaw in reverse.
3. Faust – the Debt that Must be Paid, the fate that catches up with all of us sooner or later. This is found in all its purity as the chase in O'Neill's *The Emperor Jones*. And in a completely different mood, what else is *The Cherry Orchard*?

4. Tristan – that standard triangular plot of two women and one man, or two men and one woman. *The Constant Nymph* or almost any French farce.
5. Circe – the Spider and the Fly. *Othello. The Barretts of Wimpole Street* if you want to change the sex. And if you don't believe me about *Othello* (the real plot of which is not the triangle and only incidentally jealousy) try casting it with a good Desdemona but a poor Iago.
6. Romeo and Juliet – Boy meets Girl, Boy loses Girl, Boy either finds or does not find Girl – it doesn't matter which.
7. Orpheus – The Gift taken Away. This may take two forms: either the tragedy of the loss itself, as in *Juno and the Paycock*, or it may be about the search that follows the loss, as in *Jason and the Golden Fleece.*
8. The Hero Who Cannot Be Kept Down. The best example of this is that splendid play *Harvey*, made into a film with James Stewart.

These plots can be presented in so many different forms – tragedy, comedy, farce, whodunnit – and they can be inverted, but they still form the basis of all good writing. The fault with many contemporary plays is simply that they do not have a plot.
Rory Johnston, London NW3.

☐ RORY JOHNSTON's listing of eight basic plots for plays seems very inadequate. Georges Polti, in his famous book, *The Thirty-Six Dramatic Situations*, classified these not by legendary/mythological tales of archetypes or personalities (Faust, Circe, etc.) but by the situation itself, e.g., no. 10, 'Abduction'; no. 25, 'Adultery'; no. 3, 'Crime Pursued by Vengeance', etc., etc. Nobody to my knowledge has improved on Polti's 36 possible plots, though some of his sub-divisions taken from classical models are, to say the least, tenuous (Situation 26e: 'A woman enamoured of a bull'). Confusion may have arisen with the old saying among comedians that there are only seven basic jokes.
John Pilkington, Playwright, Exeter, Devon.

☐ TO MR JOHNSTON'S eight plots for plays you can add David and Goliath – the individual against the repressive/corrupt powers of the state or community, or their rival claims. As in *Enemy Of The People*, *The Visit* and, of course, *Antigone*.
Leslie Caplan, London NW3.

□ CONSIDER the following application of Mr Johnston's eight prototypical plots:
1. Cinderella. Rick, an expat Yank bar-owner in wartime Morocco, begins as a drunken cynic but his 'essential goodness' is at last celebrated.
2. Achilles. Like the Greek warrior, the proud, 'fatally flawed' Rick – once a doer of great deeds – spends most of the story sulking in his tent. He is forced into selfless action only for the sake of the refugee Elsa, the woman he loves.
3. Faust. Rick's good looks, fame and wealth may be parochial but they are Faustian and gratuitous. Inevitably, Rick's debt is called in and he gives up his business, his girl and everything he has lived for.
4. Tristan. Manly Rick (Tristan) loves and is loved by sultry Elsa (Isolde) but she is already married to wimpish Victor Laszlo (King Mark).
5. Circe. Elsa's wiles entice Rick into her service only to destroy him.
6. Romeo and Juliet. Once, in Paris, Rick and Elsa loved and lost each other. Here, in Morocco, they get back together but are finally parted again.
7. In a concrete sense the gift taken away is a Letter of Transit which would enable Rick to go back to America but which he is forced to give up to Laszlo. More symbolically, the gift is of personal happiness and is sacrificed to political necessity, since to save Laszlo is to save the world for democracy.
8. The Irrepressible Hero is Rick personified.
There is also a ninth archetypical story-line, The Wandering Jew, which is bafflingly excluded from Mr Johnston's list. Rick is, of course, the persecuted traveller who will never return home. Thus, instead of eight (or nine) stories, there is only one, and it is called *Casablanca*.
Robin Blake, London WC1.

□ THERE are only about seven themes in fiction, and they include Love, Money, Power, Revenge, Survival, Glory and Self-awareness. It is the quest for these that makes a story. Most stories have more than one theme and it is the superimposition of themes, with the arising conflicts, that makes a story interesting. Robin Blake's suggestion that all stories can be imposed on the *Casablanca* plot is really saying that *Casablanca* contains several basic themes,

which it does, most of which are not resolved and in general are badly written. Nevertheless, the film is good because of its dramatic tension, partly created by the fact that actors were given their scripts on a daily basis, so never knew the ending themselves. It might also have been quite a different film if the original actor chosen for the lead had played the part: Ronald Reagan.
Stan Hayward, Author of Scriptwriting For Animation, *London NW2.*

QUESTION: What is the origin of the three brass monkeys with hands covering eyes, ears and mouth? Are these the same as the monkeys that suffer in cold weather?

□ I THINK they originate in Japan. In the Tosho-gu shrine in Nikko, built in the 17th century, the three monkeys are one of a series of eight carvings, meant to exemplify ideal behaviour on the part of children – they should see, speak and hear no evil, for example.
Edward Curran, London SE27.

□ IT SEEMS likely that the three monkeys (*sanbikizaru*) do have a Japanese origin, since they are in fact a Japanese pun. The word for 'monkey' (*saru* or *zaru*) is homophonous with the negative verb ending *zaru*. It is therefore a fairly obvious play on words to represent the slogan *mizaru, kikazaru, iwazaru* ('see nothing, hear nothing, say nothing') by means of three monkeys in appropriate attitudes – just as you might, if you wished, represent the English 'catastrophic, catagmatic, catalytic' by means of three cats. The word *mizaru* ('see nothing') can also mean 'three monkeys'.
G. H. Healey, School of East Asian Studies, Sheffield University.

□ THE 'suffering' of brass monkeys in cold weather has nothing to do with the castration of primates. In the days of sailing ships, men-o'-war carried cannon-balls in pyramidal heaps on the gun deck. They were prevented from rolling about by having the bottom layer enclosed in a triangular frame (like an enlarged version of the frame used to set up the balls at the start of a

snooker game) which was made of brass and known to sailors as a 'monkey'. This arrangement was very stable against all but the most violent pitching and rolling, except in cold weather. Then, the brass monkey (since it had a greater coefficient of expansion than the cast-iron cannon-balls) would shrink relative to the bottom row of balls and thrust them upward. Beyond a certain point this would put the centre of gravity of each bottom ball too high for stability. Hence the expression 'Cold enough to freeze the balls off a brass monkey'.
D. E. M. Price, Handsworth, Birmingham.

□ MR PRICE'S explanation of the cold-weather problems of these primates is ingenious but unconvincing. Over the relevant range of temperatures, the differential contraction of a brass trivet versus a pyramid of cast-iron cannon-balls is unlikely to amount to more than fractions of a millimetre. While it might just be possible with modern manufacturing techniques to replicate the effect described under laboratory conditions, it seems highly unlikely that the builders of men-o'-war were capable of manufacturing to such fine tolerances as to reliably cause the phenomenon your correspondent described.
Gavin C. Bell, Aberdeen.

□ THE myth of 'brass monkeys' aboard sailing warships has no basis in reality. In 20 years of research into men-of-war, I have found absolutely no contemporary evidence for their existence. In fact, cannon-balls were carried in wooden racks fitted to the sides of the ship beside the guns. In 1780 an order was issued by the Navy Board to replace these with holes drilled in the coamings (the raised timbers round the hatchways). Since this would have cost practically nothing, it is very difficult to see why anyone would think of using an expensive material such as brass; especially since, according to the myth, it was not very effective in cold weather. Brass ought to survive under water much better than wood or iron, yet I have never heard of anything like a 'brass monkey' being recovered from a shipwreck.
Brian Lavery, Assistant Curator (Naval Technology), the Historic Dockyard, Chatham, Kent.

QUESTION: How long is a piece of string?

☐ IT'S this long.
H. MacLean, Easdale, Argyll.

☐ I REMEMBER reading in an Arabian Nights book way back in the Thirties of a certain Caliph of Baghdad who would give his daughter to any man of wealth who could answer three questions correctly. Failure, of course, meant an early departure from the mortal coil. One crafty prince decided that a visit to the King of the Underworld was in order, not trusting the Caliph to play a straight bat. His Satanic Majesty was happy to oblige for the usual fee (the prince's soul). Two of the questions were: 'How long is a piece of string?' and 'How deep is the ocean?' The answer to the first is 'From end to end' and the second 'One stone's throw'. The third question eludes me. Incidentally, the prince won his princess but had problems with Satan later on.
W. L. Gange, Carnforth, Lancs.

☐ I DON'T know but the *Guardian* once reported that under the new schools curriculum seven-year-olds would be required to 'find a quarter of a piece of string'.
Marion Sweeney, Caerphilly, Mid Glam.

☐ I HAVE waited with some interest for a serious answer to this question but have so far been disappointed; it raises important issues. Firstly, there are questions to be answered about the determinacy of the boundaries of objects. Secondly, there are questions about the relative accuracy of different measuring instruments and methods. Thirdly, it raises profound questions about the fundamental nature of the universe, i.e. wave versus particle explanations, and the Einsteinian concepts of time and the effect of relative movement. Could someone with the appropriate qualifications be bold enough to venture the answers which I do not feel qualified to give?
Tony Faulkner, Rochester, Kent.

QUESTION: How do food companies work out the number of calories in their products?

☐ THE calorific content is measured with a device known as the bomb calorimeter. A sample of food is placed in an airtight

chamber – the 'bomb' – which is filled with pure oxygen and then placed in a tank of water. The food is ignited by an electric spark so it completely burns up. The temperature increase in the water is measured and the actual energy content of the food can then be calculated, either in old-fashioned calories or more modern joules. This method is not completely accurate, as it is rather crude when compared to the way the human body uses food. For example, proteins are completely burned up in the bomb calorimeter, whereas in the human body some of them would be used not for energy but for the production of things like skin, hair, mucus and muscle tissue. Incidentally, the subject is well covered in most biology textbooks for A-level and above, as well as in the occasional *Open University* programme on television.
Daniel Foster, Breaston, Derbyshire.

□ THE four sources of food energy – protein, fat, carbohydrate and alcohol – yield 4, 9, 3.75 and 7 calories per gram respectively. The calorie value of a food is usually estimated by multiplying the protein, fat, carbohydrate and alcohol content by the appropriate factors. Many food manufacturers do not carry out chemical analyses but instead estimate the calorie content using values for ingredients derived from tables published by HMSO. Such calculations are normally within 10 per cent of the actual value.
(Dr) Tom Sanders, King's College, University of London.

QUESTION: The idea of shipwrecked mariners sending messages in bottles has become a cliché. Are there any documented examples of this resulting in rescue?

□ ON 17 January 1876, an Austrian merchant ship was wrecked off the Atlantic islands of St Kilda. Nine crewmen were given hospitality by the islanders who were themselves in danger of starving owing to the severity of the winter. The sailors and islanders combined to launch two SOS vessels to take advantage of the Gulf Stream currents and inform the mainland of their joint distress. These 'vessels', containing a bottled message, were little canoes hewn out of log and attached to an inflated sheep's stomach. One vessel reached Orkney within nine days; the other reached Poolewe in Wester Ross within 22 days. HMS *Jackal* was despatched to

St Kilda and took the shipwrecked Austrians to the mainland. (Source: Tom Steel, *The Life and Death of St Kilda*, Fontana).
Hector Urquhart, Loughborough, Leics.

QUESTION: Is it really feasible that a chimpanzee with a typewriter and an infinite amount of time will be able to produce the complete works of Shakespeare?

☐ ACCORDING to the Darwinian theory of evolution, a chimp did just that.
George Armstrong, Silloth, Cumbria.

☐ LET'S give the chimp a chance and provide a special keyboard with just 26 capital letters, a few punctuation marks and an oversized space-bar, the size of 10 regular keys. Assuming, say, 60 words per minute and no breaks, we can expect to wait about eight hours before the word 'To' (with a space leading and following) comes into view. Extending to the phrase 'To be' would require another 12 hours of labour, while 'To be or' would warrant a lot of patience, some 140,000 years' worth, not to mention around 4,500 million pages of paper used in the process. A fraction of a sonnet, let alone an entire play, would require 'more books than could fit into the whole world' (John 21:25), as the gospel writer enigmatically puts it. Thus, for practical reasons, the answer has to be no.
Christopher R. Palmer, Department of Community Medicine, Cambridge University.

☐ ASSUME the chimpanzee has the unusual benefit of a keyboard with only 27 keys: one for each letter of the alphabet and one for space. Assume the beast hits these keys completely at random at a strike rate of one per second. And assume the chimpanzee's immediate task is to type the word 'MACBETH'. The chimpanzee has a one-in-27 chance of striking the letter 'M' with its first tap: relatively quick and easy. There are 729 (27 x 27) possible two-letter sequences: to type at random 'M' followed by 'A' with one second between each strike would take (according to the laws of probability) 12 minutes and nine seconds. 'MAC' is one of 19,683 possible three-letter sequences; and 19,683 seconds is five hours

28 minutes and three seconds. If one continues to multiply by 27 as the sequence grows, it will be found that the six letters of MACBET will, in probability, not be reached for 12 years. It will be 331 years before the word MACBETH is stumbled over by accident. Of course, a chimpanzee with an awful lot of luck could do the job in just seven seconds.
R. D. Phillips, Chorlton-cum-Hardy, Manchester.

□ IT ALL depends on what you mean by 'really feasible'. Given an infinite amount of time anything that could happen will happen. The complete works of Shakespeare produced by a typewriter-toting chimpanzee is such a possibility, i.e. it is not logically self-contradictory. Whether an infinite amount of time is 'really feasible' is the crunch question. The problem thus is not to do with the chimpanzee but with the lifespan of the universe. If the universe lasts for ever, the chimpanzee will make it. My bet is that it won't, because it isn't.
(Dr) William Johnson, Arnside, Cumbria.

□ I HAVE had this problem with apes before. As soon as they learn to type a 12-line essay, such as 'How I Spent My Summer Holiday', they think they are God's gift to literature. Before you can say 'Twelfth Night', they are off looking for something better. Those who show any real promise may make it to Hollywood as scriptwriters, where they will find there is no shortage of people prepared to slap them on the back and hand them a banana daiquiri. After a while the novelty wears off and the decline is normally rapid – from hack writer to bit parts in Tarzan films, then skid row.
Murray Allison, London N8.

□ ALL THE answers so far assume that the only restriction is the amount of time available. But ribbons and typewriters wear out, trees have to be cut down to make paper, chimps have to be fed. So unlimited resources would be needed. One thing cosmologists seem to be agreed on is that the amount of matter in the universe is finite (the great astrophysicist Arthur Eddington reckoned that it contained only 10 raised to the power of 79 protons), so even with infinite time the odds against stochastic Shakespeare are even longer than those calculated by your correspondents.
S. K. Epton, Whitby, S. Wirral.

□ THE chimpanzee must be understood as an example of randomness and the complete works of Shakespeare as an example of an enormous number of symbols of 27 different types (the letters of the alphabet plus the space bar for separating words) arranged in a specific order. Knowing how long it would take to type just one word even if working at a good speed, and knowing that the chimp will succeed in typing the complete works of Shakespeare (because given that amount of time it is necessarily so) we realise that infinity is a concept quite difficult to understand. So the answer is: of course it is feasible, but as long as you think of the chimpanzee as not being a real one and the same with the typewriter and the paper it uses. It's only a way of picturing an abstract idea.
Alex Guardiet, Fulwood, Sheffield.

□ THE complete works of Shakespeare would never occur by chance. The chimpanzee is faced with 27 keys and may press any of them. Therefore, all letters (and the space bar) would have an equal chance of being selected and in any large sample each would occur approximately the same number of times. Absolute equality would be approached more and more closely as the amount of typing increased. The letters comprising the complete works of Shakespeare are far from a random selection. In English the letters 'A', 'D', 'E', 'I', 'N', 'O', 'R', 'S' and 'T' occur far more frequently than 'J', 'K', 'Q', 'V', 'X' and 'Z'. It would be impossible for a chimpanzee to produce a lengthy, random sequence of letters that reflected this inequality. One might expect the letters towards the centre of the keyboard to be hit more frequently than those towards the ends. However, this possibility does not improve the chances of the works of Shakespeare being typed by chance. On a standard 'Qwerty' keyboard, 'A' occurs to the extreme left, whereas 'J' and 'V' are near the middle.
Gregory Beecroft, Welwyn Garden City, Herts.

□ GREGORY BEECROFT appears to have been hitting a few random keys himself when he claims that the complete works 'would never occur by chance' because the letters of the alphabet are not equally frequent in English but are hit with equal probability by the chimpanzee. Even if two events – say the typing of a 'Z' and the typing of an 'E' – are equally probable, this does not necessarily mean they will occur equally often in a given random sequence. Similarly, there is no guarantee that any sequence of tosses of an

unbiased coin will produce equal (or even approximately equal) numbers of heads and tails. A thousand consecutive heads, although exceedingly unlikely, is not an impossibility with a fair coin; neither is Shakespeare with a chimpanzee. The letter frequencies used by Shakespeare are irrelevant. Any pre-specified sequence of letters is just as likely to occur as any other, regardless of its composition. Thus a sequence consisting entirely of 'Z's is no more or less likely to be produced than any other given sequence (including Shakespeare's works). Even if Shakespeare's works consisted entirely of 'zzzzzzzzzzzzz . . .' (*A Midsummer Night's Dream*, perhaps?) the chimp's chances would not have changed.
Ben Craven, Stirling.

□ DISREGARDING practical considerations such as typewriter wear and the expiry of the universe, and assuming the chimp continues to press the keys at random, Mr Guardiet claims it will 'necessarily' produce a copy of the works of Shakespeare and Mr Beecroft that it will never achieve the feat. Both are wrong. In an infinitely long random series of typewriter symbols you can expect any finite string of such symbols – whether a short one such as 'to be' or a longer one such as Shakespeare's complete works – to occur an infinite number of times. In this case, Shakespeare's works should appear just as often in the ape's typescript as any given string of the same length containing unusual letters of the alphabet in the same proportion as common ones. However, there remains a tiny chance that the string sought will never occur. Infinite number theory gives fascinating results and it is hard to illustrate how small this chance is. If you imagine enough eternally typing chimps to completely fill a Newtonian universe of infinite size then you would still need more before probability favoured one of them omitting the works of Shakespeare from its script.
Graham Haigh, Milnthorpe, Cumbria.

□ SCANDALOUSLY, the literary implications have hardly been considered by previous correspondents. In order to produce one 'complete works' the chimp would first have to produce, in addition to millions of pages of complete garbage, thousands of incomplete works (it would also be certain to pass through several minor poets on the way). If it were possible to do it at all, then it should be possible to improve on the original. Some of the many variant versions would be free of all sexism,

racism and militarism. That would indeed be a complete edition of Shakespeare.
Gabriel Chanan.

□ PERHAPS if the problem involved a monkey producing the complete works of Jeffrey Archer people would find it easier to believe that the feat would, unfortunately, be achieved.
M. J. Moody, Beeston, Notts.

□ I AM currently engaged in trials with some chimpanzees to find out whether, given an inexhaustible supply of materials, they can produce a nuclear missile.
A. P. Eines, Southbourne, Dorset.

QUESTION: Has anyone ever died of boredom?

□ ON THE face of it, George Sanders, the suave film actor, would seem a likely candidate. When in 1972 he did away with himself with a lethal cocktail of Nembutal and vodka, the most publicised of his three suicide notes declared: 'Dear World. I am leaving because I am bored. I feel I have lived long enough. I am leaving you with your worries in this sweet cesspool. Good luck.' But Sanders had been suffering for some time from a screwed up private life, feelings of rootlessness, severe financial problems and deteriorating health. The give-away word is 'cesspool'. However stylish the form of his farewell note, 'boredom' is scarcely the word to summarise his sad decline. Since chronic boredom is closely linked with depression – is, in fact, a form of depression – it's doubtful that anyone ever died of boredom in the relatively trivial everyday sense of the word. However, when human beings are subjected to solitary confinement and sensory deprivation, they are often brought to the brink of despair and self-destruction.
Neil Hornick, London NW11.

□ DEAN W. R. Inge was accurate in his contention (see *The End of an Age*, 1948) that: 'The effect of boredom on a large scale in history is underestimated. It is a main cause of revolutions . . .' The answer has to be yes, lots.
(Rev.) Clifford Warren, Machen Rectory, Gwent.

☐ BOREDOM has certainly been responsible for a number of deaths, often by mistake. Louis XIV regularly started wars out of sheer boredom. In Chicago in 1923 Nathan Leopold and Michael Loeb plotted the murder of a schoolboy, just as a relief for their interminable ennui. Death has also been caused in trivial moments of tedium: on 2 November 1973, a passenger was killed on a DC10 because an engine exploded after a bored flight engineer had meddled with a few of the buttons in the cockpit. Although Samuel Beckett's two tramps in *Waiting For Godot* might be suffering a terminal boredom when they whine 'we are bored to death', and Nasa is worried that it may well cause serious problems on the manned mission to Mars, it's unlikely that boredom leads to the final decision to die rather than continue a life of bland indifference. In the words of Morissey, that guru of bedsit boredom: 'I think about life and I think about death, but neither one particularly appeals to me.'
John Dutton and Chris Horrocks, London N4.

☐ MY FAMILY is convinced that an actor cousin, who died sadly while in the cast of *The Mousetrap*, must indeed have died of boredom.
S. Marking, Toller Whelme, Dorset.

☐ ON 31 July 1861, whichever of the Goncourt brothers was on *Journal* duty that day asked whether their lack of success might actually mean they were failures. He then adds: 'One thing reassures me as to our value: the boredom that afflicts us. It is the hallmark of quality in modern men. Chateaubriand died of it, long before his death. Byron was stillborn with it.'
Richard Boston, Reading, Berks.

QUESTION: What causes travel sickness? Are there any cures other than pills and what is the best type of car to buy to avoid this?

☐ IN MOST cases the cause is the driver, not the car. Drivers who swoop round corners, brake from 60 mph to zero in 50 yards or take off from 0 to 60 in 10 seconds flat are the culprits.
R. Legg, Helston, Cornwall.

☐ THE brain accepts information about our position and movement from our eyes, our organs of balance in our ears and from position and pressure sensors throughout our body. Travel sickness is usually caused by not providing an appropriate visual input (it can be caused by reading in the back of a car, for example). A simple solution is to look outside, preferably forwards. In general, a car with a rough or harsh ride will cause less sickness than one with a soft, spongy suspension.
(Dr) Guy Lightfoot, West Kirby, Wirral.

☐ BEFORE driving to Italy in our wallowing Citroën I made my long-suffering 11-year-old daughter sit on a copy of the *Guardian* – as advised by our local basket-maker. After twisting and turning our way up the scenic route of the Grand St Bernard Pass in the Alps and down again, feeling very green myself, I inquired how she felt. 'I think I'm hungry', she said. After another tortuous drive that never fails to make us all ill, she answered: 'I'm fine, why?' I wonder if this works for anyone else, and why?
Christine Hare, Rooks Bridge, Somerset.

☐ HOME-MADE ginger biscuits are a very effective remedy. Make them with double the normal amount of powdered ginger and remember to save some for the return journey.
Peggy Loy, Maidstone, Kent.

☐ I AM surprised no one has so far recommended Sea Bands. These are elasticated wrist bands worn by the sufferer during journeys. They are said to work on acupuncture principles by exerting pressure, via a plastic stud, on a particular point near the wrist. My husband's is a typical success story. He had previously tried many different pills, with little effect. Wearing Sea Bands he was able to enjoy a sea trip from Ullapool in a near gale, with a stomach full of fish and chips. The bands are available from most large chemists.
Judy Jackson, Little Hayfield.

☐ NONE of the answers is wholly satisfactory. Motion sickness occurs because the brain receives conflicting information from the various organs of sense. Particularly important are the semicircular canal balance organs in the middle ear which tell if you

are standing or lying, even with closed eyes. If the eyes say you are upright, and the canals say you are leaning, then loss of lunch may follow. The way to avoid travel sickness in a car is to 'bank' into the bends as the car turns. The driver does this naturally as the steering wheel is turned and held, thus they lean to the right as they steer to the right. However, a passenger, unless they take active action, will tend to be thrown to the left during a right-hand bend. Leaning the head to the same direction as the bend means that the centrifugal force of the turn is allowed for, and the semi-circular canals only feel a downward pull, albeit slightly stronger than normal gravity. If the head is allowed to be thrown outwards, then the canals feel a lateral force akin to lying when the eyes inform them that they are vertical. Nausea will follow, and is commoner with a driver who goes faster round bends, generating stronger centrifugal forces. Whether or not there are beneficial effects to the eating of ginger biscuits I do not know, but as to copies of the *Guardian* under the posteriors of sufferers, there is more logic than may appear to this, though any newspaper will do. The point is that several sheets of paper are slightly slippery. To sit comfortably on a slippery surface in a moving vehicle requires some movement to avoid being thrown about. The natural tendency, as your bottom slides to the left, is to lean to the right, and thus produce the banking of the head so essential to avoid travel sickness. The other offerings for travel sickness, such as big cars or earthing devices, have little effect *per se*. However, belief plays a part, and perhaps faith in a concept can overcome a little centrifugal force. After all, if faith can move mountains, keeping lunch down should be a doddle.
(Dr) Stephen Seddon, Newcastle under Lyme, Staffs.

QUESTION: Why do men have fewer ribs than women?

□ MEN and women have 12 pairs of ribs (a few individuals have 13 or 11 pairs). The idea that men have fewer ribs than women is widespread but wrong, perhaps deriving from the biblical story of Eve being made from one of Adam's ribs.
Steve Harper, Lecturer in Anatomy and Physiology, Thanet Technical College, Broadstairs, Kent.

□ IT'S untrue. There is, however, a disease known as cervical rib

which produces a single extra rib at the base of the neck. This is very rare indeed and can occur in either sex.
James Mercer, Sheffield.

QUESTION: 'Bob's your uncle.' Who is Bob?

□ ROBERT Arthur Talbot Gascoyne-Cecil, third Marquess of Salisbury and Prime Minister in 1887, when he promoted (not for the first time) his nephew A. J. Balfour to be Chief Secretary for Ireland in a move widely interpreted as an unusually literal act of nepotism. Balfour himself later became Prime Minister, and later still the Foreign Secretary who made the Balfour Declaration in 1917. Originally 'Bob's your uncle' was presumably an ironic or jocular catchphrase meaning 'It's all right for you' (i.e. you've got an Uncle Bob), though now it has lost its tone.
B. A. Phythian, Keston, Kent.

QUESTION: Why, when a footballer scores three goals in a game, is it called a 'hat-trick'?

□ THE term originated in cricket and refers to the bowler's taking of three wickets in successive balls. George MacDonald Fraser (*Flashman's Lady*, set in 1843) claims the first use for Flashman. When he takes his third wicket (by cheating), the victim, Alfred Mynn, presents Flashman with his straw boater as he leaves the field with the words: 'That trick's worth a new hat any day, youngster.' More seriously, Eric Partridge (*Historical Slang*), giving 1882 as the probable date of origin, says it entitled its professional performer to a collection, or to a new hat from his club. Amateur players, being gentlemen, could, presumably, afford their own hats.
Ramin Minova, Moseley, Birmingham.

□ DAVID HARRIS, the great Hambledon bowler of the 1780s, was presented with a gold-laced hat after a fine spell of bowling, though not actually taking three wickets with successive deliveries. Around 1800 the first top hat, a white beaver, came into vogue and was awarded by some clubs to bowlers who took three wickets with successive deliveries. This practice grew until the late 1800s

when the tasselled cap, boater and pill-box cap made the top hat no longer *de rigueur*. The hat-trick was then coined by other sports to indicate a three-fold success.
Steve Pittard, Langport, Somerset.

□ WHEN football was in its infancy, and hence footballers were not professional, top scorers were not rewarded for their goals. If a player scored three goals in a match, a hat, or similar container, would be passed round for donations. I presume that only the home supporters would actually chip in.
Peter Orme, Winchester, Hants.

QUESTION: Why is the most common form of heterosexual coupling called the missionary position?

□ I MAY be wrong, but isn't the missionary position the one recommended by lay preachers?
Philip Oliver, Burton upon Trent, Staffs.

□ THIS appears to be so called not because it was used by missionaries (although that was probably the case) but because it was the position missionaries are supposed to have advocated for the 'lesser races' they were preaching to. There seem to be two reasons for this preference. The face-to-face position was thought more 'civilised' than other 'animalistic' ones and, secondly, it literally put the man on top. In this way the position embodied two key aspects of the 19th century middle-class view of the world. The evidence of sex positions in the past suggests that it was by no means the most preferred and perhaps not the most common. Presumably the missionaries encountered a situation where it was not so common otherwise they would not have had to advocate it. The rise of the missionary position, therefore, seems to be related to the intensificiation of a male dominated, imperialist, class society. But contemporary sex surveys also suggest that both men and women often get more pleasure from alternative positions. Readers sympathetic towards the Labour Party's current abandonment of class politics might like to consider the significance this has for their own lives. Not only are revolutionary positions more politically correct, they are also likely to be more fun.
Mike Haynes, Telford Socialist Workers Party, Telford, Shropshire.

☐ I AM fairly certain that Mike Haynes of the Socialist Workers Party has, unsurprisingly, adopted the wrong position over missionaries. The 'missionary position' was not advocated by them but was their conventional mode and observed as such by inquisitive Trobriand Islanders in the depth of the Polynesian night – and eventually reported to Malinovski *et al.* (q.v.). One matter is, however, illuminated by Haynes: the reluctance of SWP members to look one another in the eye.
R. A. Leeson, Broxbourne, Herts.

QUESTION: Why do your fingers go wrinkly in the bath?

☐ I ONCE asked champion swimmer Adrian Moorhouse whether he went wrinkly at the edges after hours of cranking up those practice lengths. The look of surprise on his face revealed that he had never even thought of the possibility. This suggests that whatever happens to people in their baths depends on some combination of hot water and soap.
Humphrey Evans, London N7.

☐ THE skin of the fingers is covered by a protective, waterproof layer called keratin. Under normal conditions this is translucent and flattened. However, when placed in water for some time, the protein begins to absorb water, becoming swollen and opaque. The top layer of the skin (epidermis) is tethered down to the lower layer (dermis) by means of 'papillary ridges', which form the fingerprint. The swollen keratin in the epidermis is therefore held down along the lines of the fingerprint, causing wrinkling.
(Dr) Janet Menage, Rugby, Warwicks.

QUESTION: What is art?

☐ THE definitive answer was provided 30 years ago by Marshall McLuhan: 'Art is anything you can get away with.'
John Whiting, London NW11.

☐ TOLSTOY offers the following definition: 'To evoke in oneself a feeling one has once experienced, and having evoked it in oneself, then, by means of movements, lines, colours, sounds or forms

expressed in words, so to transmit that feeling that others may experience the same feeling – that is the activity of art. Art is a human activity, consisting in this, that one man consciously, by means of certain external signs, hands on to others feelings he has lived through, and that other people are infected by these feelings, and also experience them.' (From *What is Art?* by L. Tolstoy, translated by A. Maude.)
George Crossley, Bradford.

□ THE best definition I have come across is by James Joyce: 'Art is the human disposition of sensible or intelligible matter for an aesthetic end.'
Wolf Suschitzky, London W2.

□ A WORK of art is a corner of creation seen through a temperament (Emile Zola).
C. Heritage-Tilley, Winchester, Hants.

□ ART is a stuffed crocodile (Alfred Jarry, 1873–1907, author of *Ubu Roi*).
Titus Alexander, London E17.

□ ART is 'pattern informed by sensibility' (Sir Herbert Read, *The Meaning of Art*).
Henry Burns Elliot, Colchester.

□ LIFE is serious but art is fun (source unknown).
Nathan Wood, Birmingham 15.

□ I LIKE Tolstoy's definition of art as the ability to transmit a feeling one has experienced to others through 'movements, lines, colours', etc. But surely pornography does this very effectively. Did Tolstoy consider pornography to be art?
Frank Miles, Beckenham, Kent.

□ NONE of the answers offered last week is satisfactory. McLuhan's 'Art is anything you can get away with' might admit undetected shoplifting or terrorism, neither of which would normally be considered art. Tolstoy's definitions suggest that the essential property of art is its ability to communicate the expression of emotion to a perceiver: though art often embodies this characteristic, the definition doesn't account for emotional communication,

which most people would recognise as 'outside art' in, for example, common expressions of anger or sadness. James Joyce's definition highlights the use of materials for aesthetic ends: this is quite convincing in the implication that a work of art must have been intended to be a work of art by the artist. The problem is that many works which are now widely accepted as art (such as cave paintings, ritual masks) were not made for aesthetic or artistic reasons. The hundreds of thought-provoking attempts to define art all hold true for some art but not for all art, and often are equally valid for things which are not generally understood to be art. Those who become exhausted by their attempts to answer the question with a single definition might take up the advice of the American philosopher Nelson Goodman and rephrase the question: 'when is an object a work of art?' The dynamic character of much of the most interesting art was, I think, well expressed by the artist Jeff Nuttall, who wrote in 1980, in an article entitled 'Art, Politics and Everything Else': 'Art is the skill of examining the range of our perceptions by the making of artefacts . . . Often the last place you're likely to find the perceptions being extended is in the compartment marked "art", which may have been frozen into stasis by devices like the Standards of Good Taste, Proven Criteria, the Maintaining of Tradition. In the drawer marked "art" there may well be no art at all.'
David Ainley, Matlock, Derbyshire.

☐ As Rock Hudson said in *Magnificent Obsession*: 'Art is just a boy's name.'
Hugh Raffles, London W14.

QUESTION: What is the scientific difference between plant life and animal life?

☐ The fundamental difference is in the way animals and plants take in carbon to form organic compounds. Plants are autotrophs, which means that they meet their carbon requirements solely from carbon dioxide in the atmosphere, or from water in the case of water-dwelling plants. Animals, being heterotrophs, are unable to make their own organic molecules and so must take them in ready-made by eating plants and other animals. Many of the more obvious differences between plants and animals result from

this basic difference. For example, animals are generally mobile because they need to catch prey or graze, whereas a sessile lifestyle is adequate for a plant's requirements. Despite the fact that we rarely see mushrooms running around the fields looking for something to eat, fungi, like animals, are heterotrophs. Their mobility comes from tiny spores. As each short-lived generation uses up its food source, the spores that will form the next generation are cast to the winds to find new food sources.
Tony Jobbins, Chipping Sodbury, Bristol.

QUESTION: If I say 'I always tell lies', am I telling the truth?

☐ THE human race is made up of three types of person: saints who always tell the truth, devils who always tell lies and sinners who sometimes tell the truth and sometimes tell lies. Logically a saint cannot say 'I always tell lies' since this would be a lie. A devil cannot logically say 'I always tell lies' since this would be the truth. Only a sinner can logically say 'I always tell lies', and this would be a lie.
L. Leckie, Salford.

☐ THIS is known as the Liar's Paradox. It has been around for several millennia and is usually attributed to Epimenides the Cretan, who said 'All Cretans are liars'. The quick answer is that while the question is valid from a grammatical viewpoint, from a logical point of view it is contrived contradictory nonsense. As the question is logically meaningless, any attempted answer would be meaningless also.
Mike Wallace, Glasgow.

☐ THIS is essentially the same as the dilemma faced by the barber who shaves all the men who don't shave themselves. The question is: who shaves the barber? Clearly he cannot shave himself because he only shaves those who don't shave themselves. However, he cannot remain unshaven as he would then have to shave himself. Logicians call this a circular argument or problem to which there is no solution. I therefore suggest that the questioner tells the truth all the time, so that the problem doesn't arise in future.
Gerard McEvoy, Bedford.

☐ Gerard McEvoy compares this with the so-called circular argument of the barber who shaves all men who don't shave themselves. The answer to the question 'Who shaves the barber?' is surely: 'No one. She doesn't shave.'
Mike Ashton, Welshpool, Powys.

☐ Bertrand Russell relates in his autobiography that he spent the summers of 1903 and 1904 trying to solve this contradiction, wandering the common at night and staring at a blank sheet of paper by day.
Frank Cummins, Warley, W. Midlands.

QUESTION: Why, in general, do women live longer than men?

☐ Evidence suggests that boys are the weaker sex at birth, with a higher infant mortality rate, and women seem to have a better genetic resistance to heart disease than men. The process of gender role socialisation means men are more likely to be brought up to 'shrug off' illnesses, they drink and smoke more, they are more aggressive and take more risks, are less careful in what they eat and are not socialised to show their emotions as much as women and so have less outlet for stress. Women are socialised to 'take care of themselves' more than men, and they are more likely to visit doctors, which may mean they receive better health care. Men generally live more hazardous lives than women. The more dangerous occupations, such as construction work, are likely to be done by men and they are therefore more at risk of industrial accidents and diseases. In the home, men are more likely to do the dangerous and risky jobs, such as using ladders and climbing on the roof. Men also make up the majority of car drivers and motorcyclists (63 per cent in 1990) and are therefore more at risk of death through road accidents. Men are more likely to work full-time and to work longer and more unsociable hours, such as overtime working and shiftwork, which can be harmful to health. Jobs carrying high levels of responsibility are more commonly done by men, which may cause higher levels of health-damaging stress. Men retire later than women (age 65 compared with 60) and this may also be an important factor in reducing their life expectation.
Ken Browne, Leamington Spa, Warwicks.

☐ KEN BROWNE fails to mention the most important influence on women's longevity: the tremendous reduction of death during or after childbirth in the last 100 years. Historically, women died in childbirth, men in wars, and both in agricultural accidents. Hence philosophers and nuns lived to a great age. Leaving aside the question of whether too much work is bad for you, it is not true that men work longer hours than women: all the evidence is that women have less leisure time than men because they still do most of the work in the home, whether or not they have a job. It is also an error to state that jobs carrying high levels of responsibility are necessarily more stressful. Studies of production-line workers have shown that repetitive tasks can produce high levels of stress. My grandfather, in an interview with the local paper on his 60th wedding anniversary (when both he and his wife were 90) attributed his longevity to 'hard work and eating sparingly'. They were teetotal Methodists and didn't smoke, but then not everyone would want to go 90 years without a drink.
Jacqueline Castles, London W2.

QUESTION: Am I entitled to my opinion?

☐ YOUR entitlement to your opinion is directly proportional to your ability to justify it.
Robin Boyes, Scarborough, N. Yorks.

☐ IT DEPENDS firstly on what your opinion is and secondly on what you want to do with it. The general rule, laid down in 1765, is that everything is permitted except that which is expressly prohibited: nobody may interfere with the holding or expressing of your opinions without specific authority. Thus it could be said that you are entitled to your opinion, even though there is no specific positive legal right to this effect. The difficulty with this, however, is of course that there are now several encroachments upon your 'liberty of opinion' – hence the qualified answer. You may not, for example, incite racial hatred. Neither may you blaspheme. Conversely, however, neither do you have the protection of the law against blasphemy unless you happen to belong to the correct culture or happen to hold the right religious convictions. So it's all right to ridicule some opinions or convictions (such as Islam)

but not others. Fans of Bills of Rights have yet to explain which opinions they would wish to see protected by such provisions as 'everyone has the right to freedom of thought, conscience and religion' as found in the European Convention.
Adam Tomkins, Lecturer in Law, King's College London.

□ You are entitled to your opinion so long as you voice it as an opinion and not as knowledge. Plato's opinion, as expressed in Book VII of *The Republic and Parmenides*, is that knowledge is certain and infallible, and therefore cannot, logically, be mistaken. Opinion can not only be mistaken but is necessarily so, since it assumes the reality of appearance. Thus, it is possible for there to be many opinions about one thing but only one truth. Plato could, of course, be wrong but who am I to argue with The Master?
Ruth B. Whalley, Hest Bank, Lancaster.

QUESTION: Is there a significant difference between the nutritional requirements of dogs and cats? If I feed my young tom-cat on Pedigree Chum, will he eventually turn up his toes?

□ He will eventually turn up his toes no matter what he is fed on.
N. Ashton, Neston, S. Wirral, Cheshire.

□ A cat will not thrive on any proprietary brand of dog food. Whereas dogs have catholic feeding habits and can subsist on low-protein or even meat-free diets, cats are necessarily carnivores and require relatively large amounts of animal protein. In addition, cats have other unique dietary needs. For example they require the aminosulphonic acid taurine, and are also thought to need preformed sources of niacin, vitamin A and arachidonic acid, all of which other mammals can synthesise from other components of the diet. These compounds are added to most prepared cat foods but are not usually present in sufficient quantity in dog food.
James Serpell, Dept of Clinical Veterinary Medicine, University of Cambridge.

QUESTION: What is the point of living?

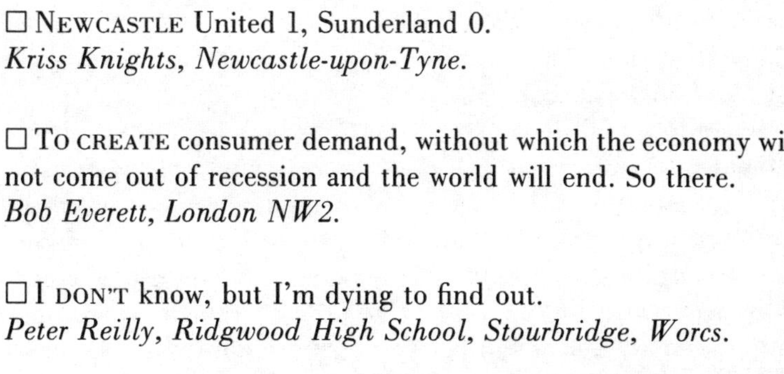

□ NEWCASTLE United 1, Sunderland 0.
Kriss Knights, Newcastle-upon-Tyne.

□ TO CREATE consumer demand, without which the economy will not come out of recession and the world will end. So there.
Bob Everett, London NW2.

□ I DON'T know, but I'm dying to find out.
Peter Reilly, Ridgwood High School, Stourbridge, Worcs.

□ SINCE Aristotle, the 'point' of life, if there is such a thing, has been taken as being its *telos* ('end' or 'aim'). Philosophy has two sorts of answer. The first is that is it not a genuine question, because 'living', like 'swimming', but unlike 'sleeping' or 'lying', can be pursued for its own sake: it doesn't presuppose somewhere to end up, nor is it the means to some further end which is part of the meaning of the idea. So a sufficient answer to 'Why are you swimming?' can be 'Because I like it', whereas to 'Why are you eating?' it would be, for example, 'Because I'm hungry'. The second approach is to look at it from the other side, and ask 'What is the point in not living?' Usually, one would reply that one has nothing to gain and no more to lose by not doing so. Neither approach is altogether satisfactory. The first reduces one's life to the sum of the thoughts and acts of a single mind and body, because it's just describing the activity of living. The second can't satisfy those who genuinely think their continued existence is too painful for all concerned to justify it. Both approaches fail because any description of a life 'from the outside' fails to capture what is most essential about it, that it is our life. Each person is left, therefore, to specify a point (or end) to their own living for themselves. It can be given to you, but only in so far as you are willing to take it on board as entirely your own. Sorry I can't be more helpful. Try drugs, and you can forget the problem; or religion, and get a made-to-measure answer.
Charles Cohen, Wadham College, Oxford.

□ THIS is easy. I understand (not being an Anglican myself) that the Church of England catechism says: 'Man's chief end is to glorify God and to enjoy Him for ever.'
Heather Lloyd, Glasgow.

☐ THE philosopher's answer:
1. 'To be is to do' (Socrates); 'To do is to be' (Sartre); 'Do be do be do' (Frank Sinatra).
2. According to Nietzsche, or I should say the wise Satyr Silenus, quoted by Nietzsche in *The Birth of Tragedy from the Spirit of Music*, there is no point to living. When hunted down and caught by King Midas, the wise Satyr Silenus, companion to Dionysus, answers Midas's question on what is the ultimate truth. 'Not to have been born, to be nothing,' he replies. 'But the second best is to die soon!' There you have it, right from the Satyr's mouth.
3. On the other hand, Albert Camus, in *The Myth of Sisyphus*, came to the conclusion that even in lives of little hope and extreme adversity, there are moments or suspended lulls in the tension when one can relax and view the world around one and one's meaning in relation to the world. Thus, Sisyphus, forced for eternity to push a boulder up to the top of a mountain only for it to roll back down the mountain again, could at least relax and recharge his batteries, and recognise his essential oneness with nature and the world around him in those moments when he had to walk back down the mountain to retrieve his boulder. By being at least conscious of the absurdity of his life, Sisyphus is happy. His consciousness ties him to the wholeness of nature and also to his essential freedom, which means that he cannot be dominated either by nature or by the gods who force him to push the boulder up the mountain: 'There is no fate that cannot be surmounted by scorn,' Camus says.
Nigel Polkinghorne, Penzance, Cornwall.

☐ THE point of anything is what comes at the end of it. The end of life is death – so death is the point of living.
(Dr) William Johnston, Arnside, Cumbria.

QUESTION: Given the availability of all known building materials and ideal rock to build on, what would be the height of the highest building that could be built today? What would be the constraining factor?

☐ WITH an infinite budget the normal limits of high-rise construction are removed. Loading can safely be distributed into the world's strongest bedrock using massive foundations. Overall

stability against wind loading and buckling will be assured if the building is allowed enough ground to be self-bracing. So, in pure structural terms, the controlling factor is the ability of the building frame to carry vertical loading. Assuming the building is a residential block (office loading is greater) and using solid steel columns of sensible style and spacing, to allow the building to be properly inhabited, an overall height of about 1,250 metres (450 storeys) is possible. A steel 'Eiffel' tower about 4,000 metres high is possible. I hope you realise that we are five years too late to get funding for this type of development.
Ian Hunt, London N10.

□ IF WE define buildings as man-made edifices above ground and containing spaces allowing humans to move about within the structure, then the pyramids of Egypt and Central America are buildings. Mount Everest is a natural pyramid; therefore, using granite blocks a conical or pyramidal building could be erected to a height of at least 10,000 metres. The actual constraining factors would be geological. Isostatic downwarping of the crust beneath the enormous weight of the structure would cause faults in the rock mass, while metamorphic processes at the core of the pyramid (melting of certain minerals in the granite due to pressure) would result in instability and collapse. These constraints could be overcome by giving the building a honeycomb or lattice structure and using a variety of lighter and more tensile materials than granite. Living spaces within the cone/pyramid could be provided, so creating a city perhaps tens of thousands of metres high. There would be increasing problems in supplying the higher levels with water, fuel, waste disposal and so forth and there would be complex ecological and climatic challenges to the architects. But perhaps the ultimate constraining factor is human nature: the general unpopularity of high-rise flats, and the biblical myth of the Tower of Babel suggest why such a conical mega-city could not succeed.
Michael Ghirelli, Hillesden, Bucks.

QUESTION: Why are Catholics sometimes called 'left-footers'?

□ THE answer lies in the rich folklore of the humble spade – and provides a good illustration of the inadequacy of calling a

spade 'a spade'. The saying turns on a traditional distinction between left- and right-handed spades in Irish agriculture. It has been used as a figure of speech and often, sadly, as a term of abuse to distinguish Protestants from Catholics: 'He digs with the wrong foot.' Most types of digging spade in Britain and Ireland have foot-rests at the top of their blades; two-sided spades have foot-rests on each side of the shaft and socket, while an older style of one-sided spade had only one. Two-sided spades may well have been introduced by the Protestant 'planters' in the 16th century. By the early 19th century specialised spade and shovel mills in the north of Ireland were producing vast numbers of two-sided spades which came to be universally used in Ulster and strongly identified with the province. One-sided spades with narrow blades and a foot-rest cut out of the side of the relatively larger wooden shaft continued in use in the south and west. The rural population of Gaelic Ireland retained the Catholic faith and tended also to retain the one-sided spade and 'dig with the wrong foot'. In fact, the two-sided spade of Ulster was generally used with the left foot whereas the one-sided spade tended to be used with the right foot. Instinctively, the 'wrong foot' of the Catholics has come to be thought of as the left foot. The figure of speech has now been extended to kicking with the wrong foot.
Hugh Cheape, National Museums of Scotland, Edinburgh.

QUESTION: Can a person like Wagner's music and still be a socialist?

□ *The Perfect Wagnerite*, George Bernard Shaw's book, argues that Wagner's *Ring* cycle is a political allegory offering a critique of capitalism. For Shaw, the Gods are to be interpreted as the aristocracy, the Giants as peasants, the Nibelungs as the proletariat and Alberich as a capitalist. Even Siegfried, the sword-wielding superman himself, is a model for a free socialist 'New Man', destined to destroy this oppressive system. Unfortunately, Shaw says, Wagner comes over all soppy at the crucial moment and the allegory collapses into a lot of gush about redemption through love. Nevertheless the *Ring* gives us some idea of what a future socialist art might be like. This may seem odd given Wagner's later association with Nazism but it must be remembered that at this time socialist and fascist ideas actually overlapped in many

areas. Wagner had some pretty unpleasant opinions, mainly in his later years, but he also believed in the prospect of an art which would recapture the relationship between popular appeal and cultural sophistication which had existed in Shakespeare's day. He wanted the widest possible audience to be in touch with the musical inheritance of Beethoven and with the power of drama which combined the achievements of Sophocles and Shakespeare. In these days of post-modern cultural fragmentation and consumer culture, that's not a bad vision of a truly socialist art.
Julie Byrne, Liverpool 18.

□ TRY listening to the works of the right-on composer of revolutionary people's 'music', Cornelius Cardew. You'll be desperate for the politically dubious pleasure of *Parsifal* in no time.
John Sheldon, Liverpool 1.

□ IF WAGNER is suspect, where does that leave Chopin (a virulent anti-Semite), Puccini (an honorary member of the Italian Fascist Party) and Stravinsky (who revered Mussolini)? As D. H. Lawrence said: 'Don't judge the artist, trust the tale.'
Jonathan Yglesias, London N10.

□ BRAHMS is known to have entertained very right-wing views, yet this did not prevent the Labour Party adopting a pop version of his First Symphony during its television broadcasts for the 1987 election. Conversely, the music of that good socialist Gustav Holst formed the background to the Tories' party political broadcasts in the same year.
Walter Cairns, Manchester 20.

QUESTION: Who invented the sash window and what are its virtues? Why did builders not adopt the inward-opening French window, which is simpler and more easily cleaned?

□ MOST probably, sash windows were not 'invented' but developed from the simpler horizontal sliding sash (known today as the 'Yorkshire' sash). They are supposed to have come from Holland in the 17th century. However, W. Horman, in his *Vulgaria*, printed in 1519, writes: 'Glasen wyndowis let in the lyght . . . I have many prety wyndowes shette with levys goynge up and down.' They were

first used conspicuously at Chatsworth in 1676–80 and then in 1685 at the Banqueting House at Whitehall, designed by Inigo Jones, where they replaced the original casement (i.e., side-hung) windows. They became exceedingly popular; earlier windows were replaced with sashes, and sashes were used almost exclusively in new buildings, from cottages to palaces, throughout Britain and the colonies, until early this century. This phenomenal 250-year success story is due to the many excellent qualities of the sash window. For instance, the opening of the window can be finely adjusted, down to a narrow gap at the top or the bottom or both, giving good control of ventilation with little danger of rain blowing into the room. A 'French' window or inward opening casement is very vulnerable in this respect, and would be quite unsuited to British weather. The sash, being hung from each of its top corners, rather than from the side as with a hinged window, is less likely to distort under its own weight. This has several consequences. Less distortion means longer life: there are many sash windows still serviceable after 150 years or more. Imagine a 150-year-old plastic window! Casement windows need wider components for stiffness. Larger casement windows need two lights (the moving parts) which necessarily meet side by side in the centre and so, from the visual point of view, give a strong central vertical emphasis. The wooden structure of the sash, on the other hand, can be made with thinner sections, giving more light and a more delicate appearance, and could be vertically divided into three panes, harmonising with the classical style and so becoming the principal feature of the graceful and elegant buildings of the Queen Anne and Georgian periods. Sash windows are less highly regarded today than they were, but they are very much victims of their longevity; that rattling, draughty but unopenable old window may well have functioned beautifully for the first 100 years of its life; but in refusing to die gracefully has become the victim of inexperienced tradesmen and heavy-handed DIYers. A new plastic window will need replacing entirely in about 20 years; in the same period a new sash window will probably only need new cords, if that.
Jacob Butler, Joiner, Bonsall, Derbyshire.

QUESTION: How is it that the vast majority of interrogative words in English – 'what?', 'why?', 'when?', 'where?', etc. – begin with the letters 'wh'?

□ ENGLISH shares with French, Latin, Greek, Russian, Sanskrit and many other mainly European languages a common origin. All these languages are held to be derived from a single unrecorded (and therefore hypothetical) language which we call Indo-European. Among the consonants which could begin a word in Indo-European was the group 'kw', and one group of words which began like that were the closely related group which come into Modern English as interrogatives and relative pronouns. Since these words were related to one another, they almost certainly consisted of a single stem beginning 'kw' to which was added a variety of forms to distinguish the different forms of the interrogative. In some Indo-European languages the 'kw' sequence remained, hence Latin *quis*, etc. However, in the development of the Germanic branch of Indo-European, to which English belongs, the initial 'k' became eventually the breathing sound 'h' (the main part of this process is known as Grimm's Law, after Jakob Grimm of the Brothers Grimm). Thus we find Old English forms such as hwa ('who'). Two later changes have taken place. Firstly, as a result of Norman influence on English spelling, the sequence 'hw' was changed to 'wh' without any corresponding change in pronunciation. Secondly, the 'h' eventually merged with the 'w' to produce a variant of 'w' which is produced without any vibration of the vocal chords. In many dialects of English this remains, so that there is a contrast between, say, what and watt, but in other dialects, including standard English, there is no contrast. The spelling system, however, very accurately shows the etymological source of each word.
(Prof.) Richard Hogg, Department of English Language and Literature, University of Manchester.

QUESTION: Has anyone got a use for the little plastic film containers? It always seems a shame to throw them away.

□ A FEW years ago I stayed at the Akhar Hotel in Agra, India, where they are used as salt and pepper pots.
Peter McFadden, Conwy, Gwynedd.

□ EACH wheel on most BMWs has a locked nut which can only be removed using a key. The lock is protected from dirt by a plastic cover. When I lost one of these a BMW dealer told me I could not

get a replacement without buying a complete new bolt at a cost of £9.78. Fortunately, I found that the top of a 35mm film container fits just as securely as the original cap.
Frank Miles, Beckenham, Kent.

☐ In his wonderfully comprehensive review, 'Penis sheaths: a comparative study' (*Proceedings of the Royal Anthropological Institute of Great Britain and Ireland for 1969*), Professor Peter J. Ucko tells us that males of the Telefolmin tribe of New Guinea 'normally wear either various types of gourds or large nuts, the latter being rarer and more greatly valued (Villeminot & Villeminot 1964: 255) but the occasional individual is to be encountered wearing instead a toothpaste container (Simpson 1963: 363), a Kodak film container or a cut-open sardine tin (*Personal Communication*, B. A. L. Cranstone)'. It is, unfortunately, hard to tell from this whether the film container referred to is the plastic pot which the questioner is concerned with or the metal device which immediately surrounds the film itself. I would guess it to be the latter but in either case such recycling is obviously praiseworthy. One wonders if the containers are worn with the labelling intact and if so whether Kodak has considered sponsorship.
Ted Polhemus, London NW6.

☐ Donate them to your local primary school: they make ideal containers for white (PVA) glue. They are airtight, so prevent the glue drying out, and hold a convenient amount for children to use.
Karen Wolff, Coventry.

☐ Oboeists and bassoonists use them as water pots for soaking their reeds during rehearsals and concerts. Perfect size, and watertight.
Rosie Collins, Padfield, Cheshire.

☐ I once sat behind a Masai on a bus in Northern Tanzania who kept a black plastic film container attached to his ear (rather like a large stud). When the conductor came to collect the fares, the man removed the container and took out a ten shilling note. I did not see where he put his ticket.
Park Sadler, Bangor, Gywnedd.

☐ THEY are ideal for re-stopping wine. They fit over the top of 1 litre and 75cl bottles as if made for the job.
Ross Gilfillan, Sudbury, Suffolk.

☐ THEY make excellent containers for urine samples to take to the doctor or hospital. They are leakproof and, unlike discarded food containers, they have no sugary residue which could contaminate the specimen.
Diana Laffin, Wokingham, Berks.

☐ A MAN I met in a pub (who I didn't know and who I haven't seen since) told me that they are useful for storing cannabis resin. Unfortunately they do have a disadvantage (he added): the resin rattles alarmingly just as one passes policemen or customs officers.
Will Corkhill, Scunthorpe, S. Humberside.

☐ AS A frequent traveller abroad, I use them as containers for foreign coins left over at the end of each trip. I label them so that when I set off on another journey I can simply grab the appropriate container. As a result I always have change for luggage trolleys, tips, refreshments, etc.
Rodney Crouch, Sevenoaks, Kent.

☐ ONE important use not mentioned so far is to fill them with water and put them in the freezer. They can then be used to cool drinks without causing dilution, as ice *au naturel* would do.
Eric Crew, Broxbourne, Herts.

☐ *THE Engineer's Mini-Notebook – Communications Projects*, by Forrest M. Mims III, published by Archer, described how to make a radio frequency tuning coil from a plastic film can, a paper and other bits and pieces. I'm not sure how useful it is, but the book is available from Tandy stores.
Seth Kay, Runcorn, Cheshire.

☐ I AND MY family have lived in Papua New Guinea off and on for over five generations and Ted Polhemus has misinterpreted the type of film container used by New Guinea natives as penis sheaths. It was the 'old-fashioned' container that they used, but more often the packaging. Early District Commissioners insisted

that the locals be properly covered when in contact with expatriates and I have seen a very interesting assortment of penis sheaths, including the gourds used in Telefomin which are known locally as 'Telefomin trousers'. It would be a sad male who could effectively cover his penis with one of the little plastic film containers.
(Mrs) L. J. Rebron, Baguley, Manchester 23.

☐ FOLLOWING the recent recommendation to use them for urine samples, I was somewhat relieved this morning to be told by the sister at the clinic that the correct container had been posted to the film laboratory after all.
Derek Taylor, Mosborough, Sheffield.

QUESTION: Who was the original buck passer and what was the buck that was passed?

☐ THE RIVERBOATS which travelled the Mississippi and Missouri rivers in the last century did more than take settlers west to join their wagon trains. They linked the major cities up and down what remains today a vital inland trade route. They also carried many less reputable travellers, including showmen and gamblers. When playing poker it is quite common for each hand to be dealt by a different player. Sometimes, as the dealer changed, so did the rules. This made cheating more difficult and the game far more interesting. As the deal moved around the group, the dealer's job was marked by placing a knife on the table in front of the man with the cards. Often this knife had a handle made from the antler of a male deer or buck: a Buck Knife. 'Passing the buck' thus came to mean passing the responsibility for control of the game to someone else. It was probably Harry Truman, a son of the town of Independence by the Missouri river, who introduced the term to the rest of the United States, with the famous sign on his Oval Office desk, which read 'The Buck Stops Here'.
Jeremiah Sheehan, London SE15.

QUESTION: Is it true that in 1647 Parliament abolished Christmas? Did this have any particular consequences?

☐ IT WAS in 1644, on the grounds that the celebration of Christmas provided an opportunity for indulgence in 'carnal and sensual delights'. Not only were all festivities outlawed, but citizens were directed to fast as a form of apology for any ungodly pleasures they or their ancestors might conceivably have enjoyed in previous years. Parliament was so taken with this concept that, in 1647, similar legislation was passed covering Easter and other festivals. The only real consequence was widespread evasion of the law, leading to much fulmination at Westminster. Oblivious of the fact that their antics simply made them look ridiculous in the eyes of all but their most fanatical supporters (some things never change), the Puritan faction even deployed the Army to conduct house to house searches for illicit Christmas dinners, which were sequestered on the spot (and, no doubt, subsequently eaten by the military).
P. M. Ray, Harrogate.

QUESTION: Under English law, is it possible for someone to bequeath all his money and belongings to his teddy bear?

☐ AS THE bear cannot draw money out of a bank and spend it on itself, the money has to be left to someone else to spend for the bear's benefit (i.e., a trust has to be set up in the will). This is simple enough but the law will not usually recognise a trust as valid unless it is for a human beneficiary, on the grounds that otherwise the trustee could spend it on himself, without anyone to protest. The major exception is if the trust is for a purpose recognised as charitable, in which case the Attorney-General would enforce it. But bestowing affection on an inanimate object, however lifelike and appealing, is unlikely to qualify as a charitable purpose. There are, nevertheless, three possible solutions. One would be to form a club for the preservation and/or admiration of the bear, and leave the money to the club. In Re Denley and Re Lipinski a similar arrangement was approved. The purposes of the clubs were less whimsical but the principle holds good. One would have to provide for the money to revert to the testator's estate in the event of the club ceasing to admire and preserve the bear. A second, much less feasible, possibility is to argue that the preservation of the bear is analogous to a small number of other purposes, such as the

preservation of graves or particular living animals. However, this small category, created only as a concession to human sentiment, is unlikely to be extended to include any kapok-filled species. The third possibility has a reasonable prospect of success but would mean that you could not leave all your money to the bear. You could leave some of your money to a charity for charitable purposes, on condition that the charity also undertook the preservation of the bear.
A student of the Middle Temple (name and address supplied).

QUESTION: Who was the first socialist?

□ FIGURES such as Jesus Christ or the English Civil War radicals John Lilburne and Gerard Winstanley can be seen as socialists by virtue of their beliefs but they are really only socialists by implication, having been given that title by posterity. The first socialist in the sense of that word being applied to him by contemporaries was Robert Owen, whose schemes for creating a 'New Moral World' involved the establishment of communities where property would be held in common. The word 'socialist' first appears in the London *Cooperative Magazine* of November 1827, defining Owenite communitarians as 'Communionists or Socialists'. J. F. C. Harrison, in his book *Robert Owen And The Owenites In Britain And America*, points out that by 1840 socialism was virtually synonymous with Owenism. This led Marx and Engels to prefer the title 'communist' or 'scientific socialist' to differentiate themselves from what they regarded as 'utopian socialism', which neglected class conflict. The fact that Owen was a paternalist who took the idea of utopian communities from his own benevolently despotic rule at his cotton factory at New Lanark in Scotland has led to his being regarded as an inappropriate originator of socialist thought in Britain and he is now somewhat neglected in this respect.
Harry Cocks, Brighton.

□ CHRISTOPHER Columbus, who in 1492 embarked on a quest without really knowing where he was going, under-estimated both the time it would take and the cost, and did it all on someone else's money.
Patrick Kewell, Clevedon, Avon.

☐ SPARTACUS, who led the slave revolt in 73–71 BC, laid down the fundamental principle that the toilers will only be liberated by their own actions.
Derek McMillan, E. Grinstead, W. Sussex.

☐ GOD . . . who had the extraordinary idea that all men are equal.
Bill Longman, Cambridge.

☐ IT'S the wrong question. Socialism came first, and private property later. So the question should have been 'Who invented private property?' Ancient Jewish tradition blamed Cain. Not only a murderer, he committed the second crime of instituting private property in land: he 'set bounds to fields'. The ancient world looked back with longing to the Golden Age of Saturn when all things were held in common: 'No fences parted fields, nor marks nor bounds Divided acres of litigious grounds, But all was common.' Virgil, *Georgics* I (125–128) Plato applauded simple communism but said it would fail because of the lowest part of human nature. Lactantius, in the reign of Diocletian, condemned private property, and the early Christian Fathers like St Cyprian, Clement of Alexandria, Tertullian, etc., all advocated common ownership.
Karl Heath, Coventry.

☐ AROUND AD 532, during the rule of Khosro Anoushirvan, the king of the Sasanians, a man called Mazdak founded a communistic sect which made headway among the people, especially the poor. Mazdak demanded that the rich should live less luxuriously and should distribute their wealth among the poor. Khosro condemned the Mazdakites, who were butchered in 528 by planting them in the soil upside down or cutting off their heads.
Behrouz Kia, Istanbul, Turkey.

QUESTION: We are constantly assured that certain diseases cannot be caught from a toilet seat. Are there any that can?

☐ INDOLENCE.
Peter Barnes, Milton Keynes.

☐ POST-inebrial cranial septicaemia (infected bruise caused by lavatory seat falling on patient's head while throwing up).
A. E. Baker, Kettering, Northants.

☐ I WAS once informed by my father and elder brother, both of whom served in Her Majesty's forces, that the only people who could catch sexually transmitted diseases from a toilet seat were officers or the padre.
Stephen Griffiths, London N20.

☐ YOUNG children hold on to the toilet seat to stop themselves falling into the pan. This, coupled with thumb sucking while performing and a dislike of hand washing after the event, encourages the spread of enteric diseases such as dysentery. Others with similar unhygienic practices may also unsuspectingly eat that which has come out of a previous occupant's behind and fall prey to the same illnesses.
(Dr) Lorraine Lighton, Consultant in Communicable Disease Control, Tameside and Glossop Health Authority.

QUESTION: So what?

☐ JUST so.
Tony Stevens, Telford, Shropshire.

☐ SO THERE.
Graeme S. Smith, Maidenhead, Berks and Julie Farrington, Bedford.

☐ So lution.
Andrew J. Penman, London NW1.

☐ So in love . . .
'Cole Porter', London.

☐ BE it; far so good; forth; to speak; so much for a silly question.
Michael J. Smith, Swaffham, Norfolk.

☐ A FRIEND of mine was once in a London taxi. The driver said

excitedly: 'Do you know who has just been sitting where you are, sir? Lord Bertrand Russell, the philosopher. But when I asked him, "Well, Lord Russell, what's it all about, then?", do you know, guv, he didn't know.'
Bill Davies, Knutsford, Cheshire.

□ THE QUESTION is a logical contradiction: 'so what?' challenges the question-and-answer format as being relevant to discussion while, being in the form of a question, explicitly accepting it. The questioner has a point, though. If we are seeking the truth then everything in thought is a mere approximation, and not the *real* thing by definition.
Rick Carless, Nottingham.

□ 'SO WHAT' is the title of one of Miles Davis's finest compositions, an anodyne version of which recently became the first jazz record to reach the charts in the UK for about 30 years when recorded by Ronny Jordan.
Keith Leedham, Harrow on the Hill, Middx.

□ IF NOTHING really mattered, the questioner would not have asked; the question negates itself. Pseudo-sceptics should consider the unconscious dialectic of Jean de la Fontaine's dictum: 'Nothing is useless to the man of sense.'
Peter Mahoney, London SE22.

□ IN HIS wonderful unfinished autobiography, *The Strings Are False* (Faber & Faber), Louis MacNeice's opening sentence is made up of this question. He goes on to reply: 'This modern equivalent of Pilate's "What is truth?" comes often now to our lips and only too patly, we too being much of the time cynical and with as good reason as any old procurator, tired, bored with the details of Roman bureaucracy, and the graft of Greek officials, a vista of desert studded to the horizon with pyramids of privilege apart from which there are only nomads who have little in their packs, next to nothing in their eyes.'
F. R. Powell, London EC1.

QUESTION: There are 5,500 members of the Glyndebourne Festival Society. I am a 53-year-old male, and am now 2,563rd

on the waiting list. What are my chances of being offered membership before I die?

☐ THE questioner will be offered membership if he is still alive when only 5,499 of the 8,062 (5,500 members and 2,562 would-be members) are still on the roll. If we assume all these other people are also 53-year-old males, in equally good health, and they all remain lifelong members, then the chance for him is 5,500/8,063 (68 per cent). By using mortality tables we can broaden the approach. The chance of him becoming a member is the probability that he survives the expected time it takes for the group to reduce in number from 8,062 to 5,499. The older the other members and would-be members, the greater his chance. For example, if they were all 60-year-old males, he would need to survive 15 years, which gives him an 83 per cent chance (using mortality tables). Conversely, if the others were all 40–year-old males, he has to survive 32 years and his chance reduces to a mere 28 per cent. We can also compare the mortality of the sexes. If all the group were 53-year-old females, the questioner's chance of becoming a member would drop from 68 to 50 per cent – an indication of how much longer women live than men. So, assuming he is about average age for the rest of the group, and there are roughly as many men as women, his chance is between 50 and 68 per cent, say 60 per cent.
Martin Sandford, Den Haag, Netherlands.

QUESTION: I have heard that it is impossible to fold a square piece of paper more than seven times. My own attempts appear to bear this out. But is it true?

☐ NO. IT depends on the thickness and size of the square of paper. I folded a 45-inch square of newsprint (just about) eight times but it would have been less of a struggle if the original sheet had been bigger and thinner. I am sure that better scores than eight are possible but, unless you are prepared to pay for half an acre of tissue paper and the hire of a football field, don't ask me to prove it.
A. E. Baker, Pytchley, Northants.

☐ THIS experiment was carried out by a Canadian current affairs TV programme, *Live It Up*, using a piece of paper measuring 100 yards by 100 yards, laid out on a football pitch. Surprise,

surprise, they managed not seven but nine folds. It must be mentioned, however, that they had to sit on the paper to maintain the ninth fold, but certainly the eighth was accomplished naturally. Considering that they quashed the accepted belief regarding this doctrine, their remarkable discovery has had negligible impact on the world as we know it. Typical of Canadian achievements.
M. J. Mortimer, Toronto, Ontario.

QUESTION: What is the purpose of sneezing, and what triggers it when it is useless? Medical works refer to my uncontrollable bouts of sneezing as non-specific allergic rhinitis, but it's difficult to imagine what it could be an allergic reaction to?

☐ NON-SPECIFIC allergic rhinitis is a nonsense term. Allergic rhinitis can only be specific, because it must be caused by an allergen. The term is implying that superficial questioning has not elicited any clear causal relationship between exposure to an allergen and the sneezing. Although it fulfils the fundamental definitions of an allergy, allergic rhinitis may not involve the type of antibody classically concerned in allergy, immunoglobulin E (IgE), and the cause or causes are often masked so that active steps have to be taken to uncover them. It may be due to house dust mites, or foods (different in different cases), but it may also be due to chemicals, mainly modern synthetic chemicals to which exposure has been increasing dramatically in the 'developed' world, especially since the Second World War. It is interesting to note that the prevalence of hay fever increased in London over a period when the pollen count actually dropped. The physiological purpose of sneezing is to free the nose of irritants, but if the nasal irritation results from the consumption of a non-tolerated food, sneezing serves no useful purpose.
D. J. Maberly and H. M. Anthony, Airedale General Hospital, Keighley, W. Yorkshire.

QUESTION: Over the past 2,500 years, some of the best brains that mankind has produced have studied the problems of philosophy. What problems of relevance to everyday life have they solved?

☐ BEFORE the 19th century, there was no science and there were no scientists, and what we would now call science was done by philosophers. Democritus contributed the atomic theory of matter; Archimedes his screw (still used in jacks and pumps as well as to propel ships and aircraft); Pascal the theory of probability; Copernicus modern astronomy; Newton the dynamics which is still universally useful in engineering; Hobbes artificial intelligence (thinking as calculation); and so on. Today, when we don't know how to set about solving a problem (when there is no established scientific method) we have to step back a pace and do philosophy – we have to think about the way we think until we can come up with a new scientific method or even a completely new science. Then we can get back to work and stop philosophising until we get stuck again. Indeed, anybody who finds himself in difficulties in work or life and stops to think about the way he is working or living, instead of pressing on in the old way, is doing philosophy.
Grahame Leman, London W3.

☐ PHILOSOPHERS are sometimes criticised for arguing amongst themselves, but artists and scientists argue amongst themselves too. Artists have brought you costume drama, scientists have brought you television, but philosophers have brought you the right to vote; the right not to be sold into slavery; the right to trial by jury and equality before the law; freedom of speech . . . Sufficiently relevant to everyday life?
Michael Hampson, Harlow, Essex.

☐ THE questioner should ask, first of all, if he/she would even be able to pose the question without the study of philosophy.
Edward Carter, Department of Artificial Intelligence, University of Edinburgh.

☐ PHILOSOPHERS do not solve problems, but create them in forms ever more difficult to solve, thus perpetuating philosophy. This is not unique; economists, sociologists and politicians behave in exactly the same way with corresponding consequences.
(Prof.) Sir James Beament, Queen's College, Cambridge.

☐ AS THE last lecture of my moral philosophy course our professor said: 'Don't think you're no further forward. The value of studying

philosophy is that you've reached a more informed state of ignorance.'
Alan Brown, Glasgow.

QUESTION: Who rules the bar code? Who grants, administers, controls the allocation of lines and numbers? Soon, it seems, every article on sale will carry a bar code. No doubt human beings, for convenience, will get their own. Shall I be allowed to choose my own and sign myself thus, making redundant the cumbersome signature?

☐ THE most familiar bar codes are administered by EAN International which was established in Brussels in 1977 as the then European Article Numbering Association. The now international article numbering system, or EAN as it is still known, is used in over 65 countries and administered in the UK by the Article Number Association. Each national numbering authority allocates blocks of numbers to its members, who then use these numbers (shown as bar codes) to identify their products. The bar codes contain no information; all the product details are held on a database which uses the article number as a reference. If individuals were ever bar coded, the numbers would have to be allocated centrally so you would not be able to choose your own. Certain specific numbers associated with people – some passport numbers, for example – are already bar-coded. However, a universal and unified system for the identification of people, similar to EAN's universal and unified numbering of products, is not a prospect.
A. T. Osborne, Secretary General, Article Number Association, London WC2.

QUESTION: Considering (a) changes in the laws covering rights of assembly and strike action; (b) the growth of quangos staffed by unelected Tory place men; (c) the extent of the Official Secrets Act; and (d) the electoral system, is Britain now a dictatorship?

☐ BRITAIN is described as a 'parliamentary monarchy'. In theory, at least, elected members of Parliament speak/act/vote on behalf

of the people of this country (their constituents). But since we do not operate under a system of proportional representation, the voice of the people is not always heard or heeded. MPs and civil servants, like anybody else, can be corrupted with offers of money or other benefits. Unfortunately, we hear about far too many incidents of this kind, particularly among government ministers. Beyond a doubt, our rights and civil liberties have been eroded so much over the last 15 years that George Orwell would have been spot-on had he entitled his book *1994*. By European and American standards we live in a kind of police state and are at the mercy of the establishment and bureaucrats. Our 'Freedom of Information' Act is a farce. If we had real freedom of information, there would be no censure of the press; matters of government would be open to public scrutiny; and we would be able to obtain details of everything, from the exact ingredients of bangers to the names of both defendant and plaintiff in all cases. On the other hand, a 'dictatorship' is the office of someone invested with absolute authority, who presumably has the right to do anything he wants within his own country without having to answer for it. Somehow, I don't think John Major could walk into the Bank of England and be given cash for his Spanish holiday, or have Mrs Thatcher shot for slagging him off. It is true that we don't have a great many liberties, but we do not live in a dictatorship.
M. Roy, Battersea, London.

☐ THE correct term is 'Oligator ship'. The Oligarchs are the City, the owners of the right-wing press, directors and organisations who subscribe to Tory funds etc. They lurk beneath the surface, largely concealed from the public on whom they are preda-tory. The alligators and crocodiles are the oldest surviving relatives of the dinosaurs.
Peter Rowland, Dulwich, London SE24.

QUESTION: How many sheets of A4 paper would I have to recycle to save a tree?

☐ TWO. One to write to the Mailing Preference Service requesting that they arrange to stop all unsolicited mail deliveries to your address; and the second to make an envelope for the first.
P. G. Waterson, Bishopbriggs, Glasgow.

☐ IT IS a fallacy to assume that paper is made from trees growing wild which will be spared to live out their full natural life if not used to make paper. In fact, all the trees required to make paper for use in the near future have already been planted, and will be made into paper regardless. If more paper is recycled, the price of unrecycled paper will drop in order to maintain demand. However, this reduction in price will reduce tree planting to meet anticipated future demand. So if you love trees for their own sake you should not recycle at all but on the contrary use as much unrecycled paper as possible.
Mike Scott, Chester.

☐ A SIMPLISTIC answer to this would be 15,000 sheets. This assumes that it takes between 10 and 17 trees to form the raw material for one tonne of paper, and that the weight of the paper is $80g/m^2$, standard for most printing and photocopying papers. It is true, as Mike Scott says, that most of the trees used for paper manufacture are grown for the purpose, and that the felled trees are replaced. However, the demand for paper has meant that old forests – which are more valuable for wildlife – have been replaced by managed plantations. So recycling paper does help to protect some wildlife habitats. It also has significant environmental benefits through energy savings and reducing emissions of pollutants. It is not possible to recycle paper indefinitely, as it gradually degrades in the process, so the input of some virgin fibre into the production process is necessary.
Penny Pitty, Waste Watch, London SW1.

QUESTION: If you were run over by a hovercraft would you be seriously injured?

☐ SPEAKING as one to whom this has happened, I can relate that the experience is fairly unremarkable. One is aware of the passing of the flexible bow skirt over one's body; there follows a period of comparative calm as the hovercraft passes overhead; and then the stern skirt brushes over. The cushion pressure inside the skirt of a small commercial hovercraft is low, usually less than 3 ounces per square inch above atmosphere (the pressure inside a car tyre is typically more than 200 times higher than this).

This low-pressure air is enough to support the 'hard' structure of the hovercraft about 18 inches above the ground. The skirt which contains this 'cushion' of air, usually made of flexible rubber, is designed to conform to uneven surfaces and allows the craft to negotiate obstacles without harming them. A previous employer of mine who built small hovercraft used to routinely run employees over to demonstrate the principle to potential clients. I should add that the experience is not particularly enjoyable, since the bottom of a hovercraft is one of the wettest and muddiest places I know.
Russ Bagley, Griffin Hovercraft, Southampton.

QUESTION: How do we know the correct way to pronounce a dead language?

☐ WE ask a ghost writer.
David Leah, Liskeard, Cornwall.

☐ OLD languages don't die. They just fade into new languages (at least most of them do). While the entire sound system of an ancient language rarely survives intact, fragments can usually be found scattered around its various daughter languages. For example, many traits of Latin pronunciation are directly observable in Italian, French, Spanish and Romanian. The job of the linguistic historian is to try to piece these various bits together. The most tried and tested technique is comparative reconstruction, which focuses on the systematic sound correspondences that emerge when we compare the same words in different sister languages. Where this exercise turns up different sounds, it is usually possible to trace them back to a common historical source. For example, many English words beginning with 't' correspond to words beginning with 'ts' (spelt z) in the sister language German; compare English *ten, to, time* with German *zehn, zu, Zeit.* On the basis of this and many similar correspondences, we can reconstruct a common Germanic parent language in which the older sound in this particular instance is the knowledge that each type of sound change takes place in one direction only. On the strength of what happens in many other languages, we know that 't' at the beginning of a word can turn into 'ts' but not vice versa.

The more widely we cast our comparative net, the further we can reach back into the mists of time. The 't' of early Germanic itself derives from an even older 'd' – contrast English *two* and *tooth* with, say, Italian *due* and *dente*. Ultimately we arrive at the sound system of an ancient Indo-European tongue, the common ancestor of languages as apparently diverse as English, French, Russian, Irish, Greek and Urdu.
John Harris, Department of Phonetics and Linguistics, University College, London.

QUESTION: Who changed the name of Richard to Dick? Why?

□ THIS came about, first, through the very common shortening of names – for example, Will for William, Sim for Simon, Gib for Gilbert, and Wat for Walter. These short forms were then subjected to rhyming process. Some examples are: William – Bill; Robert – Hob, Bob; Roger – Hodge; Molly – Polly. Dick is one of the earliest to be mentioned in records, in 1220. During the 13th to 15th centuries, it is probable that the majority of peasants were called these short and rhyming forms. Such names resembled the Old English names which had been generally used before the Norman Conquest. Because these forms were usually for the peasants, they gave rise to use as common nouns, such as: jack/dick – man/fellow; hodge – country labourer.
Ann Addison, Nuneaton.

QUESTION: Who first 'lost his bottle'?

□ SHAKESPEARE wrote about lager louts in the early 17th century in *The Tempest*, Act IV Scene 1. After a drunken and fruitless chase across wild marshland led by the 'monster' Caliban, the bedraggled Trinculo bemoans the fact that he and Stephano have sunk so low as 'to lose our bottles in the pool'. Stephano agrees – 'There is not only disgrace and dishonour in that, monster, but an infinite loss.'
Colin Morley, Totteridge, London N20.

☐ THE 'bottle' is, in full, the Cockney rhyming slang 'bottle and glass'. The 'loss' refers to the control of the anal sphincter in moments of great danger or stress. From this, we can deduce that Adam was the first to experience this unpleasant occurrence, when called to account in the Garden of Eden.
Joseph Cramp, Clayhall, Essex.

QUESTION: A recent television advert suggests that it is possible to fit the entire world's population on to the Isle of Wight. How true is this statement?

☐ THE Isle of Wight has an area of 381 square kilometres. It is possible to squeeze about 10 average British adults into one square metre, and thus 3.81 billion of them on to the island. The world's population, at present, is in the order of 5.56 billion. If (a) the average person requires only 90 per cent of the space required by the average Briton; (b) 12 per cent of the population, being aged four or less, require no space at all; and (c) a further 20 per cent, aged between 5 and 14, require only half the amount of space occupied by adults, the potential capacity of the Isle of Wight increases to 5.34 billion. Hence, the original question can only be accurately answered after detailed analysis of the demographic and anthropometric make-up of the world's population.
Geoffrey Taunton, Portsmouth.

☐ IT IS highly unlikely, because of the limited running of the Red Funnel Steamers and the other non-too-frequent ferries. The first few million to arrive would have eaten everything available, probably have blocked the sewage systems, and would undoubtedly have died before the last visitors had even gained an entry Visa.
Richard Trim, Narborough, Leics.

QUESTION: Is there any evidence to suggest that the Soviet Union ever contemplated the possibility of making a military assault on Western Europe?

☐ ACCORDING to secret documents seized from the military archives of the former East Germany, the Warsaw Pact planned a modernised version of Hitler's *Blitzkrieg* against the West, using spearheads of tanks and tactical nuclear weapons. These documents, covering the period from the 1960s to the mid-1980s, were made public in March of this year. They convinced German military planners and historians that the Soviet bloc not only seriously considered an assault, but also had achieved a far higher level of readiness than Western intelligence had assumed. The Warsaw Pact intended to push forward on five fronts to reach the French border in 13–15 days, according to the documents. Having conquered West Germany and the Low Countries, Soviet-bloc forces would then push through France to reach the Spanish border and the Atlantic coast within 30–35 days. A training exercise in 1980 developed a strategy for supporting the advance of the first front with 840 tactical nuclear weapons (targeted on Schleswig-Holstein, East Lower Saxony, North Hessen and East Bavaria). Warsaw Pact exercises were offensive and rarely practised defence against a NATO attack, as this was regarded as unlikely by the East's military planners. Soviet-bloc planning for a military offensive against the West was so detailed and advanced that the Communists had already made street signs for Western cities, printed cash for their occupation government, and built equipment to run Eastern trains on Western tracks. Furthermore, an estimated 8,000 medals ready for an offensive against the West were discovered in the former East German defence ministry headquarters. This secret decoration for bravery was known as the Blücher Order, after the Prussian field marshal who helped Wellington to defeat Napoleon at Waterloo.
Tony Martin, Nunhead, London SE15.

☐ AS IS usual in anti-Soviet stories, Tony Martin does not enable us to check the authenticity of his sources (which in any case should be Soviet, not German, to hold any water). My fascination with this question began when we re-armed Germany in 1951, to the great dismay of our former ally – Germany being a power that had twice been our mortal enemy and which had spread death, destruction and genocide across Europe and Russia on an unprecedented scale. In my compulsive quest for information, I failed to find one piece of cast-iron, irrefutable evidence that the Soviet Union could have contemplated such a step. They lost

20 million, plus countless wounded, which must have left cruel mental scars on the surviving population. Material destruction was on a scale unimaginable, even to those of us who remember the bombing of our cities. The Soviet Union was striving to prove the superiority of a planned economy. One can hardly imagine them being diverted into military gambles. Mr Martin could not quote a single Russian leader from Lenin onwards who ever nursed such an idea. The reverse is true: the West did contemplate an assault on the Soviet Union, from John Foster Dulles and his 'Roll back Communism' through to Reagan's 'Star Wars' which, it was hoped, would allow a successful first strike. As stated by A. J. P. Taylor in *The Russian War* (1978): 'The greatest crime of the Soviet Union in western eyes is to have no capitalists and no landlords.' Now that these are being reinstated we can be buddies. Incidentally, they have been running through-trains from Moscow to Ostend and return for many years. They simply crane up the coaches and change the bogies at the frontier.
John L. Beasley, Penzance, Cornwall.

QUESTION: Why is the control area of an aircraft called the cockpit?

☐ A COCKPIT was a small dugout circle enclosed by wooden rails and used for cock fighting, a popular 17th-century sport. Similar structures came to be called a cockpit by analogy: for example, the Cockpit Theatre, which would often feature bloody scenes on its confined stage. Later, the back part of the orlop deck of a man-o'-war became known as the cockpit. It was narrow and deep, with wooden railings, and there was another connection with blood – during battle, wounded sailors were transferred to it. This opened up new meanings for cockpit linked to travel, while retaining the idea of a confined space. In some ship designs the cockpit was also used for navigation. Travel in narrow, deep spaces was a feature of early aircraft. And the language of flying picked up many terms from seafaring – aeronautics, knots, navigation. So the 'cockpit' was borrowed to refer to the confined space in the fuselage for crew and passengers. Later it was specialised to mean the pilot's area.
Doug Gowan, Hornsey, London N8.

QUESTION: According to encyclopaedias, the rhinoceros has roamed the earth for 70 million years. If dinosaurs became extinct about 60 million years ago, why did the rhinoceros survive?

☐ IT IS probably simplistic to assume that dinosaurs (there were more than 100 families of them) died out suddenly 65 million years ago, destroyed by asteroids or meteorites. The most likely explanation is a gradual decline brought about by climatic change, which mammals like the ancestors of the rhino were able to exploit to their advantage. Mammals evolved from mammal-like reptiles between 250 and 200 million years ago, so dinosaurs and mammals co-existed over a period of nearly 200 million years. In this time, many dinosaur families – the anchisaurids, brachiosaurids, diplocids etc. – simply died out. So mammals, birds, reptiles and amphibians are dinosaurs that have adapted to changing conditions. The evolution of the rhinoceros may provide part of the answer to this evolutionary conundrum. The rhinos of Africa and the tapirs of South America are related: their common ancestor was possibly *Indricotherium* from Asia, which was 18 feet high at the shoulder and weighed 32 tons. It died out in the Miocene period. Later in the Miocene, the horned rhino evolved: sub-species included the Woolly Rhinoceros and the *Brontotherium*. These latter were ecologically replaced by the giant rhinos of the late Oligocene, about 35 million years ago.
Robert Turpin, Peverell, Plymouth.

☐ BOTH the question and the given answer are in error. Rhinoceroses have certainly not 'roamed the earth for 70 million years'. Ancestral rhinoceroses have been found in deposits of late Eocene age (about 40 million years old), whilst the dinosaurs died out 65 million years ago at the end of the Cretaceous Period. Therefore a gap of about 20 million years separates the dinosaurs from the line of mammals that gave rise to the rhinos of today. Rhinos and tapirs are closely related, but *Indricotherium* was not the 'common ancestor' of the two groups. *Indricotherium* was in fact an early offshoot of the lineage that gave rise to modern rhinos. Also, the Woolly Rhino (*Coelodonta*) could not have been ecologically replaced by the '. . . rhinos of the Oligocene', as the Woolly Rhino lived during the Pleistocene, 21 million years after the end of the Oligocene! Although dinosaurs were on the decline before they finally became

extinct, we cannot, at present (if ever), assign this to a single cause. The world's climate was changing at the end of the Cretaceous Period, and there is good evidence of an asteroid impact 65 million years ago. However, the relative importance of these factors (and other environmental and biological changes occurring at the same time) is a matter of great contention. Finally, the following statement: 'So mammals, birds, reptiles and amphibians are dinosaurs that have adapted to changing conditions,' is just not true. The dinosaurs were a distinct group of animals. It is thought that some small carnivorous dinosaurs are ancestral to birds, but living mammals and amphibians are only distantly related to the dinosaurs. In fact it is thought that dinosaurs are more closely related to birds than to living 'reptiles' (turtles, lizards and snakes, and crocodiles).
Paul M. Barrett, Department of Earth Sciences, University of Cambridge.

QUESTION: Why do red peppers cost more than green peppers?

☐ RED PEPPERS are ripened green peppers. The high cost of the former reflects the additional cost of delaying harvesting and marketing until the immature green-skinned pepper matures to a sweeter red-skinned pepper.
Philip Roberts, Preston.

QUESTION: Why does the surface above an underground nuclear test sink, to form a crater, without any material appearing to be blown out of the hole? Air-to-ground filming of such tests appears to show that an implosion, rather than explosion, takes place. What has happened to the missing soil?

☐ UNDERGROUND testing of atomic bombs contains the explosion and radiation. For this reason the depth to which the bomb is buried varies from 5–600 feet to 2–3,000 feet, depending on the size of the bomb. When the bomb is detonated, the temperature of the blast is around 100 million degrees centigrade and the pressure many millions of atmospheres. This has the effect of melting the surrounding rock and blowing it up into a huge

underground bubble several hundred feet in diameter. Shortly after the explosion, the temperature and pressure drop, leaving a void into which the overlying rock collapses. This is manifested on the surface as a crater.
Chris Waller, Yate, Bristol.

QUESTION: What does 'Twenty-twenty vision' mean and what is the measurement scheme it comes from?

☐ THERE are several methods for the measurement and recording of vision, but all are based on the angular subtense at the eye of the smallest object (typically a letter) that can be resolved. In the UK and US it is customary to use Snellen's notation, where Vision equals the actual distance from the test chart divided by the distance at which smallest letters read subtend an angle of 5 minutes. The testing distance employed in the UK is usually 6 metres (a 3–metre consulting room with a plane mirror), and below each row on the test chart is printed the distance at which the letters would subtend 5 minutes of arc. Once a person has read as far down the chart as he/she can, the vision is recorded in a fractional form. For example, if only the large letter at the top of the chart can be resolved, the vision is recorded as 6/60. A vision of 6/6 (six-six) is taken as a good standard of vision, although many people perform better than this. As a comparison, the characters on a standard British car number plate, at a distance of 54 metres, would be almost the same angular size as a 6/6 letter. In the US the testing distance is usually 20 feet, so a vision of 20/20 is equivalent to 6/6. Thus a person with 'twenty-twenty' vision is considered to have good eyesight.
(Dr) Eve Pascal, Vision Sciences Department, Glasgow Caledonian University.

QUESTION: Why was it decided that 999 should be the telephone number of the emergency services in Britain? Who made this momentous decision, and when?

☐ THE emergency code had to be easily remembered, and standard across the country. To work in London, a three-digit code was much to be preferred and, to be usable on the figure-only dials

used in most places, the code needed to be a real number. A letter code like 'TIMe' and 'ENGineer' – perhaps 'HELp' – was never in with a chance. '000' was out – '0' was the code for the operator, and the whole point of this was to provide a by-pass for emergency calls, ensuring an immediate answer. In the end, '999' was pretty much forced on the designers. Callers had to be able to dial the code with as much ease in a payphone as on any other line, and this meant being able to do so without needing to insert any coins. The Button A/B payphone was such that the dial was useless until the correct local call fee had been prepaid. The digit '0' was an exception, and could be dialled straight away, without coins, to raise the operator. It was a relatively simple task to modify things to extend coin-free dialling to the next dial number, namely '9'. Hence '999'. The service was introduced in London in July 1937. It is convenient to assume that the person who made this decision was a faceless civil servant in the Post Office engineering department. However, matters of such public interest rarely went ahead without the authority of the responsible minister – the Postmaster General – and so it is much fairer to say that the ultimate decision was made by a politician.
Neil Johannessen, Manager, BT Museum, London EC4.

QUESTION: Some time ago Alistair Cooke mentioned in his 'Letter From America' that before the end of the century, the UK had to repay the US for war loans made during the 1939–45 war. Have these loans been repaid and, if not, how much do we owe and when is repayment due?

□ THIRTY billion dollars' worth of ships, tanks, guns and planes were supplied, under Lend-Lease and free of charge, to the British Commonwealth. In exchange, Britain paid for the subsistence of US servicemen stationed in the UK and the building of bases in Britain, Australia and India – estimated at $7.6 billion. Britain's repayment of loans to the US had nothing to do with Lend-Lease during world war two. On 6 December 1945, Attlee's Labour government requested two loans from the Americans to pay for post-war development including the cost of the National Health Service. According to HM Treasury figures, the total sum outstanding at 31 March 1993 was $1.357 billion. On 31 December each year, Britain makes two payments, one on each

loan. The payments made on 31 December 1992 totalled $115 million principal, $22.5 million interest.
Tony Martin, Nunhead, London SE15.

☐ TONY MARTIN says that 'Attlee's Labour government requested two loans from the US to pay for post-war development, including the National Health Service'. This accusation, that the US was financing Labour's welfare state, was widely believed, especially in America, then and later. It is totally false. The money was borrowed to cover the UK's balance-of-payments deficit, not domestic spending. And this deficit was mainly caused by the UK's continuing high overseas military spending, at a time when America was vigorously cutting back its own.
Peter Stephenson, London NW3.

QUESTION: Is evolution a theory still waiting to be proved by the discovery of 'missing links'?

☐ NO. EVOLUTION is known to happen; there are sequences of 'links' without missing bits. Moreover, we can see evolution happening. The best-known example is a type of moth in which, originally, most individuals were pale and camouflaged against the bark of birch trees. There were always a few darker individuals. When industrial pollution stained the trees, white moths were easily seen and picked off by birds but dark ones were now well camouflaged. The population evolved from being predominantly white to being predominantly dark. If the questioner was referring more specifically to human evolution, then we scientists must be more careful. Although there are fossils showing parts of the evolutionary pathway, and although there is other evidence (we share something like 98 per cent of our genetic code with chimpanzees), we cannot prove scientifically that humans evolved from something non-human. A belief in evolution is the only known scientific way of making sense of the evidence but it would be arrogant and unscientific of us to state human evolution as a fact.
(Dr) Peter Cotgreave, Department of Zoology, Oxford.

☐ LIKE all good scientific theories, this theory is framed in such a way as to be eminently falsifiable: the discovery of the bones of

a horse or baboon in the same geological stratum as the remains of a dinosaur, for example, would comprehensively demolish it. Despite this, no such contrary evidence has been found and all that we have learnt from genetics and molecular biology, two sciences unknown to Charles Darwin, has supported the theory – though there is still room for debate about the details (is natural selection the only driving force; is the rate of evolutionary change constant?). Use of the words 'missing link' suggests a fundamental misconception of what the theory states. Evolution cannot be likened to a simple linear process, like a ladder with distinct rungs that have to be slotted in in a particular sequence. A better model would be a continuously branching tree. From this we can see that our nearest biological relatives, the primates, are all as far along their particular branches of the tree as we are along ours and our relationship to them, from the close to the not-so-close, can be shown directly. The theory does not require a 'link' at some notional man–ape boundary.
Michael Hutton, Camberwell, London SE5.

QUESTION: The symbol of Christianity in the early centuries was the fish. When did this change to a cross bearing the figure of Christ and why?

☐ WHEN the early Christians were persecuted they used the arcane, coded symbol of the Fish. Its Greek translation *Ixthus* was an acronym for *Iesus Xristos, Theou Uios, Soter*, meaning Jesus Christ, Son of God, Saviour. Later, when Christianity was expediently combined with the Almighty Apollo and Mithras cults to form the official Roman religion, it became safe to display the crucifix openly, although the Emperor Constantine in AD 312, allegedly seeing the conquering sign XP (*Chi Ro*) in the sky was obviously still reading in Greek, not Latin. The fact that the Greek *Chi*, for Christ, coincidentally was an 'X' helped to associate it with the Cross.
Benedict Sandham, Mannamead, Devon.

QUESTION: Where do you draw the line?

☐ PLIMSOLL got it right. If you ignore him, you're sunk.
David J. Nicolle, Bexley, Kent.

☐ YOU draw the line – or you used to draw the line – in the prize ring in the days of *alfresco* prize fighting. A line was scratched in the turf for each of the fighters to 'toe the line' at the beginning of each round. Fighters were not allowed to 'overstep the mark'. Fights were fought to a finish, and if a fighter was unable to toe the line because he did not feel 'up to scratch' he lost the contest.
Harry Humphreys, Lytham St Annes, Lancs.

QUESTION: Does anyone know where the phrase 'the world's oldest profession' to describe prostitution originates? Is it *really*?

☐ THERE is a similar phrase in the morality play *The Fall of Righteousness* (*c.* 1340). Cain, having been exiled, is wandering in the wilderness when he is visited by Lilith, an agent of Satan. Her function is to explain to him the nature of the post-Fall society he is to encounter and, during her description of this world of sin, she claims: 'Whoredom is the original business of woman.' This should probably be taken less as a statement of fact than as an example of medieval misogyny.
Alwyn W. Turner, London NW5.

☐ A GARDENER, an architect and a politician were discussing which is the oldest profession.
'Horticulture,' said the gardener. 'Who made the Garden of Eden?'
'No,' said the architect. 'It must be architecture, for God created the Earth and the Heavens out of Chaos.'
'Yes,' said the politician, 'but who created the Chaos?'
Anna R. Cooper, Bournemouth.

☐ OF COURSE prostitution is not the world's oldest profession. For 90 per cent of our history, humans have lived as hunter-gatherers, and I have encountered no instance of prostitution in societies organised in this manner. Prostitution is better seen as a recent aberration in human history – though one could argue the same for professionalisation. Midwifery is really the world's oldest profession. Shamanism probably runs it a close second; occasionally the two are combined.
Roxana Waterson, Singapore.

QUESTION: What is the origin of the term 'Third World'?

☐ THE term comes from the 'original' world (i.e. the Middle East, Mediterranean Europe, Mainland Europe, British Isles) being termed the 'Old World' when the 'New World' (i.e. the Americas) was settled by Europeans. This left the rest of the world (i.e. Africa, Asia, etc.) which was renamed the 'Third World' in the latter part of this century.
David A. Dix, Newcastle under Lyme, Staffs.

☐ I DISAGREE with Mr Dix's explanation. The term is a translation from the French *Tiers-Monde* created by the late economist and demograph, Alfred Sauvy. Modelled after the *Tiers-État* of the pre-1789 era (meaning those who weren't aristocrats or church members), the *Tiers-Monde* was applied to those countries who weren't part of the western world (which the English renamed the First World) nor the communist world. The term had a wide success because, just as the *Tiers-État* was the power behind the French Revolution, the third world could become a new revolutionary actor. Since these times, a new term, the *Quart-Monde* (Fourth World) has appeared in France, and it comprises all those who are poor in rich countries (unemployed, tramps, etc.).
Xavier Leroy, Johannesburg, South Africa.

☐ I HAVE always thought the term originates from the car insurance industry. In a car accident, the innocent victim is called the third party. Thus 'Third World' refers to the idea that it is an innocent victim of a collision between the capitalist First World and the communist Second World.
John Anderton, Weaverham, Cheshire.

☐ YOUR correspondent Xavier Leroy has the right translation of Third World as coming from the French *Tiers-Monde*. However, I think he misunderstands the actual English meaning of it. *Tiers* means third in the sense of 'the fraction one-third', not in the sense of 'third in a sequence'. Thus, by inference, *le tiers monde* means the third of the world which does not enjoy the same standard of living as the remaining two thirds. There are thus no First or Second worlds.
D. R. Allum, Towcester, Northants.

QUESTION: Where do the terms leftwing and rightwing come from?

☐ THE political terms right and left date from the early days of the French Revolution, and derive from the seating arrangements in the National Assembly in 1789. In the Estates General in May, the Nobility sat in the place of honour on the right-hand side of the Chair. In the Constituent Assembly in July, the supporters of the Old Regime also sat on the right-hand side of the Chair, and their opponents therefore sat on the left-hand side, with the moderates in between. The result is described by Thomas Carlyle in *The French Revolution* (1837): 'Rudiments of Methods disclose themselves; rudiments of Parties. There is a Right Side (*Côté Droit*,) a Left Side (*Côté Gauche*); – sitting on *M. le Président*'s right hand, or on his left: the *Côté Droit* conservative; the *Côté Gauche* destructive. Intermediate is Anglomaniac Constitutionalism, or Two-Chamber Royalism.' This pattern has continued in French and other assemblies, especially those with a circular or semi-circular hall. Left and right 'sides' later became left and right 'wings', as the image of seats in a hall was replaced by one of units in a battle, and conventional political terminology was fixed for ever. In the English Parliament, the Government sat on the right-hand side of the Chair but it continued to do so whether its politics were 'Left' or 'Right'. This pattern has continued in assemblies copied from the British model, especially those with two sides facing each other in a rectangular hall.
Nicolas Walter, London N1.

☐ THE terms come from the physical make-up of the parliament in post-revolutionary France. The revolutionaries sat on the left side of the house (denoted by the colour red), the bourgeoisie sat in the centre (denoted by white) and the royalists sat on the right (denoted by blue) – a make-up which can be recognised in the design of the French flag.
Ann Moody, London SW6.

☐ USE of the terms left and right in fact predates the French Revolution by over a century. They were used in the 1680s by the Societies United in Correspondence ('Convanters'). The Societies used them in the opposite sense to ours, Right being extremists and Left moderates. In the late 19th century the American and

French revolutions and the first English working class political organisations were influenced by the tradition handed down from the Societies of the 17th century. It is probable that the French Assembly adopted the phrase from this tradition, and in it the extremists sat on the right and the moderates on the left. But when the chairman called on a speaker he called him from his right or left hand, with the result that the meaning of the words reversed.
C. Wason, Bridgwater, Somerset.

☐ THERE is no connection between the layout of the seats in the French Assembly and the development of the red, white and blue tricolour, as suggested by Ann Moody. It's true that red was associated with the left and a red flag hung outside the Jacobin Club, and that white was the colour of the monarchists (it was the livery colour of the Bourbons). There is also a case to be made for identifying the colour with the three Estates. But the development of the *Tricolore* was completely coincidental, and was based on colours originating in the municipal arms of Paris, combined with the Bourbon white. In any case the *Tricolore* was established well before the 'post-revolutionary parliament'. The cockade was officially adopted on 31 July 1789, and the tricolour flag on 24 October 1790, but the first revolutionary assembly did not open until 1791.
William Crampton, Director of the Flag Institute.

QUESTION: A friend recently told me that the term for a group of ravens is 'an unkindness'. What's the origin, and are there any other similarly bizarre names for groups of animals?

☐ THE ORIGIN of the term is presumably related to an old (now obsolete) sense of the word 'unkindness', meaning 'unnatural conduct'; the raven was traditionally regarded as a bird of evil omen and mysterious or unnatural conduct. The word as used for a flock of ravens dates from the mid-15th century, and is included in a list of 'proper terms' in the *Book of St Albans* (1486). Other group terms include: 'a hastiness of cooks', 'an observance of hermits', 'a shrewdness of apes', 'a cloud of flies',

'a blush of boys', 'a piteousness of doves', 'a desert of lapwing' and 'a bevy of ladies'.
Judy Pearsall, associate editor, Oxford English Dictionaries, Oxford University Press.

□ JUDY PEARSALL defines an 'observance' as the group name for hermits. Surely a group of hermits constitutes a contradiction in terms?
Greg Mackay, Rome, Italy.

□ THE collective term for our financial advisers must be 'a wunch of bankers'.
David Lambert, Harlow, Essex.

□ NO-ONE has yet mentioned James Lipton's *An Exaltation Of Larks*, which includes not only this but a comprehensive catalogue of collectives. Some of the other ornithological ones are delightful: a charm of finches; an ostentation of peacocks. Others are racy, humorous, sardonic or serendipitous, like: a wince of dentists; a piddle of puppies; a stampede of philatelists.
(Mrs) Else Pickvance, Northfield, Birmingham.

□ HOW about 'A Morbidity of Majors' included in the 'Groups of a Kind' listed in the 1990 Penguin edition of the *Quickway Crossword Dictionary*?
Tom Egan, Eglwyswrw, Dyfed.

□ I WAS once told by college lecturers that the collective noun for a group of college principals was 'a lack'.
Ian Lucraft, Sheffield.

□ I WAS speaking to a professor of psychiatry some years ago, who candidly explained to me that the collective noun for him and his clinical colleagues was 'an absence of professors'.
Len Ratoff, MBE (retired general practitioner), Cressington Park, Liverpool.

□ MY research has elicited the following: sac – a group of gastroenterologists; colony – a large group; bellyfull – a large group in a small room; appendix – a splinter group; rumbling appendix

– a noisy splinter group; burst appendix – a splintered splinter group; abdomination – a group of splinter groups; eructation – the hot air generated by an abdomination.
John Hazlehurst, Cumbria.

QUESTION: Why does 'bastard' as a term of abuse apply only to men?

☐ BASTARD as a term of abuse can be traced back to the figure of the illegitimate malcontent of Elizabethan and Jacobean drama and culture (e.g., Edmund in *King Lear*, Don John in *Much Ado About Nothing*). This type, enviously plotting the downfall of his legitimate siblings and peers, is necessarily male as it is the male illegitimate child who most obviously challenges and is excluded from the ruling power structures and lines of inheritance. Typical characteristics are deviousness, unscrupulousness, ambition and a complete contempt for the rules and codes of society. Although there are many more positive images of bastards in European culture, where he becomes self-made hero rather than Machiavellian schemer, the male bastard is still seen to inherit his parent's subversive sexual energy, to be untrammelled by society's rules, and this feeds into the half-hostile, half-admiring meanings of 'bastard' today.
Jenny Bourne Taylor, London N8.

☐ THE term bastard is an indirect insult to women as it implies that 'your mother is a slut'.
Lucia Asnaghi, London NW2.

QUESTION: Why are the primary colours of transmitted light red, blue and green, when the primary colours of pigments are red, blue and yellow?

☐ COLOUR perception is the eye's reaction to a narrow band of electromagnetic radiation. Green and yellow occur at roughly the mid point of this range. Primary colours are so-called because other colours can be obtained by mixing them. Apart from blue and red at the ends of the scale, a third colour, green or yellow from the mid-range, is required. Two forms of mixing are involved here –

subtractive in reflected light and additive in transmitted light. In pigments mixed on a palette, colour is generated by subtracting (absorbing) all but a narrow range of wavelengths from the white light that strikes the surface. The wavelength of the reflected light then lies between that of the colours used in the mixture. Subtraction in a mixture of blue (wavelength 450 nanometres) and yellow (610nm) gives green at 510nm, while a mixture of yellow and red (750nm) yields orange at 680nm. Green (blue plus yellow) added to red gives brown, not yellow. Accordingly, for colour generated by reflection from pigments the primaries are blue, yellow and red, as can be shown by mixing water colours, for example. In additive or optical mixing, the light reflected by two or more differently coloured surfaces is blended at the retina of the eye; this gives a quite different impression of colour from that of the components. For this mixing, the coloured points must be so closely spaced that the eye cannot resolve them. For example, a film of small, coloured particles deposited on glass will transmit rays of different wavelength that are mixed when they reach the eye. Yellow is then obtained by blending red and green light at the retina. This can be verified by inspecting the screen of a colour TV with a magnifying glass. Areas that seem yellow at a distance will be revealed to be made up of tiny blobs of red and green colour. White areas contain blue, green and red dots.
Allan Brown, West Lulworth, Dorset.

QUESTION: What action could be taken if we had several months' warning that a comet was due to crash into the Earth? Has any serious consideration been given to this, and are there appropriate bodies to plan for such an emergency?

☐ In 1991, Nasa conducted a series of studies of the asteroid (or comet) impact threat to the Earth, and ways in which to avoid it. These were followed up by a Near-Earth Object Detection Workshop which concluded that over 2,000 objects larger than one kilometre across lie in Earth-crossing orbits. Luckily, the Nasa team also concluded that it was feasible to avert similar catastrophes by deflecting the path of the object. Deflection methods would either involve a 'kinetic-energy impact' – i.e. a series of non-nuclear missiles shot at the object – or, for larger objects, a huge nuclear explosion close by. However, the team also

decided not to proceed beyond the theoretical because of the high cost in the face of a low risk factor.
Jeff Craig, Edinburgh.

☐ COMETS, asteroids and rogue satellites heading for England and Wales are a responsibility of the Home Office, which funds emergency planners in metropolitan districts, fire and civil defence authorities, London boroughs and county councils. Our job is to get city, town and county halls in shape for the next disaster. We do what we can, but the obliteration of Mother Earth is not a priority right now. There are quite enough disasters around already before we ransack municipal basements to find the old civil defence plans for survival after World War Three.
Simon Turney, Emergency Planning Unit, South Yorkshire Fire and Civil Defence Authority.

QUESTION: 'An event has happened, upon which it is difficult to speak, and impossible to keep silent.' What was Edmund Burke referring to?

☐ HE WAS referring to the case of Warren Hastings. This was a great public scandal until its lengthy duration resulted in most people losing interest. Hastings was a British governor-general of India until he was impeached in 1786 and then tried before the House of Lords. Burke, who made the comment in 1789, was a prime mover in the case against him. The charges ranged from fighting unnecessary wars to maladministration and financial impropriety. The trial lasted seven years (1788–95), at the end of which Hastings was acquitted.
Mark Pack, York.

QUESTION: Exactly when will the world's oil run out, and will there be any alternative convenient energy available at that time?

☐ THE rate of consumption of oil is not constant. Fuel efficiency measures may decrease the rate of consumption, or, more likely, increases in use in less-developed areas will increase the rate of

consumption. Also, it is not known exactly how much oil exists. Geographers usually distinguish between a resource – that is, the total amount of oil on the planet – and a reserve, which is the total amount of oil we know about and can extract economically. Clearly, the reserves of oil are always changing with new finds, or improvements in technology, or changes in price. At best, all that can be said is that current reserves at current rates of consumption should last until at least 2030. Undoubtedly, however, oil will run out some day if we continue to use it at anything approaching current rates. Whether we have an alternative depends on many factors. One thought is that as oil becomes more scarce the price will increase, which will force industry and governments to act to find alternatives. The sceptics argue that even if there is sufficient foresight for this to happen, the transition may well be difficult with increased potential for conflict as organisations fight (perhaps literally) for the remaining reserves.
Mark Payne, Montacute, Somerset.

□ REGARDING alternatives, the main uses for which oil is particularly convenient are transportation – uniquely so, in the case of aviation fuel, for which no real substitute has yet been found – and certain grades of lubricants, which as yet have not been recreated synthetically. However, for all other purposes, oil is going out of favour, primarily on environmental grounds. In almost all instances, including motor transport, the substitute fuels will be natural gas (methane), which is cheap, plentiful (it exists in greater quantities than oil), safe, and far cleaner than coal or oil.
Nicholas Perry, Croydon.

QUESTION: Is anything unthinkable?

□ NOT that I can think of.
Bob Livermore, London E3.

□ THE dictionary definition of thinking is 'to use the power of reason' – we assume thinking has a purpose about it. In that sense, dreaming is unthinkable as we cannot 'think' dreams. It is the unstructured nature of dreams that makes them hard to recall or describe. Aspects of the future are unthinkable in the sense

that Bach could easily have played jazz but was unable to think in those terms because he didn't have the relevant musical concepts to think with. The process of thinking entails an objective to reach and the appropriate mental images to attain that objective. If these are missing then the concept is unthinkable.
S. Hayward, London NW2.

QUESTION: Is it possible to carry out a genuine altruistic act, bearing in mind that it ceases to be so at the slightest feeling of pleasure or satisfaction?

☐ SPONTANEOUSLY laying down one's life for another must surely count as such.
Anthony F. Bennett, Chichester, W. Sussex.

☐ I WOULD imagine that standing for the Tories in a 'safe' Conservative seat at a by-election is truly altruistic. There surely could be no pleasure or satisfaction in either the campaign or the result.
Vincent Quirk, Skelmersdale, Lancs.

☐ ALTRUISM, as 'regard for others as a principle for action' (*OED*), is in the act, not in the gratification or otherwise which one might feel in doing the act. Regard for others, although maybe the priority in altruistic acts, does not necessarily exclude regard for yourself.
Adam Thompson, Brussels.

QUESTION: Is 'A question sender' the most appropriate anagram of Notes and Queries?

☐ DO INANE requests; send a risqué note.
Steve Dungworth, Harrogate, N. Yorkshire.

☐ INSANE quest doer.
P. F. McGinley, Wakefield, W. Yorkshire.

☐ O, SEND a request in.
Jack Griffiths, Ferring-by-Sea, W. Sussex.

☐ SEND a note, Squire.
C. Campbell, Fleet, Hants.

☐ ENQUIRERS' sad note.
Andrew Peel, Canterbury, Kent.

☐ REQUEST non-ideas; sender so antique.
Gerry Abbott, Chorlton-cum-Hardy, Manchester.

☐ ENQUIRE, as stoned; I end reason quest.
Claire Whieldon, Keele, Staffordshire.

QUESTION: Why did Hitler not invade Switzerland?

☐ BECAUSE a stable, working Switzerland served him better, providing a base for business deals, an important railway link to Italy, a safe haven for spies and securing diplomatic contact with enemy forces. 'Six days a week the Swiss work for Hitler, on the seventh they pray for victory of the Allied forces,' went a joke in those times. The German share of Swiss exports (mainly weapons, ammunition, high-tech machinery, food) increased from 15.5 to 42 per cent between 1937 and 1942. Not only civil goods made their way from or to Germany through Switzerland: weaponry was transported up to October 1941, and forced Italian labour as late as 1943. The allied forces even considered bombing the Gotthard line in 1944. Money robbed by the Nazis during the war was transferred into Swiss bank accounts. Although aware of the fate of those fleeing the death camps in Germany, the Swiss authorities refused to take in more people. Germany really had no reason for invading Switzerland, as this country worked so well for the Nazis. If there was a winner in the Second World War, it was the Swiss.
Thomas Schwager, St Gallen, Switzerland.

QUESTION: Next year I shall be attending an international school in Hong Kong. A part of this will require me to display English culture, including national costume, songs, dances and recipes. Any ideas?

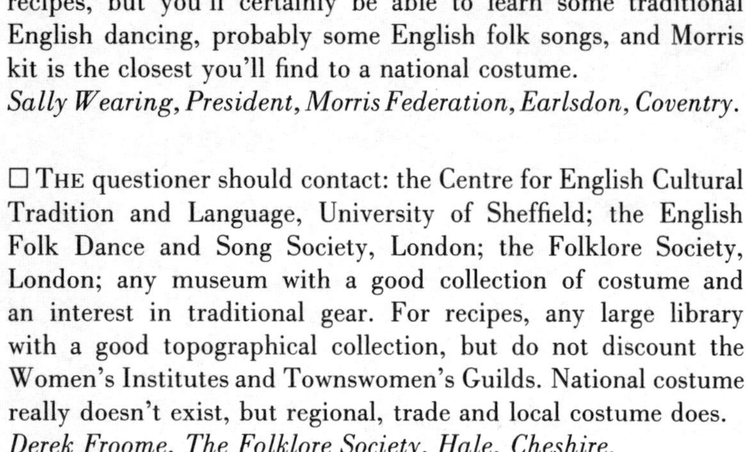

□ JOIN a Morris team. They may not be able to help with the recipes, but you'll certainly be able to learn some traditional English dancing, probably some English folk songs, and Morris kit is the closest you'll find to a national costume.
Sally Wearing, President, Morris Federation, Earlsdon, Coventry.

□ THE questioner should contact: the Centre for English Cultural Tradition and Language, University of Sheffield; the English Folk Dance and Song Society, London; the Folklore Society, London; any museum with a good collection of costume and an interest in traditional gear. For recipes, any large library with a good topographical collection, but do not discount the Women's Institutes and Townswomen's Guilds. National costume really doesn't exist, but regional, trade and local costume does.
Derek Froome, The Folklore Society, Hale, Cheshire.

□ 'ENGLISH' culture perhaps existed between the departure of the Romans from the British Isles and the arrival of the Danes. Since then, England – which can only have a geographical meaning – has been under permanent foreign (British) domination. Our most famous rulers, Knut (Danish), Richard Lionheart (French), Henry VIII (Welsh), George I (German), and now the Greeks, have left the area of land called England without any culture of its own. We have no costume, songs, dances and recipes that have amused our British rulers and therefore been allowed to survive. Our language is a 'mish-mash' of Danish and French with just about anything else we can take on. Our football yobs wave the British flag at 'English' matches. Our national drink is tea – brought back by the British. Our ancestors were press-ganged into the British navy, conscripted into the armies, and died in British pits and factories to make the British owners rich. The Irish, Welsh, and Scottish were further away from London, more protected by their mountains and sea. They still have a culture.
Andrew Moss, Greiveldange, Luxembourg.

□ SALLY WEARING may not be aware of the non-European origins of the Morris dance. J. A. Rogers, in his book *Nature Knows No Colour Lines* (1952) cites a number of authorities to show that the name 'Morris' is a corruption of 'Moorish', and hence that the dance has an African origin. Dr Johnson's dictionary (1755),

for example, has 'Morris dance, that is Moorish or Morrice dance'. Shakespeare used the term 'Moor' to refer to all black Africans, as was the common usage since long before his time. The African origin of the Morris dance is further reinforced by the fact that, in times gone by, white dancers blackened their faces to dance it. The main argument of Rogers's book is that there has long been a black presence in England – and in much of Europe – which has left many marks on our culture, including this, the most English of dances.
Charlie Owen, London N4.

☐ ONE traditional English dance might be appropriate. It requires 12 Englishmen, 11 clad in white and the 12th in a white coat. The dance starts with one of the 11 screaming at the man in the white coat. The latter replies by solemnly raising the index finger of his right hand. The 11 in white then leap in turn into the air with the man who uttered the initial scream, slapping hands and displaying unreserved ecstasy. After one minute of this display, the 11 suddenly stop and begin to clap rhythmically, all the while staring into the mid-distance. They are joined in the applause by the audience for approximately one more minute. The dance then ends. This dance is called 'The Dismissal Of The Australian Batsman' (sometimes also called 'The Waugh Dance'). It is performed at most four times every five days during periods of the English summer.
Stuart Newstead, Oxford.

QUESTION: Why did World War I produce better poetry than any other war? Is it only true of Britain?

☐ THE British poetry of World War I is uniquely powerful because the circumstances of the war contrasted with the imagery which contemporary writers and politicians had developed to describe an ideal England. The 'heart of England' was a network of rural pathways, ancient ruins and markers of buried pre-history. The trenches in France and Flanders were like a terrible inversion of this ideal national landscape. British First World War poetry was the distillation of the best aspirations of Victorian culture meeting the worst consequences of the modernity which the culture had generated. The special resonance of that moment could never recur.

(Dr) Paul Barlow, University of Northumbria, Newcastle upon Tyne.

☐ THE best German war poetry never became as well-established because, when the anthology of First World War German poetry was due to be published as part of the national collection, the Nazis took over and the original editor was replaced by a party member more interested in the *Heldentod* (dying for the Fatherland) than any anti-war experience.

John Warren, Oxford Brookes University.

☐ HOW ABOUT the *Iliad*? Or numerous Sagas and Border Ballads, and *The Cattle Raid Of Cooley*?

N. MacDonald, Lenzie, Glasgow.

QUESTION: Is a fourth – or higher – spatial dimension a reality that exists but eludes human senses and imagination, or is it an abstract concept for which there is no room in the real universe?

☐ THE fact that we cannot comfortably fit our right-hand foot into our left-hand shoe is evidence that space has only three dimensions. Consider a two-dimensional experiment: two paper shapes are laid out on a table, one in the shape of an R, the other a mirror-reversed R. By simply moving the shapes around on the two-dimensional surface of the table, you cannot make them exactly coincide. (The reason being that they have no axis of symmetry. In contrast, an E, which does have an axis of symmetry, can be made to coincide with its mirror-image). However, if you let one shape move in the third spatial dimension, by lifting it up and turning it over, you can make it coincide with its mirror-image counterpart. The apparent differences between these two-dimensional objects disappear once they are allowed to move in three spatial dimensions. The three-dimensional right foot and left foot are just like these shapes: they cannot be made to coincide as things are (having no plane of symmetry). But were they able to rotate in a fourth spatial dimension, their differences would disappear. Nature is

full of objects which have no plane of symmetry. A molecule of adrenaline, for example, has no plane of symmetry, and can occur in either a 'right-handed' form or a 'left-handed' form. The fact that these different forms have different physiological properties should convince us that there is no fourth dimension of space.
(Dr) Robin Le Poidevin, Department of Philosophy, University of Leeds.

□ THE fourth spatial dimension is simultaneously at right angles to any direction in which we care to point. However, being 'trapped' in the three dimensions we can't actually point in this direction. Also, even if we could detect the extra dimension, we would not be able to 'see' it because our retinas are two-dimensional surfaces and to see a four-dimensional object in its entirety, we would need three-dimensional retinas. The best we could hope for would be to see three-dimensional slices of the objects in series as we scanned it, just as hospital scanners are used to view slices of the human body. There exist some computer programs which show the projection of, say, a hypercube (the four-dimensional analogue of an ordinary cube) rotating. The images are perplexing and some people claim to be able to get an idea of the appearance of the actual hypercube through watching these real-time images. According to some of the latest theories in physics, space consists of many more dimensions than we can actually detect. The fourth and higher dimensions are postulated to be a physical reality.
(Dr) Khurram Wadee, Ealing, London W13.

□ THE contradiction between the two respondents can be resolved by analysing what we mean by 'space'. Dr Le Poidevin's symmetry examples certainly show us there are only three dimensions to our everyday, common-sense kind of 'space', the 'space' we can perceive and move our feet in. Physicists dealing with superstring theory, however, have developed persuasive theories using an extra six spatial dimensions. These higher dimensions, however, are curled up into tiny circles, or similar closed surfaces, and are so small they are invisible on casual inspection (something in the range of $1/10^{33}$ across). This curling up of dimensions is analogous to our observing, say, a piece of string from a distance and seeing it as a line, then moving closer and observing that it actually has an extra, circular dimension. If we could observe any point (say, a subatomic particle) at a large enough magnification, we would

similarly see that it is not a point, but has further dimensions in unexplored directions.
Mark Howard, London NW6.

QUESTION: What is the difference between right and wrong?

☐ IN A logically sound language, there would be no such adjectives as 'right' and 'wrong': these words do not describe objective qualities but attitudes. Any meaningful statement about right and wrong implies someone's approval; either your own, or that of the circle in which you move, your religion, your god, a consensus of opinion via democratic process, etc. The use of such words as 'approved' and 'disapproved' has the advantage that it helps us clarify our minds on whose approval we are referring to.
Richard Benjamin, Ethical Society, London WC1.

☐ THE present government has demonstrated that the right can almost invariably be wrong.
Ted Tranter, Birchington, Kent.

☐ RICHARD BENJAMIN is wrong to simply assume that 'right' and 'wrong' do not refer to objective qualities – this is still a hotly contested issue in moral philosophy. If, as I expect, Mr Benjamin is working with a conception whereby the only objective properties are the ones turned up by physicists, then no doubt he is right. However, under this conception not only would the adjectives 'right' and 'wrong' have to disappear from Mr Benjamin's 'logically sound language', but so too virtually every other adjective we commonly use. This ought to make Mr Benjamin suspicious that maybe there are objective criteria relating to human conduct that make certain adjectives, including right and wrong, objectively applicable. Biting someone's face off just does seem objectively wrong, given the sort of lives we might intelligibly be expected to want to lead as human beings. Secondly, he seems to be peddling a long-since discredited 'emotivist' theory of moral discourse by identifying 'right' and 'wrong' with 'approval' and 'disapproval'. It is simply false to claim that a sentence such as 'I believe euthanasia is right' means the same as 'I approve of euthanasia'. I might well approve of euthanasia but the question whether euthanasia is right surely remains to be answered. Similarly, the fact that whole

communities might approve of certain behaviour – for example, capital punishment, enslaving other cultures, etc. – does not mean that such behaviour is right.
Robert Avon, School of Humanities and Social Sciences, University of Wolverhampton.

☐ ROBERT AVON fails to recognise that the right road for one traveller is the wrong road for another. It has nothing to do with the objective quality of the road. 'Right' and 'wrong' are used together to measure the quality of something, just as 'hot' and 'cold' are used to measure temperature, and 'north' and 'south' to measure directions. Used independently of each other, they are meaningless, the toys of philosophers.
Sam Micklem, Eldwick, West Yorkshire.

QUESTION: Did Adam and Eve have navels?

☐ IN *Genesis* 1.26, God (displaying his own disconcerting tendency to plurality) says: 'Let us make man in our own image, and let them have dominion over the fish of the sea.' So 'man' was a collective being from the beginning. As for Adam and Eve, the names occur much later on in the text, after the fall, and mean something like 'red' or 'earthy' and 'living' or 'lively'. So they're symbolic qualities, and were presumably consciously attached to symbolic persons. It took a later, less-aware culture to start treating these allusive stories as literal histories. So the first humanity wasn't very different from present-day humanity, belly-buttons and all, and the power of creation stories can still be recaptured by those who gaze beyond their own navels.
David Newton, Chelmondiston, Suffolk.

☐ 'YES' is the short answer. It could be argued that the Adam created in God's own image was navel-less: sexual reproduction only came on to the scene after the expulsion from Eden, and the navel is a mark of our fallen state. In the last century a creationist rearguard action against Darwinism centred on Adam's navel. Philip Gosse's book *Omphalos* (Greek: navel) argued that, although Adam was created, his body looked as if he had once been born; similarly, although the animals in the Garden of Eden were created as adults, they looked as if they had been

born and grown in the normal way. Gosse's master-stroke was to extend the argument to the Earth itself, which 'appeared' as if it dated back millions of years. However, neither creationists nor evolutionists were impressed with this, and the case for a scientifically respectable creationism duly perished.
Phil Edwards, Manchester.

☐ MY THEORY is that when God had finished making man he realised that Adam just didn't look right with that expanse of smooth featureless abdomen, so he created the belly button. Later, when placentation became just the thing, it was the perfect place for the umbilical cord to attach to the foetus.
(Dr) Kitty Smith, London N8.

QUESTION: What is the origin of the phrase 'taking the mickey'?

☐ MICHAEL BARRETT was the last man to be publicly hanged in Britain – for an explosion at Clerkenwell Jail in 1867, which was an attempt to free a leader of the Fenians, Richard O'Sullivan Burke. Irish immigrants were to become known as 'Michael Barretts', a term of derision later shortened to 'Micks'. The stereotype of the Irish being stupid gave rise to the term 'taking the mickey'.
David Glinch, London SE6.

☐ ACCORDING to both James Macdonald's *Dictionary Of Obscenity, Taboo And Euphemism* (Sphere, 1988) and R. W. Holder's *Dictionary of Euphemisms* (Faber, 1987), 'Mike Bliss' or 'Mickey Bliss' was cockney rhyming slang, and 'taking the Mickey' was therefore 'taking the piss'. E. J. Burford, in *The Orrible Synne: A Look at London Lechery . . .* (Calder-Boyars, 1973), also reports that 'micgan' was Old English for piss, from the old Norse 'migan', and that this was the root of the expression.
P. Cross, Highbury, London N5.

☐ P. CROSS is right to identify the origin of the phrase in Cockney rhyming slang. However, to suggest that it owes something to the Old English 'micgan' is to overlook the medical term for the same process, micturition.
Neil Grant, Kings Heath, Birmingham.

QUESTION: When not in use, what is the correct position to leave the toilet seat, lowered or raised?

☐ IF THE loo in question is used by both sexes, lowered please. The unexpected contact of bare flesh and cold porcelain is traumatic.
Anne Bryson, West Kirby, Merseyside.

☐ SO NOW we know! Anne Bryson reveals the real reason women get mad when men leave the seat up – they don't bother to look before they plonk themselves down! Right, now let's settle this: we'll all leave both seat and cover down after use and then we'll all have to check before the action starts.
Christopher Turner, Sevenoaks, Kent.

☐ THERE need be no gender war – seat and lid should both be replaced! Every time the toilet is flushed, fine droplets of probably harmful bacteria explode upwards over an area of four cubic feet. Wise people limit infection.
Margaret Williams, Isleham, Cambs.

QUESTION: Somewhere in a field in the north of England there used to be a sign saying 'Please do not throw stones at this notice'? Are there other examples of this kind of helpful public information?

☐ THERE is a sign at the back entrance to the botanical gardens in this town that says: 'Slow Down – You are entering a work zone.'
Paul Mestitz, Geelong, Victoria, Australia.

☐ IN A coffee-bar in Sincelejo, northern Colombia, the following is displayed: 'Bread with butter: 100 pesos. Bread with margarine: 80 pesos. Bread without butter: 60 pesos. Bread without margarine: 40 pesos.'
Bernardo Recamán, Bogotá, Colombia.

☐ SEEN in a field in West Yorkshire: 'Beware of the Bull. Entry Free. Bull Will Charge Later.'
(Mrs) Ray Tantram, Great Bookham, Surrey.

☐ SEEN at the tip of Great Camanoe Island in the British Virgin Islands (1962–64): 'No trespassing without permission.'
A. S. Batham, Taupo, New Zealand.

☐ I AM told that in Belize, in a place called 'The Dump', there was a football field with a sign saying: 'Anyone throwing stones will be persecuted.'
R. E. G. Smith, Maseru, Lesotho.

☐ OUTSIDE Shap Abbey in Cumbria stands this notice: 'Admission Free. Special terms for parties.'
Marcus Cousterdine, Blackpool.

☐ IN RECENT years there was a blue heritage plaque on a house in Zinzan Street in Reading which stated: 'William Hogarth (1697–1764) never lived here.' It has since disappeared. Maybe they found out it wasn't true?
Maxine Wicks, Bishopston, Bristol.

☐ MY FAVOURITE road sign is in Chesham, Bucks, where the highway authorities – having spent large sums of taxpayers' money to build a relief road with two lanes in each direction – now instruct motorists: 'Use Both Lanes.'
Geoffrey Allen, Pavia, Italy.

☐ WHEN we lived in Massachusetts in the 1960s, I distinctly remember a sign on a high-tension electricity pylon saying: 'To climb this structure means instant death. Anyone found doing so will be prosecuted.'
Nicholas O'Dell, Phoenixville, Pennsylvania, US.

QUESTION: Are there any valid arguments, other than religious ones, as to why it would be better for the planet for the human race to continue rather than to become extinct?

☐ THE questioner asks whether or not it would be better for 'the planet'. This is a problem of values. The planet, insofar as it is a material object, clearly has no values of its own, since values are a product of consciousness. The planet could no more experience pleasure in the continued existence of life than it would lament its

passing. It therefore follows that any positive attributes the planet is thought to possess only exist because of their presence in the mind of a living being capable of experiencing them. So far as we know, humans are able to experience more complex and varied responses to the world than any other animal. This opinion may be no more than 'speciesist' vanity, but the existence of anything approaching human levels of creative thought in other animals is so far unproven. In any case, whatever other animals think, we can only answer this question from within our own value system. To this extent it answers itself. The beauties and pleasures of the natural world which we experience are only recognised as such because we are here to do the recognising. If we didn't exist, neither would these experiences. The planet is only valuable as long as someone is here to value it. Our existence is thus a necessary condition for the continuation of the planet itself as something which is meaningful.
(Dr) P. Barlow, Sunderland University, Tyne and Wear.

☐ DR BARLOW'S answer is based on the assumption that '*better*' necessarily means '*morally superior*': this makes nonsense in the context. In the English language it can also mean 'in a superior physical condition', as when we say that someone is better after an illness. In this sense the planet would obviously be better without the human race. In these days of efficient contraception and when there are few family businesses left to keep going, the main motives for perpetuating the human race must be to satisfy the parental instinct, to attempt to achieve some sort of immortality, or to keep *Debrett's Peerage* in business. However, it may surprise the questioner to know that two Christian sects, the Albigenses and Cathars in the 11th–13th centuries in southern France and elsewhere, condemned procreation on the grounds that it increased the amount of evil in the world which they saw as a battleground between spiritual good and material evil. They were condemned as heretics and became the victims of a crusade led by our Simon de Montfort.
Robert Sephton, Oxford.

☐ IT WAS not *our* Simon de Montfort, Earl of Leicester, born in 1208, who led the merciless crusade against the Albigenses and Cathars in south-west France. It was Simon IV le Fort, Sire de Montfort, who was appointed to lead the crusade in 1209, following

the assassination of the Papal Envoy, Pierre de Castelnau, near St Gilles. Meanwhile, *our* Simon de Montfort was a babe in arms.
F. Paul Taylor, Frodsham.

□ I WONDER if Robert Sephton realises that by introducing the Albigenses and Cathars into the debate, he undermines his own argument. These sects, like other forms of Manicheism, believed that all matter was evil. For them, the world would be a better place if all biological life was extinguished. By this logic, a healthy planet is a dead planet. So keep up the good work, all you polluters out there!
Flavia Dunford-Trodd, Liverpool.

□ IF IT is acceptable and rational for a parent to step in front of a speeding bullet to save a child, which most people would agree on, then it is also acceptable and rational to wish for my/our extinction in order to save the planet. All one needs to do is give a plausible defence of what one is trying to save. If there are two alternatives – the complete extinction of all life on Earth or the extinction of all human life – which do we choose? According to Dr Barlow, who says that 'the planet is only valuable as long as someone is there to value it', one might as well make the decision with a pin. This I cannot accept. The second alternative leaves the planet intact and with a wealth of biological diversity, whereas the first leaves just another dead planet. There is a difference. The real question is, is this the alternative that faces us?
Giles Radford, Ashford, Kent.

QUESTION: Can the temperature of a vacuum be measured? If so, what is it the temperature of?

□ YES, with a thermometer. Suspend it in a hollow sphere, pump out the air and heat the sphere until it is red hot. The thermometer soon approaches the temperature of the walls. Not in contact with any matter, it is measuring the temperature of radiation – mostly infra-red and some visible light. Alternatively, point your thermometer out into space, as has indeed been done. It reads –270°C, which is the temperature of the microwave background radiation from the glowing embers of the Big Bang.
(Dr) John Samson, Department of Physics, Loughborough University of Technology.

□ WHAT Dr John Samson is measuring in his experiments is the temperature of the residual molecules, since an absolute vacuum is not achievable. Radiation has wavelength, frequency, intensity and direction but not temperature.
Edward Gulbenkian, Mitcham, Surrey.

□ THE temperature of something is a measure of the average kinetic energy of its molecules. In the theoretical perfect vacuum, there are no molecules and hence the idea of temperature is without meaning.
David Henderson, Nuthurst, W. Sussex.

□ RADIATION most certainly does have temperature because it has energy, measured by the vibrational frequency of its photons. Photons can be treated as particles in a manner akin to atoms and molecules. You measure the temperature of a vacuum cavity by taking the energy spectrum of the radiation flying about inside it. In fact, the temperature of outer space as measured by the 'background radiation' is taken as evidence for the Big Bang hypothesis of the origin of the universe. Since then the expansion of the universe has diluted the original high temperatures down to a background of about 4° 'Absolute'.
Peter Rowland (MSc, PhD), Dulwich, London SE24.

QUESTION: The *Collins English Dictionary* of 1979 features the word 'pornocracy', defined as a 'government or domination of government by whores'. What events, historical or otherwise, brought this word into being?

□ DURING the 9th and 10th centuries, with the break-up of the Carolingian empire and the resultant internecine wars, foreign invasion and the rise of local feudal lords, the Papacy became marginalised and lost its political authority and spiritual prestige. Between AD 914 and 963, the landed aristocracy under the leadership of a Roman senator Theophylact, his wife Theodora and their daughter Marozia came increasingly to dominate the Curia. Marozia, mistress of Pope Sergius III and mother of his son, the future Pope John XI, took control of Rome. In a move characteristic of her egregious family, the Crescentii, who held

power on and off throughout the 10th century, she had her Pope son imprisoned until her other son, Alberic, took up the reigns of power (AD932). This period is known as the 'Pornocracy'. Whether Theodora and Marozia were whores in the true sense of the word is a moot point. One suspects, however, that to a male-dominated church the very idea of women being in control of the Curia must be anathema and, by its very definition, an obscenity.
Colin Andrew, London NW1.

QUESTION: An article on climate and weather in the *Fortean Times* mentions that Eskimos visited Scotland during the 'little ice age' of the mid-18th century. Is this true?

□ IN ABERDEEN there are two kayaks in the Anthropological Museum of Marischal College. In an exhibition there a few years ago several accounts of Eskimo visits to Scotland were recounted. During the late 17th and early 18th century there were several records of strange men in canoes seen fishing off the Scottish coast. They were called 'Finmen' in the belief that they came from Finland. Around 1730 an Eskimo kayaker came ashore near Aberdeen but died soon after, and his is one of the canoes now in the museum. A century later an Eskimo named Enoolooapik was brought from Labrador to Aberdeen aboard the ship *Neptune*. He stayed for about a year, becoming a popular figure around town and occasionally giving kayaking demonstrations on the River Dee.
(Dr) Warren L. Kovach, Pentraeth, Anglesey.

QUESTION: What, according to orthodox Christian teaching, happens to the souls of the dead? There seem to be two opposing views. One has it that the souls (after a possible spell in Purgatory, some say) go pretty directly to Heaven, the other that they remain with their bodies until the last day, when Christ will come in judgment.

□ ORTHODOX Christian teaching certainly seems to hold two irreconcilable views. The Scriptures, however, are clear that man, far from possessing an immortal soul, has 'no pre-eminence above a beast . . . all go unto one place; all are of the dust and all turn

to dust again' (*Ecclesiastes* 3:19). In truth, the whole notion of the soul is generally misunderstood as being a sort of disembodied spirit. As the earliest use of a word in the Hebrew Bible can often throw light on its later use, it is instructive to look up the first reference to a '*nefesh*', the Hebrew word that is frequently translated as 'soul'. 'And God said: "Let the waters bring forth abundantly the moving creature that hath life [*nefesh*] and fowl that fly above the earth in the open firmament of heaven".' (*Genesis* 1:20). There is no ambiguity here; if the creature were to die, it would no longer have 'life' or a 'soul'. The claim, therefore, that the soul goes to Heaven (or Purgatory – a place-name unknown in Scripture) has no foundation in the Bible. God has, however, promised that those who have heard the message of the Gospel and understood the promises made to Eve, Abraham, Isaac, Jacob and David (see *Galatians* 3:8) and thus are responsible, shall be raised for judgment at the coming of Jesus, the Messiah: 'And at that time shall Michael [Hebrew: 'Who is like God'] stand up, the great prince which standeth for the children of thy people . . . And many of them that sleep in the dust of the earth shall awake, some to everlasting life and some to shame and everlasting contempt' (*Daniel* 12:1,2). The 'everlasting life' promised to those who are counted worthy, is described in the *Book of Revelation*: 'They shall be priests of God and of Christ and shall reign with him a thousand years' (20:6). This millennium will culminate in all things being subdued unto God and 'then shall the Son also himself be subject unto him that put all things under him, that God may be all in all' (1 *Corinthians* 15:28).
K. Ritmeyer, Skelton, York.

□ Mr Ritmeyer's biblical quotations are misleading, in that they are used to support a very human argument, and ignore the spiritual. In *Acts*, Chapter 7, the martyr Stephen, a man 'full of the holy spirit and wisdom' says in his dying moment: 'Lord Jesus, receive my spirit.' In his parable of the rich man and Lazarus, the Lord Himself speaks of afterlife (*Luke* 16). My advice to the questioner is to accept the definition that 'soul' is the amalgam of a physical body and an intelligent life-force ('spirit'). The Bible makes it absolutely clear that when the physical frame expires, the 'spirit' goes into the custody of the Lord of Creation, Jesus Christ.
James Fasey, Toton, Nottingham.

QUESTION: Can anyone provide information about the fire at Alexandria in Egypt which destroyed the great library there among other things? When was it, do we know what was lost, and what were the consequences?

□ THE library was the first research institute in world history. Alexander the Great's successors as rulers of Egypt, Ptolemy I and II, developed it in the 3rd century BC. It contained the greatest collection of handwritten papyrus scrolls in the ancient world, perhaps numbering over 700,000 and a foundation for the systematic study of the arts and sciences was established. Even the Old Testament came down to us from mainly Greek translations made in the library. The library was deliberately burnt down by a mob circa AD 420 as classical civilisation disintegrated and the Dark Ages closed in. All that survived was a tiny fraction of its work and a cellar of the Serapaeum, the library annexe. The loss was incalculable but we do know, for example, that the work of Eratosthenes, a library director who had accurately calculated the size of the Earth, and Aristarchus of Samos, who had postulated a heliocentric universe, the axis-rotation of the Earth and its revolution around the sun, had to be rediscovered by Columbus and Copernicus a thousand years later. Of the 123 plays of Sophocles only seven survived (one of which was *Oedipus Rex*). Much the same happened to the work of Aeschylus and Euripides.
Tony Martin, London SE15.

QUESTION: Hasn't this question about *déjà vu* been in Notes & Queries before?

□ PLEASE refer to my previous answer.
Stephan Harrison, Tottenham, London N17.

QUESTION: Why is there a United States naval base at Guantanamo Bay in Cuba?

□ IN 1898, while Cuba was still a Spanish colony, the United States defeated Spain in a war that happened in the midst of a revolutionary struggle for Cuban independence. After the war,

a convention was set up to frame a constitution for Cuba. The US attached a proviso to the constitution that deprived Cuba of real independence: this became known as the Platt Amendment (reproduced in full in the book *From Columbus To Castro – History Of The Caribbean 1492–1969* by Dr Eric Williams, former Prime Minister of Trinidad). This clause basically made Cuba a colony of the United States and required that country to maintain a military presence on the island. The convention initially refused to accept the Platt Amendment but the United States made it clear that they would not withdraw from Cuba until the Platt Amendment was accepted, and so the convention backed down. In 1903 the United States 'leased' bases at Guantanamo Bay and Bahia Honda, agreeing to pay an annual lease of $2,000 which was to run for 99 years; in 1912 they surrendered Bahia Honda in return for a larger base at Guantanamo Bay for a rate of $5,000 annually. Incidentally, the Platt Amendment governed American relations with Cuba until the advent of Fidel Castro.
(Mrs) V. P. Connell-Hall, Peckham, London SE15.

□ MRS CONNELL-HALL is correct that the US base at Guantanamo in Cuba traces its origins to the Spanish American War of 1898. This occurred when the US – for reasons which are hotly debated – chose to intervene in the Cuban war of national liberation against Spain. As a condition for subsequent withdrawal, it required 'independent' Cuba to accept the Platt Amendment, which justified subsequent US interventions in order to protect 'life, property and individual liberty' (*sic*). However, she is wrong to say that the Amendment remained in force until the revolution of 1959, for it was abrogated in 1934 by F. D. Roosevelt, whose 'Good Neighbor Policy' involved a renunciation of direct intervention in Latin American countries – not least because, in Cuba and elsewhere, such interventions had proved costly and counter-productive (see Bryce Wood, *The Making of the Good Neighbor Policy*). Conversely, the post-1934 Cuban regime was generally congenial to US strategic and economic interests. Castro's revolution changed all that, and his regime has had to suffer some less-than-good neighbourly policies. However, it did not have to abrogate the Platt Amendment, which was long dead, nor did it challenge the US presence at Guantanamo.
Alan Knight, Professor of Latin American History, Oxford University.

QUESTION: Why is a mirror image not upside down as well as being the wrong way round?

□ THE short answer is that a mirror image is not the wrong way round (in the sense of a left/right reversal). Try this experiment: instead of designating your hands 'left' and 'right', place a glove on (say) the right hand and call them 'gloved' and 'ungloved'. Now stand in front of a mirror so that you are facing north. Your (right) gloved hand points east. So does the mirror image's gloved hand. Your (left) ungloved hand points west. So does that in the mirror. Your feet point down and your head up – so do those in your reflection. What has changed? You face north – your mirror image faces south. This is the only reversal.
R. Thomson, Brighton.

□ CONSIDER looking at a book in a mirror. The key is that one has to turn it round to face the mirror. If you turn it around its vertical axis, right and left are reversed, so you get 'mirror' writing. If you turn it around its horizontal axis you do not get mirror writing: it is upside down, and not right–left reversed in the mirror. In every case, you see what you have done to make the book face the mirror. The same holds for yourself. Usually you turn around vertically to face a mirror – but you can stand on your head, then you are upside down and not right–left reversed. The history of this ancient puzzle dating back to Plato, and its solution, are discussed in *Odd Perceptions* by R. L. Gregory (Routledge, 1986) and in the *Oxford Companion to the Mind* (OUP).
(Prof.) Richard Gregory, CBE, FRS, Department of Psychology, University of Bristol.

□ I TRIED various contortions with books in front of mirrors trying to fathom Professor Gregory's reply. All I got when I turned the book on its horizontal axis was mirror writing which was also upside down. Maybe I don't know my Plato from my Aristotle but I think the Prof. is pulling our legs. It all depends on how you define 'wrong way round'. A mirror simply reflects every point straight back. There is no left–right inversion and also quite consistently no top–bottom inversion either. Our feet remain on the floor, our heads remain in the clouds, our left hands remain on the left and our right hands remain on the right. Inversion only

occurs if we imagine ourselves to be our mirror images . . . maybe that's where Prof. Gregory's speciality – psychology – comes in.
Brian Homer, Gwynedd.

☐ PROFESSOR Gregory is certainly not 'pulling our legs', as Mr Homer suggests. Quite the reverse(!). Mr Homer claims that he saw mirror writing which was also upside down, which would be a refutation of the original question. Writing seen in a single mirror can be either upside down or the wrong way round but it cannot be both. Write the word 'bow' on a piece of paper. Turn it around a vertical axis to face a mirror. In the mirror it looks like 'wod', which is right–left reversed. If the paper is instead turned around a horizontal axis to face the mirror, the word looks like 'pom', which is upside down but not right–left reversed. The word Mr Homer would claim to see is 'moq'. It would not be possible to observe this with only one mirror. The rest of Mr Homer's answer is sensible and is not inconsistent with Prof. Gregory's perfectly reasonable answer. This question is a speciality of the professor's, as can be judged from his contributions to *New Scientist* a few years ago. Nevertheless, the really intriguing question is psychological: why do we think of people or objects seen in mirrors as being the 'wrong way round' and why do we find it disturbing to see them? It is contrary to our perception of the 'real' world, where people greet each other by shaking their right hands, and the hands of a clock go round in a clockwise direction. It is as disturbing as the clever TV ads for Tennants Pilsener, where the tape is run backwards but still almost makes sense in 'real' time.
(Dr) Roger Owens, Wedmore, Somerset.

QUESTION: Is there an easy way to make money?

☐ YES! For further details send £1,000 to Peter Andrews, Finance Department, Vencourt House, London W6.
P. Andrews, London W6.

☐ WHILE I would not endorse such activity, my own antics as a child come to mind. I would sometimes accompany my father to the supermarket, wearing a big coat. While his gaze and that of anybody else was elsewhere I would slip a block of pre-packed cheese into my pocket. The following day I would return it, saying

it was mouldy, and gain a refund. When I was a little older, I got a paper round. The man who ran the shop would go into the back to fetch the newspapers. During this time I would slip a few packets of cigarettes and some men's magazines into my holdall, which I later sold at school to the joy and titillation of the fifth formers.
O. Hemingway, Prestwich, Manchester.

☐ THE questioner should try getting others to do work in a project for which he gets the payment. One option would be to start a newspaper column which involved some readers sending in questions that other readers then answered.
Neil Nixon, Maidstone, Kent.

☐ A CHARACTER in *Good As Gold*, Joseph Heller's satire on Washington politics, came to own a string of supermarkets. When asked his secret for the Midas touch, he maintained that it was very simple: find a loophole in the law.
Paul Becke, Edinburgh.

QUESTION: What is happiness?

☐ IT IS the name of the hit single by Ken Dodd in 1964. The refrain line, 'I thank the Lord that I've been blessed with more than my share of happiness', confirms that happiness refers to the state of enjoying unusually low tax payments. A chilling warning that such a state is inevitably transient was provided by his hit single the following year: 'Tears'.
David Wirth, Twickenham, Middx.

☐ HAPPINESS is wanting to be where you are, when you are.
A. J. Evens, Southsea, Hants.

☐ HAPPINESS is 'a warm puppy' (Charles M. Schulz: *Peanuts*); 'a warm gun' (Lennon & McCartney, 1968); 'being single' (car bumper sticker); 'good health and a bad memory' (Ingrid Bergman); 'seeing Lubbock, Texas, in the rear-view mirror' (anon); 'a warm earpiece' (British Telecom ad); 'yes, but ecstasy is a warm codpiece' (graffito); 'a cigar called Hamlet' (cigar ad); 'egg-shaped' (egg ad).
Colin M. Jarman, London N22.

☐ HAPPINESS is having your complete answer published in Notes & Queries.
David Farrell, Cardiff.

☐ HAPPINESS is recognising the utter futility of responding to Notes & Queries.
David Hunter, Sheffield.

☐ THE brief responses you have so far printed do not answer the question. It is easy to see what happiness is not. Happiness is not being wealthy, for even those in possession of wealth may be vulnerable; it is not having good health, for even those sound of body may be disconsolate; it is not being loved, for even those in receipt of love may desire more; it is not in pleasure, for pleasures are transitory and unlikely to be appreciated by those lacking happiness. Obviously these things can be conducive to happiness, yet plainly are not sufficient for it. Happiness is a way of being. One is happy when one is able to flourish. One flourishes by developing and expressing one's abilities in activities and causes which one finds meaningful or just worthwhile, though one may in fact not know that one is flourishing and thereby happy.
(Dr) Keith Seddon, Director of Studies, The Philosophical Society of England, London SW19.

QUESTION: A Cambridge graduate recently claimed: 'Six of the 12 most important discoveries since the birth of Christ were made within half a mile of my rooms.' Assuming the claim is valid, what were the 12, and which were the six?

☐ IF THE 'importance' of a discovery is measured by the extent to which it altered the world, here is my list of 12, none of which has very much to do with Cambridge. Moveable type; heliocentric solar system; human blood circulation; electromagnetic induction and radiation; explosives; antibiotics; mechanical clockwork; telephony; vaccination; mercantile capitalism; digital computing; genetic inheritance and plant and animal breeding. You will notice, of course, that at least four of these were 'discovered' by people with close Scottish connections.
(Dr) Iain Stevenson, London WC2.

☐ Dr Iain Stevenson notes that 'none' of his list has very much to do with Cambridge. I disagree, as discoveries at Cambridge include: theory of gravity; DNA; atomic theory; Darwin's theory of evolution; digital computing; electricity and electromagnetic induction. The other six discoveries were: heliocentric solar system; internal combustion engine; printing; mechanical clockwork; explosives; antibiotics.
Douglas Ellison, London SE16.

☐ Douglas Ellison's list of six 'discoveries at Cambridge' is wide of the mark. Electricity: Galvani, Volta, Ampere, Ohm, Oersted and Franklin, had no connection with Cambridge, or even England. Electromagnetic induction: the discoverer, Faraday, worked at the Royal Institution in London. Digital computing: Babbage was at Cambridge but produced no functioning computer, so could he really be the discoverer of digital computing? The credit seems really to belong to IBM at Harvard and Ferranti at Manchester. Theory of evolution: after three undistinguished and rather wasted years at Cambridge, Darwin had a five-year voyage in HMS *Beagle*. On his return he married and settled in Kent where between 1837–44 he formulated his theory of evolution. Atomic theory: the scientific atomic theory (as opposed to speculation) is due to John Dalton, Manchester in 1803. DNA: the discovery was shared between Cambridge and King's College, London. Theory of gravity: the famous apple tree was in the garden of Woolsthorpe Manor, near Grantham, where Newton spent the plague years 1665–67.
Norman Thorpe, Whalley, Lancs.

QUESTION: Why do humans have hair only on certain parts of their body and why those parts?

☐ We are naked apes because, at a crucial stage in our evolution, to protect ourselves from faster and stronger predators, we chose to live near lakes and rivers and became good swimmers. Since hair increases water drag, it was selected against a part from where it provided heat protection for the one part of the body to remain above the surface of the water – the head. Once bi-pedalism became established, initially because it enables a water-located primate to scan its environment, head hair continued in its heat-protecting

function. In the aquatic stage of evolution, we developed our uniquely human system of temperature control in the form of millions of eccrine sweat glands. These largely displaced the scent-emitting apocrine glands of our non-aquatic primate ancestors. However, we retain a residual quantity of apocrine glands, concentrated under the arms and in the pubic area where the vestigial patches of hair serve to conserve and concentrate the gland's secretions.
Christopher Hill, Highbury, London N5.

□ FURTHER to Christopher Hill's note, the millions of eccrine sweat glands also exude salt, as do our tears. We know how salty they taste. This suggests the crucial stage in our development was near the sea and our diet excessively salty. Perhaps our species was isolated by the sea for a long period leading to memories of seas engulfing the world (Noah), an isolated paradise with the growth of self-awareness and the recognition of nakedness (Adam and Eve) and a sea being divided to lead the tribe back to the promised land (Moses). Elaine Morgan's book *The Scars Of Evolution* sheds much light on the possibilities.
B. W. Campbell, Bainton, Lincs.

QUESTION: How careful do you have to be in hitting an intruder over the head if you want to cause unconsciousness without killing him/her?

□ AS SOMEONE who has practised various martial arts for over 10 years, and now teaches both self-defence and ju-jitsu, I can testify that there is no easy answer to this question. Practically, the answer depends on four factors: (i) the variation in the strength of the target skull. Some people have very thick skulls, some paper-thin. (ii) Assuming an averagely strong skull, one must then consider exactly where on the head you hit. Any strike on or around the base of the skull or upper neck is more effective, and thus potentially more fatal, than a simple 'klonk' on the top. The safest (but therefore least effective in KO-ing terms) place to hit the head would be downwards onto the front 'corners' of the skull. (iii) The next factor is what you hit them with. Unless specifically trained, or unusually strong, a blow, punch or chop with an empty hand is unlikely to render someone immediately unconscious, although

it may stun them for long enough for other action to be taken. Using a weapon of any sort greatly increases the effectiveness of the technique and therefore the danger of killing someone. As a rule of thumb, though, the harder and sharper the weapon, the more dangerous it would be. Remember also that victims could equally damage themselves as they fall on the floor: contact with the edge of a table can be enough to kill. (iv) Finally, consideration of the legality of your actions is important. The law preaches a doctrine of reasonable use of minimum force. I would advise anyone confronted with an intruder to use force as an absolute last resort. Quite apart from the fact that the intruder will probably be better prepared for, and more inclined to use, extreme violence, avoiding the encounter and calling the police are far more sensible courses of action. If cornered, however, and with no other choice, by all means grab the poker or a golf club, but consider striking for less potentially fatal though equally debilitating areas of the body – the groin, elbows and kneecaps, for example.
Robert C Avery, Maidenhead, Berks.

□ HAVING spoken to a policeman over a theft, I mentioned that I kept a Number 2 wood handy in case of finding an intruder at a sufficient disadvantage. He then warned me of the problem of using too much force. I suppose the answer must be to use a 9 iron.
A. C. Cook, Middlesbrough, Cleveland.

QUESTION: If Henry VIII founded the Church of England to legitimise his divorce, why is it now against the canon law of the Church? Can the present head of the Church reverse this?

□ THE question contains three fallacies:
1. Henry VIII did *not* found the Church of England. It was in existence centuries before the Norman Conquest brought it under the political control of the Bishop of Rome. The Church was reformed, not founded, in the 16th century in response to growing pressure from within the Church itself for greater freedom from Roman interference. The king gave his support to this movement because he, too, had his own problems with the Roman authorities.
2. Henry VIII neither sought nor obtained a divorce. He sought to

have his 'marriage' to Catherine of Aragon annulled on the grounds that the then rules of kindred and affinity had been broken. There is no doubt that the Pope would have granted such an annulment had he not been a prisoner of Catherine's nephew. After all, he had previously granted annulments to European monarchs on far flimsier grounds. But the annulment was refused, so Henry obtained one from Canterbury. His later 'marriage' to Anne of Cleves was annulled on the grounds of non-consummation, as some marriages are today. The bride and groom couldn't stand the sight of each other and spent their wedding night playing cards. An annulment means that a marriage never existed in the first place, as opposed to a divorce which recognises that a marriage did exist but does so no longer. The Church's canon law, based on the teaching of Christ Himself, forbids remarriage of divorced persons.

3. The monarch is not the head of the Church. That position belongs to Christ alone. The reigning monarch is 'supreme governor' of the Church of England and, as such, cannot constitutionally impose her (or his) will on the Church.

A. Tomlinson, Congleton, Cheshire.

□ It is a general principle that canon law is subordinate to theology, and therefore cannot be changed in a way that implies an alteration in the fundamental doctrines of the Church, which ultimately derive from the word of God as witnessed in scripture. In the western Church, this has been taken to allow annulment and forbid divorce – although divorce is allowed in canon law in the eastern (Orthodox) tradition. Annulment is not a way out of the monarchy's current difficulties; firstly because the children of the annulled marriage would be debarred from succession to the throne, and secondly because there are no grounds for questioning the original validity of any of the current marriages. Catherine of Aragon, by contrast, had previously been betrothed and then married to Henry's deceased elder brother Arthur – both bars to a subsequent valid marriage with Henry. The marriage had only been able to proceed because the Pope had 'dispensed with' the application of canon law for this union. The issue under contention in the 1530s was whether the Pope had authority to make such a dispensation – which led in time to a denial of papal authority altogether.

Tom Hennell, Withington, Manchester.

☐ I REALLY must protest at the outrageous statement: 'Henry VIII did not found the Church of England. It was in existence centuries before the Norman Conquest brought it under the political control of the Bishop of Rome.' Wasn't it the Bishop of Rome (Pope Gregory) who sent Augustine to preach to the English? Was Bede an Anglican? Was it Anglicanism that Boniface took to Germany? The notion of an autocephalous Saxon Church is on a par with the belief that the Holocaust never happened. Henry VIII usurped the Pope's authority in England and appointed Cranmer as Archbishop of Canterbury to give him a divorce from his wife. He plundered the Church mercilessly. A movement for reform did not come from within the Church. Subsequently both Lutheran and Calvinist doctrines entered the new 'Church of England'. Then, under Elizabeth I, the 39 articles finally established the protestant nature of the Church of England . . . and we blame the Communists for rewriting history.
Adrian Jarvis, Bickington, Devon.

QUESTION: Is it now accepted that dowsing, or 'water divining', really works? If so, has it been explained scientifically?

☐ IN THE late Sixties, I joined Lancashire County Council's School Playing Fields Service as a technical officer, building and maintaining a vast acreage of school grounds. I noticed that all their area supervisors carried two copper welding rods in their cars. The last seven inches of the rods were bent at a right-angle to form a handle. They were used to detect old land drains which, if left uncoupled to the new sports field drainage, would cause trouble, as even land bulldozed to form a flat surface for the games pitches can continue to 'bleed' to these earlier agricultural drains. The technique is to walk arms forward with the welding rods held loosely, in line with the outstretched arms. When passing over a drain, the copper rods swing inwards and cross. It seemed to work for about half the people willing to try it and was highly regarded for its accuracy and for saving time in not having to search through old plans, or dig long trenches across soggy sports fields. On one occasion, I learnt that the borough engineer of Middleton, near Manchester, was unable to locate a buried manhole on one of their playing fields. I walked the field with the two copper welding rods

and, by planting garden canes wherever they crossed, I was able to plot the line of two old sewers. The missing manhole was found at the point of intersection. We never knew why it worked but most agreed that the rods were locating cavities rather than running water. We called it 'dowsing' and never used the technique for 'divining' water.
Alan Barber, parks management consultant, Nailsea, Bristol.

□ ACCORDING to Terence Hines, a New York psychologist and critic of parapsychology, there has never been any evidence to show that dowsing really works, despite extensive controlled studies. He puts the movements of the dowsing rod down to small unconscious muscle twitches in the diviner's body. Most evidence for dowsing consists of anecdotal eyewitness reports, which are notoriously unreliable and are further complicated by the fact that witnesses tend to recall selectively only those dowsing attempts which are successful. Furthermore, dowsers frequently predict that water will be found at several locations. As well-drilling usually stops after the first success, other predictions which may have turned out to be wrong won't be tested. Also, vague predictions about depth may at first appear successful on the basis that digging deep enough will usually produce results. Add to all this the geological clues in the land which a dowser may pick up, albeit unconsciously, and you have a case for dowsing which appears not to hold water.
Jacqui Farrants, Romford, Essex.

□ BIOMAGNETISM – the interaction of living matter (e.g., bees, carrier pigeons, whales) with the ambient magnetic field – has developed as a recognised science over the past quarter-century. At first, independently of that, Yves Rocard, professor of physics at Paris and a wartime resistance hero, used a dowser's services when needing water for a seismic laboratory in Normandy 35 years ago, and then sought an explanation of his success. In his four books (1962 to 1991) he attributed the effect to small differences between the Earth's field at the right and left sides of the dowser's body. The hazel-twig or pendulum is not the detector but amplifies and indicates a muscular reaction. Although water is not magnetic, groundwater may correlate with magnetic anomalies – e.g., a ferruginous component of soil may be gradually deposited and concentrated. Despite the many difficulties in getting reproducible demonstrations, dowsing has achieved some respectability

in garden and church archaeology (e.g., *Dowsing And Church Archaeology* by Professor R. N. Bailey *et al.*, 1988).
(Dr) J. C. E. Jennings, London N6.

□ WHILE with the Ministry of Defence, R. A. Foulkes conducted experiments to see if buried metal or plastic objects could be located by diviners (see *Nature* vol. 229, 15 January 1971, p. 163). On a 400-square grid, each square measuring 20ft by 20ft, he buried metal (dummy) mines, plastic mines, wooden blocks, concrete blocks and blanks. Twenty-two experienced dowsers were convinced they could sort them out but none did better than chance. Other experiments on water dowsing at Chatham were a little less rigorous but with the same negative result. Their last test included a search for a 42-inch water main eight feet down carrying a flow of 80,000 gallons an hour.
(Dr) A. Selwood, Harrogate, N. Yorks.

□ UNTIL I saw the letter from Dr Selwood, I had always assumed that diviners were able to detect metal under the ground. But I have never heard of a diviner who has come through a test to detect water. A prize of $10,000 was once offered by an American water association for detecting water flowing from a central tank through pipes buried beneath the ground. There were several pipes of different materials and water could be directed along any, or all of them, via a series of valves. The task of the diviner was to detect which pipes carried water. I never heard that anyone ever won the prize. This begs the question as to how diviners survive. Water diviners do not have much of a challenge in this moist country of ours. A borehole drilled virtually anywhere in Britain will encounter water eventually and in most cases it will be within a few tens of metres from the surface. It is upon this that the diviner relies, unconsciously or otherwise. I would not wish to give the impression that all water diviners are charlatans, because I expect that most who work at it for long enough build up useful experience. However, I am convinced that the performance with the 'rods' is nothing more than mumbo-jumbo. The difference between a diviner and a professional hydrogeologist is this: put a diviner in an area outside his/her experience and the diviner is lost; in contrast any half-competent hydrogeologist will be able to provide reliable advice virtually anywhere in the world. The catch is that the professional advice is usually expensive. Many

diviners work in conjunction with a small drilling company and it is astonishing how frequently water is 'found' just by the track, and convenient for the rig. I used to work for one of the water authorities, and it was not uncommon to receive requests for advice about water from hill farms and other households remote from the nearest water main. One day a farmer in the Lake District asked for information. It was clear from the address of the farm that it was situated on a rock formation known as the Bannisdale Slates which have no useful water-bearing capacity (they would not, after all, be much use for roofing otherwise). The farmer explained that a diviner had told him there was water below ground and a driller was standing by to construct a borehole to reach it. The advice sent to him was against drilling but the farmer ignored it, the borehole was drilled and found to be completely dry. The farmer was about £3,000 out of pocket.
(Dr) K. J. Vines, Plymouth.

QUESTION: What is a tune?

□ THE orchestral player immediately recognises a tune and concocts a ribald lyric to fit it. Tchaikovsky wrote many tunes, Beethoven relatively few. Perhaps the classic symphonic tune is the occurrence of the Heinz beans advertisement, 'A million housewives every day . . .', in Mendelssohn's *Hebrides Overture.*
Laurence Payne, Seven Kings, Essex.

□ A TUNE is a series of sounds whose frequencies bear specific ratios to one another and whose durations bear specific ratios to one another. It must be so defined because its identity does not depend, within reason, on the actual frequency, called pitch, or on the actual rate of sound production. The durations usually relate to a repeated time unit called rhythm. In most western music, the available frequency ratios are set by reference to a scale found, for example, in the ratios of the sounds from a keyboard instrument and the commonest ratios are those provided by the 'white' keys. However, more readily recognisable and memorable tunes usually contain sequences in which the ratios of the successive notes approximate to simple fractions such as ⅔ or ⅘, or suggest that they may be related to sounds which contain a set of such simple ratios heard simultaneously. These multiple frequency

units are called 'chords', a succession of which is often called harmony. A tune need not suggest a harmonic basis, and more than one such basis is acceptable with a given tune, but many of the sound sequences which are rememberable as tunes do have their harmonic basis. A common feature of many tunes is that the pattern established by the initial set of sounds is imitated in the continuation of the tune. But for those apparent requirements, one could devise more than 16 million tunes of eight successive sounds, using eight adjacent 'white' notes of a keyboard, each of which could also have various duration patterns. Use 12 notes and the number is astronomic. Yet a thematic index of every reasonably well-known tune contains about 16,000. An alternative definition of a tune is 'that which an arbitrary group of old grey men can whistle after they have heard it once'. A title derived from that idea was given to a long-running television programme containing remarkably little which would have satisfied this test.
(Prof.) Sir James Beament, Queen's College, Cambridge.

QUESTION: There are many public houses called The Lamb And Flag. What is the origin of the name?

☐ IT AROSE from the Crusades: the lamb was a symbol of Christianity (the Lamb of God) and the flag was a military banner. Thus the name has the same sort of bloodthirsty pedigree as the Saracen's Head (which was presumed to be cut off by the noble Crusaders). No doubt the same Crusaders refreshed themselves at these pubs before setting off to do their worst.
Gyan Mathur, London WC1.

☐ THE earliest hostelry names were drawn for the most part from chivalric and ecclesiastical heraldry and originally reflected patronage and/or property of knightly families or of the Church. The Lamb of inn names is the *Agnus Dei*, the Paschal lamb, which was the emblem of St John the Baptist. It was also a blazon of the Knights Templars, a military order founded *c.* 1118 to protect pilgrims to the Holy Land. In both chivalric and ecclesiastical heraldry, the lamb was often represented bearing the staff of the Cross upon which flew a banner, itself decorated with a cross motif, hence the hostelry name The Lamb and Flag. The earliest example

of the sign of The Lamb of which I am aware is a Norwich instance recorded in 1504, but the elaborated sign of The Lamb and Flag seems to have been current only from the 19th century.
(Prof.) Barrie Cox, Department of English Studies, University of Nottingham.

QUESTION: I heard recently that in the 1930s there was a property in Bolton called Sod Hall, which my grandfather wanted to buy. Did it, or does it, exist?

☐ SOD HALL was a property off Clegg's Lane, Little Hulton, an old district still referred to as 'near Bolton, Lancs'. It is shown on the Ordnance Survey map, published 1 November 1950. The hall is not mentioned in local guidebooks published by the Old Little Hulton UDC, though many local people recall that a Victorian or earlier building was there until a few years after the Second World War. This was called Sod Hall Farm and was occupied by several generations of the Shaw family. The farm was bulldozed in about 1960 to make way for new housing. The old name was revived by a tradesman who opened the Sod Hall Mini-Market and General Store almost opposite the original site, but the store closed a few years ago.
B. Rogerson, Swinton, Manchester.

☐ I CAN'T help the questioner, but on the Kent approaches to the Dartford Tunnel there is a house proudly called 'Llamedos'. I conclude that the owner is not Welsh but merely has an inverted sense of humour.
Peter Bourne, Ketton, Lincs.

☐ ON THE same lines, there is an ex-police house, now in private ownership, in the village of Hollesley, near the Suffolk coast. Its name these days is Evening Hall.
David Mackness, Ipswich.

☐ IN THE village Wisbech St Marys in Cambridgeshire, there is a fancy house built a few years ago by a local entrepreneur with a reputation for doing regular battle with the authorities (particularly the planning department). The house is called Fockham Hall.
John Webb, New Romney, Kent.

QUESTION: Postmodernists say there is no objective truth. Why should anyone believe them?

☐ AS THE question suggests, postmodernism is self-sabotaging, like all sufficiently radical forms of scepticism and reductionism. Unlike some earlier forms, however, it is based on an elementary confusion between truth and certainty: although no person or group can justifiably claim complete objectivity, it does not follow that there is no truth, just that we should not place anything beyond the possibility of revision. Since postmodernism is a fashion statement rather than a philosophical position (I think many postmodernists would accept this), it need not be taken seriously intellectually. It is, however, morally pernicious: if there is no objective truth, then it is not objectively true that 'The Protocols Of The Learned Elders Of Zion' is a forgery, or that the Gulf war took place – Baudrillard has in fact denied that it did. Postmodernism also demonstrates, under the guise of opposing all-encompassing views of the world, the most extreme self-importance and intellectual imperialism: claiming as it does that the world consists only of texts, it implies that literary criticism encompasses all other disciplines.
Nick Gotts, Leeds.

☐ IN RESPONSE to Nick Gotts, what possibly needs clarifying is the belief that postmodernism denies truth. Certainly there is within the field of postmodernism a rejection of any single objective 'Truth' leading to ultimate enlightenment and so on, but there is still an acceptance, indeed the promotion, of many subjective 'truths' rather than none at all. Truth thus becomes contextually reliant rather than all-encompassing. Reality is another matter entirely: I think that what Baudrillard was probably saying was that the Gulf war wasn't a war as such, more a kind of movie war, choreographed for the cameras. As to postmodernism being a fashion: well possibly, but only insomuch as the dominant theories of any epoch are fashionable. Finally, I believe that it confuses matters to think of postmodernism as an 'it' as there are many conflicting theories employing the term trying to get a hold of a complex theoretical spatial temporality: the here and now.
Andrew F. Wilson, London E7.

QUESTION: What was the good news that they brought from Ghent to Aix?

☐ Aix is besieged and about to surrender; the good news is that help is on the way. This is the implied meaning of line 46 of Robert Browning's poem, 'the news which alone could save Aix from her fate'. The explanation is Browning's, but he gave it with reluctance; he always insisted that the ride itself was what mattered. He said that he wrote the poem 'on board ship off Tangiers', when he 'had been at sea long enough to appreciate even the fancy of a gallop'. There is no historical foundation for the episode: according to Browning it reflects a 'general impression of the characteristic warfare and besieging that abounds in the annals of Flanders'.
D. Karlin (co-editor, with John Woolford, of The Poems of Browning, *Longman Annotated English Poets, 1991).*

QUESTION: Makers of mains radio and television sets recommend unplugging if the house is to be left unattended during a holiday. A fireman has recommended that they be left plugged in but switched off at the mains socket to provide a route to earth should a condenser discharge. Which is correct?

☐ The fireman is wrong. Condensers, correctly known as capacitors, store electrical charge. In a TV or radio they would only ever discharge through their associated circuitry within the television, and not to earth. In any event most televisions nowadays are not earthed – note the two-core (live and neutral) mains cable.
Charles Turner, Stockport, Cheshire.

☐ Most mains sockets only have the live terminal wired up to the switch, so if the socket has been wired incorrectly (i.e. live wire to neutral terminal), when the plug is left inserted and the socket switched off the appliance remains live even though it won't operate. Even with the socket wired correctly, the condition of the switch could make the appliance unsafe if left. The safest way would be to turn the plug upside down and insert only the earth pin into the socket (this is possible because of its longer length).

Even though the pin cannot be inserted fully, there will still be a connection because the earth terminal in the socket is close to the surface. Also remove connection leads to outdoor aerials in case of lightning.
Peer Czerwinka, Eccles, Manchester.

QUESTION: What happened to the only British serviceman to refuse repatriation at the end of the Korean war?

☐ THE MARINE, Andrew Condron, was indoctrinated in a Chinese prisoner-of-war camp in Korea. The Chinese initially convinced him that the Americans had used germ warfare, and this seems to have influenced his decision to live on in China. As a result of this Chinese propaganda coup, the British Foreign Office was concerned to know 'the state of Condron's mind' with a view to persuading him to return to the West. However, this plan was foiled when Lt-Col J. L. Lindop of the Intelligence Division of the Admiralty confirmed to A. L. Mayall of the Foreign Office that the Navy 'regard Condron as a deserter and . . . he is liable to be arrested and charged with desertion . . .' Unsurprisingly Condron stayed on in China. By 1959, however, the Foreign Office considered Condron to be an embarrassment to the Chinese and monitored his conduct – and the Chinese reaction – with the greatest glee. The British Embassy in Peking reported that Condron was becoming disillusioned with the Chinese regime and uncontrollable. The embassy official spoke of 'song and drink on a fairly hearty scale' and concluded that 'while he is here, particularly if he is indeed becoming disgruntled, there is a chance of his becoming quite an embarrassment to them'. Drinking was not the only activity that the Foreign Office considered a potential embarrassment to the Chinese: Condron had 'involved two Chinese girls in serious political difficulties when he became "too friendly" to them'. The obvious relish of the Foreign Office at this was soon to turn to their own embarrassment when Condron began a relationship with a Jaqueline Hsiung-Baudet, the illegitimate daughter of Philippe Baudet, a leading French diplomat. I am not sure what happened to Condron after 1959. I believe he married Jaqueline but I cannot confirm this. He faced arrest from the Admiralty if he returned to the West. He was disillusioned with the Chinese regime, unable to keep down a steady job and had

vague plans to move to Czechoslovakia 'because it has the highest standard of living in the socialist bloc . . .' His girlfriend was being questioned for 'consorting with an Imperialist'. Indeed, the only positive thing to come out of Condron's experience, according to the Foreign Office, was that 'his Glasgow accent seems to have vanished'. This information was compiled from diplomatic files available at the Public Records Office, Kew. Wherever he is now, I wish Marine Andrew Condron the best of luck.
Patrick Dransfield, London NW3.

□ PATRICK DRANSFIELD seems to have left his critical faculties at the front door when he visited the Public Records Office. Marine Andrew Condron was not persuaded to stay on in China because of rumours of the Americans' use of germ warfare; he was basically motivated by an admiration for the Chinese as a nation. Also present in the equation was a youthful spirit of adventure. Under the terms of the ceasefire treaty, any prisoner on either side was entitled to remain with his captors. Some 25,000 North Koreans took this opportunity, as did 22 UN personnel. Several more of his fellow British POWs wanted to stay but were dissuaded by the Chinese (who also tried to persuade Condron to return home). During his time in Peking, he applied for, and was given, all of his back-pay for the period of his incarceration and in 1961 he received an honourable discharge from the Royal Marines with the conduct rating 'very good'. This is the highest classification that a Royal Marine can achieve. The British Embassy's glee at the 'scandal' they uncovered about Mr Condron's liking for a few drinks and the company of attractive members of the opposite sex makes one wonder what planet they were living on. As he was a vigorous 27-year-old, who had recently been released from three years' imprisonment under very harsh conditions, it would have been very surprising if his thoughts had turned in any other direction. It is now strange that the 'legitimacy' (a rather outmoded concept) of Mr Condron's girlfriend, who later became his wife, is called into question. Her father, Philippe Baudet, later French ambassador in Moscow, always maintained that he had married her mother in church, although perhaps the Chinese authorities did not recognise the union. It is unfortunate that this rather tasteless insinuation is made now. Mr and Mrs Condron returned to Britain in 1962 and have lived here ever since. In 1986, Mr Condron was at a reunion in the Royal Marine Commando School at Lympstone

near Exeter and he has attended several other gatherings. Some of his fellow POWs recommended him for a decoration on their return from captivity in recogniton of his efforts, while a prisoner, to save lives and improve living conditions. Needless to say, these suggestions fell on deaf ears.
Michael McDermott, Abergavenny, Gwent.

☐ IN ABOUT 1963 a man came to our door selling the *Encyclopaedia Britannica.* He was extremely nice, my parents bought the encyclopaedia and we became friends. This was Andrew Condron. The former serviceman showed us newspaper cuttings about himself and talked about his life in China. By this time he was married to Jaqueline (who was working as a producer for the BBC World Service) and they had a son, whose name was, I think, Simon. We remained friends for a few years and I think Andrew returned to journalism. In the mid-1970s I bumped into Jaqueline on a bus. She was still working for the BBC and their son was planning to go to Cambridge. By this time Andrew and Jaqueline had divorced. I can confirm that Andrew liked to drink spirits but the files quoted are wrong when they say that he had lost his Glasgow accent.
David Freedman, London NW2.

QUESTION: Why German measles? Why not French or English?

☐ IT IS a corruption of 'germane', meaning 'like or akin to' measles.
(Dr) (signature illegible), Blandford, Dorset.

QUESTION: Why are 'inverted commas' only inverted on one side?

☐ AS THE question implies, to describe quotation marks as inverted commas is only half true. The reason is that printed characters have evolved from hand scripts. If you draw curved quotation marks by hand with an old-fashioned (thick and thin) pen nib, the opening commas will be thicker at the base and

the closing ones thicker at the top, due to the different angles of the pen strokes. Printers' typefaces usually imitate this effect. Incidentally, office typewriters save a key by having neutrally orientated marks which can be used at either end of the quotation. Neither of these is inverted but neither, perhaps, are they really commas.
Trevor Denning, Birmingham.

QUESTION: Why do many people confuse left and right (when giving directions, for example) but not up and down? Is it simply because of gravity?

□ YES. We evolved from little wormy things swimming about in the sea where a sense of up and down was important – to swim up would result in reaching the surface, to swim down would eventually mean crash-diving into the seabed. But whether to swim to the left or to the right was hugely unimportant – one encountered still more sea in either direction. As we made it on to dry land, gravity gave us a top and a bottom and locomotion gave us a front and a back. We can easily distinguish top from bottom thanks to gravity (top is furthest from the centre of the Earth) and we can determine our front from our back since our sense organs are fixed facing front where they can tell us where we're going rather than where we've been. We cannot, however, determine our left from our right without resorting to a variety of conventions unique to this planet (and not easily communicable to alien intelligences). The notion of left/right implies asymmetry and plenty of natural examples exist to establish this convention – the anti/clockwise twists and helixes of certain molluscs and plants, Maxwell's Corkscrew Rule in electromagnetics, the 'handedness' of certain molecules and crystalline structures, etc. Most of us can remember the convention by virtue of our own inbuilt left or right dominance, whether we are in the dextral majority or in the sinistral minority. If one tends towards ambidextrousness it becomes more difficult and one has to resort to established asymmetric conventions such as checking the button-hole on the left side of a jacket. But for such a person, naked and without recourse to any form of asymmetric object the problem is still more difficult since our external appearance is essentially

bilaterally symmetrical – apart from the male whose left testicle often hangs lower than the right. I make absolutely no correlation between this and the male's ability or otherwise in giving left/right directions.
A reader, London SW1.

□ I RAISED this very question with my wife nearly 30 years ago because I am one of those 'many people'. She told me it was because I had not had the benefit of a Roman Catholic upbringing. Apparently, making the sign of the cross acceptably depends on conquering the confusion.
(Prof.) Alan Alexander, Hellensburgh, Scotland.

QUESTION: If the three wise men from the east followed a star to their east (*Matthew*, Chapter 2) how did they reach Bethlehem? They would have needed to follow a star to their west, surely.

□ CORRECT. The Magi did follow a star in a westerly direction, but let us not forget that they were, after all, wise men, and therefore probably not given to hasty actions. The Greek word 'anatole' used by Matthew implies 'the direction of rising', so in rendering this as 'east' it should be understood as a general direction rather than a precise heading. It is not too fanciful to infer that they made further observations and deliberations over a lengthy period before concluding that the star (or whatever) was so portentous as to warrant following. By this time the object could well have been setting in the west, the direction in which the Magi eventually travelled.
Alan Linfield, Tring, Herts.

□ IT IS a basic misunderstanding of navigation to imagine that one actually 'follows' a star. Imagine you are walking on the moors and can see a single tree some miles off. By walking towards it, you will remain on a constant compass bearing and eventually reach it. On the other hand, if you knew you wanted to head east, you could navigate by walking away from the tree, keeping it on a constant bearing on your compass. With the tree (or indeed a star) you follow a bearing rather than the object. Anyone can use a star to

steer by. If you know you want to go north, just keep the pole star (Polaris, which happens to be almost exactly above the north pole) ahead of you. If you want to go south, keep it on your back. East and you must keep it on your left shoulder. This is not very accurate, but for short distances it might be good enough. Proper celestial navigation is more complicated, because all heavenly objects are in motion relative to an earthbound observer. The stars will appear to whirl round the sky because the earth spins daily on its axis. They change their apparent position with the seasons, as the earth tilts on its axis. They will seem to alter position according to the observer's latitude. The calculations required to compensate for their motions are very tricky. You will need a very accurate watch, a sextant, an almanack, a magnetic compass, a view of the horizon at sea level and knowledge of the equations to work it all out. The Three Wise Men had none of these.
Marcus Palliser, London W14.

QUESTION: I am told that one should not eat potatoes that have started sprouting. Why?

□ ALL PARTS of the potato plant contain glycoalkaloids, a group of toxic compounds also present in Deadly Nightshade. Glycoalkaloids are part of the potato plant's natural defensive system, and particularly high levels are found in the leaves and sprouts. Symptoms of 'potato poisoning' include severe gastrointestinal disorders and neurological disturbances, and fatalities have been reported in extreme cases. Glycoalkaloids are also found in the peel of the potato tuber, where they may be accumulated as a response to bruising, rotting or light; the latter also causes greening. It is for this reason that green, sprouted or otherwise damaged potatoes should not be used in food preparation or food processing. Glycoalkaloids are intensely bitter, a property which should minimise accidental poisonings.
(Dr) G. R. Fenwick, Agriculture & Food Research Council, Norwich.

QUESTION: What does the 'PG' in PG Tips stand for?

□ IN THE 1930s tea was sometimes sold on its supposed medicinal

properties – indeed, one blend had become successful through a campaign directed towards doctors and nurses and was even sold in chemists' shops. To challenge this competition, Brooke Bond introduced a brand known as 'Digestive'. After the Second World War, however, the Ministry of Food would not allow 'Digestive' as a trade description of tea, so Brooke Bond changed the name to Pre-Gestee with, on the label, a disclaimer to the effect that 'Brooke Bond do not claim any medicinal, nutritional or dietary value for their tea'. Parcels of the tea (24 x 1/4 lb packets, wrapped in brown paper for delivery to grocers) bore the letters PG as an identification and so the tea became known as PG Tips, a name that has remained since its first use in 1950–51.
Julie Winters, Brooke Bond Foods, Croydon.

QUESTION: How easy would it be for the security services or others to fix the result of a general election?

□ IT WOULD need the co-operation of the Presiding Officers and clerks at polling stations. At the close of the poll, these officers would be able to identify, from the marked copy of the Register of Electors, those who had been eligible to vote but had failed to do so. Some of those electors' numbers could then be entered on the counterfoils of spare ballot papers and the papers marked to favour the candidate whose election was desired. Were this illegal procedure to be followed in all marginal seats, the effect on the outcome of a general election might well be decisive.
John Ellis, Spilsby, Lincs.

□ SPECIFIC to the 1992 election, the 11 seats the Conservatives won with the smallest majorities were instrumental in giving them a parliamentary majority of 21. Statistically, the degree of manipulation of votes needed to have prevented those seats falling to the candidate placed second in the official returns would have been minimal. Between Vale of Glamorgan (majority 19) and the 11th narrowest Tory victory in Southampton Test (585), a cumulative total of only 1,241 votes needed switching from the runner-up's tally (i.e. 10 switched from Labour to Tory in Vale of Glamorgan, 23 in Bristol NW and so on). These 1,241 votes represent just 0.000036 per cent of the 34

million cast nationally and in the constituencies in question the hypothetical switch represents proportions of the local electorate ranging from 0.0002 per cent to 0.005 per cent. Psephologists often point out that swings in marginals are quirky and fail to reflect wider trends. They therefore appear to offer an element of camouflage for introduced inconsistencies. It is a fact that as I coloured in my *Guardian* 'DIY Election Results Table' only 44 per cent in the first column of Tory marginals came out red or yellow whereas 63 per cent did so in the second 'safer' column. Even stranger, only three out of 35 Labour or Lib-Dem vulnerables turned blue. In a situation where opinion polls point universally to a close contest, it has to be allowed that the possibility exists for illicit forces to consider methods of improving the chances of one or other party. Whether it could happen must be judged in relation to any evidence for similar activities in other democratically sensitive areas, together with society's constraints both in enforcing and demonstrating proof of fair play. What seems certain, though, is that any system which invests a block, albeit incidentally, of 0.000036 per cent with a potential to effectively disfranchise 58 per cent for five years is deeply suspect in conception, even before you examine its susceptibility to covert abuse.
S. Paul-Ross, Lyndhurst, Hants.

QUESTION: What would be the smallest possible nuclear explosion? I seem to remember that in Isaac Asimov's Foundation trilogy a nuclear booby trap destroyed someone's bedroom.

□ If all the uranium in an amount the size of a sweet, fissioned it could destroy a building. However, such small nuclear fission explosions are impractical because a chain reaction cannot be sustained in such a tiny amount. The minimum amount of fissile material required is called the critical mass and this depends on the design of the device. It is thought by some that the critical mass for a conventionally-designed booby trap made from uranium is about 10kg, which is a lump about the size of an orange. But if the design were improved the quantity could be much less.
Tayakan Kapinakhish, Balsall Heath, Birmingham.

□ The smallest nuclear delivery system was the US Army's

Davy Crockett rocket-powered projectile, which was deployed in Germany in 1962. It had a warhead of about 0.5 kilotons yield and a blast radius of between 200 and 600 yards. The complete system (launcher, sights, rocket motor and warhead) weighed 68kg. Nuclear reactions can take place between hydrogen atoms, neutrons, etc., so I imagine there is no theoretical minimum size of an explosion but there may be practical limits due to the complexity of trigger mechanisms. The incident referred to in Dr Asimov's works occurred in *The Stars Like Dust*, where Biron Farrill's bedroom is occupied by a radiation bomb that later turns out to be a fake.
John Waters, Port Talbot, W. Glamorgan.

□ THE Davy Crockett project was eventually vetoed by President Kennedy on the grounds that it might lead to soldiers of NCO rank taking the decision to 'go nuclear'.
Roger Sabdell, Richmond, Surrey.

QUESTION: I have just finished reading a novel in which an elderly man is murdered by being suffocated with a pillow. Is this really possible, and wouldn't it be spotted by a pathologist?

□ IN MY novel, *A Kind Of Healthy Grave* (1988), an old man dies as a result of being smothered by a pillow. I was assured by an experienced forensic scientist that this was plausible.
Jessica Mann, Truro, Cornwall.

□ THE SHORT answers are 'yes' and 'perhaps' respectively. In fact the example of an elderly person as the victim of such a method of asphyxiation is very appropriate, since it is most often either the old or small children and babies who are killed in such a fashion. Asphyxia causing death is achieved in five distinct ways:
1. Mechanical, such as suffocation with a pillow or the forced flexion of the head on to the chest (in a rugby scrum for instance); strangulation with hands (quite difficult to do unto death); with a ligature (easier); hanging; or crushing (such as at Ibrox, Heysel or Hillsborough).
2. Toxic, where there is plenty of oxygen but it is prevented from linking with red blood cells. The commonest example is carbon

monoxide poisoning, either in exhaust pipe suicides or in caravans with poor fire ventilation.

3. Environmental, where there is simply not enough air, such as in a locked freezer, a submarine or a confined space where someone has let off a carbon dioxide fire extinguisher.

4. Medically induced, which is done partially by an anaesthetist before an operation. When the balance of oxygen/drug intake is wrong, the result may be asphyxia.

5. Pathological, where a disease restricts oxygen flow from the lungs to the organs. Oedema (fluid) on the lungs, mucus from a dose of bronchitis may do this, especially with older or weaker people. Paraquat poisoning causes death approximately 10 days after contact (licking some will do), as the lungs gradually scar over and breathing becomes progressively impeded.

That it is more vulnerable persons who are most often killed by suffocation with a pillow is no coincidence: the nervous reflexes which cause us to cough, sneeze, roll over or wake up would, in attempted smothering, cause most of us to kick like a mule. When a person is weaker, through age, infirmity, drink, drugs or disability, the act is more easily accomplished. This 'struggle' or 'force' factor bears upon the likelihood of detection of such acts too. If the nose and mouth are obstructed by hand, say, then it is more likely that a bruise may be left on the points of contact with the victim's face (at times this can show a highly obvious pattern and even the likely size of the killer's hand). With a pillow, a bruise is less likely. This is not necessarily the end of the road, however (except for the victim). People who take longer to die are likely to show small 'pinhead' haemorrhages on the forehead, hairline and eyes. These burst blood vessels are the result of the body going into its final fall-back position: when blood or oxygen supply is restricted, all areas are potentially sacrificed in an attempt to keep the grey matter topped up. In this case, unless death came quickly, the oxygen would be sucked from these blood vessels, causing them to burst, and leaving the smallest but most telling signs. I think the Inspector should be told.

Craig W. Cathcart, Edinburgh.

QUESTION: In the *Book of Genesis*, Adam and Eve's sons, Cain and Seth, both marry. Where did their wives come from?

☐ THE SHORT answer is that they married their sisters, something which Israelite legislation forbade, but which was probably acceptable in extremis (*cf.* Lot and his daughters in *Genesis* XIX 30–38). However, such a literalistic reading of *Genesis* is wooden, overlooking the fact that the stories at the beginning are 'myth' or 'saga'. That is not to say they are fairy-tales. Rather, they are ancient stories, set in primeval time, told to explain how things come to be as they are, often with an astute analysis of the way human beings tick. Thus the characters are representative figures. Adam in Hebrew means 'man' or 'mankind'; Eve possibly means 'living'. The story of the farmer, Cain, and his murder of his shepherd brother, Abel, whose offering was acceptable to God, reflects the victory of agrarian society over the ideal simplicity of the nomad. Cain and his descendants subsequently build the first cities, which are later perceived as dens of vice. Seth represents a new beginning and fresh hope. In view of the deep symbolism of the stories, to question the origin of Cain and Seth's wives is to follow a false scent.
(Rev.) David Bryan, Abingdon, Oxon.

QUESTION: By what criteria can the extent to which a country is civilised be assessed? Which are the most civilised countries?

☐ THIS can be easily determined by whether or not the state practises capital punishment. The degree of civilisation can be measured by the elapsed time since the last execution and by the percentage of the public that is against the return of the death penalty. Thus the UK is now moderately civilised, but precariously so.
Toby Moore, Canberra.

☐ 'CIVILISATION' derives from the Latin *civis* and *cognates*, meaning citizen and relating to concepts of city-dwelling. So, the criterion by which civilisation could be measured is the extent to which a country's population lives in cities. Thus, Britain would be more civilised than, say, France; and the United States and Japan would probably be amongst the most civilised countries. Of course, in practice, civilisation is really a loaded assessment of moral and cultural superiority, which also derives

from European perceptions of classical antiquity and the early Mediterranean city states. It is therefore useless as an objective framework for thinking about societies. A recent trend has been to associate 'civilised' with 'humanitarian', but this is no more helpful, since only wealthy nation states can usually afford to be humanitarian to their neighbours.
J. Dronfield, Cambridge.

□ IN THE words of Mahatma Gandhi: 'A nation's status of civilisation can be measured by the way it treats its animals.'
Ute Cohen, Las Vegas, Nevada.

□ PROBABLY the best answer was provided by the late Norbert Elias in 1939 (*The Civilising Process*, Blackwell, Oxford, 1995). Elias shows how 'civilisation' was originally a French term which connoted a process. Gradually, however, it came to express the self-image of the dominant classes and countries in the West, acquiring in that connection the meaning of a state of affairs which had already been achieved. It also came to imply, as a corollary, antithetical pair-terms such as 'barbarism' which were used to denigrate non-western countries and peoples, weaker western countries and, for a long time, the lower classes in the West itself. Elias also shows how, in the course of their rise to world power, people in countries such as Britain and France underwent 'civilising processes' as measured by such criteria as: the formation of relatively stable and internally pacified states; growing wealth; moves in the direction of the democratisation of political institutions; the establishment, starting with the upper classes, of forms of manners and etiquette through which greater regard for others is expressed; and the emergence of forms of conscience in terms of which overt violence is abhorred. Elias regarded these processes as reversible and did not believe they had gone very far. He speculated that people in a more civilised future, should it be achieved, will probably regard even the most advanced peoples of today as 'late barbarians'. In *Studien Über Die Deutschen* (1989), Elias showed how the dominant trend in the development of Germany did not follow this generally 'civilising' path. Germany did not become a unified nation-state until 1871 and did so under the leadership of the militaristic Prussians. This meant that forms of authoritarian rule became entrenched, leading to opposition to democracy as 'un-German',

a brutalisation of large sections of the middle classes through a cult of duelling in the universities, and eventually to a breakdown of civilisation in the Weimar years. It was in this context that the extremely 'de-civilising' rise of Hitler and the Nazis and the Holocaust occurred.
Eric Dunning, Professor of Sociology, University of Leicester.

□ THE quotation from Gandhi related this to the treatment of animals. But there is a serious objection. In a South African coastal city many years ago, whites erected a large statue to horses, with a plaque bearing Gandhi's words. The area was notorious for black labourers' deaths on its farms.
Len Clarke, Uxbridge, Middlesex.

□ EQUALITY of income, quality of life and influence on the decision-making process. Using these criteria no 'developed' country is either civilised or seeking civilised status, with the possible exception of Iceland.
Matthew Beeching, Bridport, Dorset.

QUESTION: Has anyone on *The Antiques Roadshow* ever obtained the market value quoted by the experts for their exhibits?

□ THERE have been numerous occasions when the price estimates have been achieved and exceeded in subsequent sale. A painting of cats by Henrietta Ronner, bought at a car boot sale for 50p and estimated on the Inverness Roadshow at £15,000 was subsequently sold at Christie's for £22,500. Successes of past series include a lost painting by the Victorian artist Richard Dadd estimated at £100,000 and subsequently bought by the British Museum for slightly more.
Christopher Lewis, executive producer, Antiques Roadshow.

QUESTION: What could we do if it became obvious that either the Queen or the Prime Minister had gone completely mad?

□ THERE are precedents for both situations. Monarch: tolerate the situation until the public demand action, then appoint a Prince

Regent. Prime Minister: tolerate the situation for two general elections, then appoint John Major.
Colin Taylor, Aughton, Ormskirk.

□ THE questioner implies a 'terminal' event, but the reality would be less dramatic. If the Queen or Prime Minister developed a mental illness they would be able to seek treatment in the normal way. If they lacked the insight to do this, they could become the subject of a Mental Health Act Assessment. If this resulted in temporary detention in hospital, there is an obligation in the case of the Prime Minister (or any MP) for the speaker of the House to be informed. No special provisions exist for the Royal Family. The political consequences of such an event occurring in the case of the Prime Minister can only be surmised; but clearly they are related to the duration, severity and likely prognosis of the condition as well as to the current political situation. In the case of the Queen, apart from other members of the Royal Family taking on some of her duties during any period of illness, I doubt whether there would be any cause to remove her: although were the illness a chronic one she might be persuaded to abdicate.
D. S. Allen (consultant psychiatrist), High Wycombe, Bucks.

□ HARDER to answer is what do you do with an electorate which appears to have gone the same way?
Roger Davis, Pontypridd, Mid Glamorgan.

□ IN ANSWER to Roger Davis, Parliament should follow Brecht's advice: dissolve the electorate and elect a new one.
A. Rudolf, London N12.

QUESTION: In an article on the Froncysyllte aqueduct, the *Guardian* quoted Telford as stipulating no more than three narrow-boats to be on it at one time. Why? Surely the number of boats does not make any difference to the weight on the piers?

□ THE questioner is correct. A barge floats due to the Principle of Archimedes. That is to say, the volume of water displaced by the vessel weighs the same as the barge and its contents. Consequently, everything is in equilibrium. Incidentally, when the aqueduct was

opened on 26 November 1805, six boats crossed the structure in a procession. The engineers were in the fourth one, suggesting they had a fair degree of confidence in their aqueduct.
Philip Parker, Senior Project Engineer, British Waterways, Northwich, Cheshire.

□ I EXPECT they had in mind the weight of the draught-horses on the towpath!
T. Bolton, Orrell, Lancashire.

□ THE questioner should stop thinking about pier pressure. If the aqueduct contains more than three boats there will not be enough water left in the trough to allow them to progress efficiently. Taken to an extreme, if the aqueduct had narrow boats nose to tail along its length, there would be an almost total displacement of water.
R. A. Stewart, Hanwell, London W7.

□ R. A. STEWART is surely wrong when he says that 'if the aqueduct had narrow boats nose to tail along its length there would be an almost total displacement of water'. The displacement of water would indeed be equal to the combined weight of the boats, but it would be spread along the total length of the canal, making no significant difference to the depth of water on the aqueduct.
Harry Rushton, Cheshire.

□ BOATS would increase the weight on the piers if the aqueduct were sealed tight by lock gates at each end, and the boats lowered into the water from a crane; then all the displaced water would stay in the channel and the weight on the piers would increase. This doesn't happen normally when a boat enters the aqueduct as the displaced water flows out into the canal at either end. If we could compute the total pressure exerted on the bed of the whole length of the canal we would find that any extra boat in the water adds to the pressure briefly until the displaced water flows out of the nearest overflow – or indefinitely if the water level is lower than the maximum. The aqueduct, being a part of that canal bed, must take a share of that extra pressure, however small and insignificant in practice.
David Nelson, Dunfermline, Fife.

□ ARCHIMEDES' rules are OK for barges if there is no motion.

The problem arises when they are moving – particularly if an over-zealous bargee speeds up behind a second slower-moving barge. A wave of water may then be trapped between the two barges which is deeper than the previous equilibrium depth. Hence a barge race could lead to overloading. This is probably what Telford had in mind.
John Hallett, Reno, Nevada.

QUESTION: Can plants develop cancer?

☐ ABNORMAL growths are common in plants but they are rarely the creeping malignant types associated with animal cancers. Common forms are the various cankers (same etymology) usually manifested as abnormal bark growth on trees. These are caused by parasitic attack, usually fungal. The bizarre growth distortions known as plant galls are perhaps the most familiar examples of plant cancers. These are caused by parasitic agents ranging from viruses to insects and parasitic plants. The gall is an abnormal growth of host tissue stimulated by the parasite infection and is usually structured to provide some service (usually shelter and/or food) for the parasite.
Jonathan Briggs, Nailsworth, Glos.

☐ TOBACCO is well known for the cancers it helps to develop.
Simon Walsh, Braintree, Essex.

QUESTION: Seventh Heaven. What are the other six?

☐ IN THE Cabbala, a Jewish mystical system of technology and metaphysics developed, mainly between the 9th and 13th centuries, it was maintained that there are seven heavens, each rising in happiness above the other. In this cosmology the lower heaven was the region of the stars; the highest, also known as the heaven of heavens, was the abode of God and the most exalted angels. This classification passed into Islamic theology in which the first heaven is of silver and in it are the stars, each with an angel warder and strung out like lamps on golden chains. This is the abode of Adam and Eve. The second heaven is of gold and the domain of Jesus and John the Baptist. The third is of pearl and

allotted to Joseph; here Azrael writes the names of new-borns in a large book from which he expunges the names of the newly-dead. The fourth heaven, of white gold, is Enoch's. Here dwells the Angel of Tears, who ceaselessly sheds tears for the sins of man. The fifth heaven is Aaron's and is of silver. The sixth heaven, which is of ruby and garnet, is presided over by Moses; here dwells the Guardian Angel of heaven and earth, half-snow and half-fire.
Geoffrey Taunton, Portsmouth.

□ GEOFFREY TAUNTON'S answer was informative, but the Cabalistic version of the cosmos he describes was itself co-opted from an ancient Greek concept. Their six concentrically nested heavenly spheres were supposed to be composed of an essential, crystalline substance, and to each was fixed one of the known heavenly bodies: Sun, Mercury, Venus, Mars, Jupiter and Saturn. The moon occurred in the corrupted earthly realm, as evidenced by its visible blotches (the maria), and so was not accorded its own sphere. Seventh heaven, which became associated with the Judaeo-Christian Empyrean, occurred above the ultimate sphere encompassing and directing all the rest – the *Primum Mobile.*
Jim Costa, Museum of Comparative Zoology, Cambridge, Mass.

QUESTION: Did John Logie Baird (or his descendants) profit from his invention of television?

□ IN HIS notes for an autobiography, published in *Sermons, Soap And Television* (Royal Television Society, 1988), Baird states that his company, Television Limited, went into receivership, and his share of what was left amounted to £3,000. At one time his paper holding in the company was worth a quarter of a million pounds. He made and spent a lot of money during the days of TV Ltd; and the Baird Television Company, of which he was to become president, paid him £4,000 in 1937. Shortly after the declaration of war in 1939 the company called in the receiver and Baird's contract was terminated.
Tom Singleton, Shere, Surrey.

□ UNFORTUNATELY John Logie Baird did not 'invent' television and probably nobody outside Britain has even heard of him. The fundamental part of any television system is the scanner –

the device that breaks the picture into elements which can be converted into electric impulses. Baird used a scanner invented by the German Paul Nipkow over 40 years earlier, and linked it to photo-electric cells. But his system was incapable of anything more than poor quality picture definition and was prone to mechanical breakdown. Despite this, towards the end of the Twenties the BBC was persuaded to adopt the Baird system for experimental transmissions. There was little or no chance of long-term success with it, but it believed there was some kudos in being the first to televise anything at all. Meanwhile, others had been working on a completely different system of electronic scanning using an adapted cathode ray tube. The Russian-born American Vladimir Zworykin was a leading inventor in this field, and this system eventually became the basis of today's television.
Don Benlow, Wisbech, Cambs.

□ DURING the 1930s my father received a good salary as a director of the Baird Television Co. We had a large house at Sydenham, near the company laboratories at Crystal Palace. But as your correspondent Tom Singleton states, Baird never made a fortune from shares or royalties. After he died in 1946 my mother received a modest pension from the Baird Company. That was about it as far as 'profits' were concerned. Controversy rages on about whether mechanically scanned TV was 'the real thing'. It was certainly the only viable form of television from 1925 until about 1935. Your correspondent Don Benlow errs in saying that Baird's name is unknown outside Britain. The Americans recognise Baird as the first with television, and I have given lectures to interested audiences in the US and Canada. The first television transmission across the Atlantic, in 1928, was reported with banner headlines in the *New York Times* and it was a great spur to television research in the US. As far as other countries are concerned, a friend has sent me a long article about Baird in China's television magazine. Australia's major television awards, the Logies, are named after my father.
Malcolm Baird, Department of Chemical Engineering, McMaster University, Ontario.

□ HOW sad that no-one mentioned Alan Dower Blumlein who, having sorted out all the fundamentals of stereo sound in the 1930s, headed the team at EMI which produced the first television

pictures using electronic scanning. He was a true engineer and inventor, and audio and video systems still make use of the basic elements of his work.
Chris Woolf, Liskeard, Cornwall.

☐ THE claim that Baird cannot be credited with the invention of the television because he did not invent the scanner is untenable. It is akin to claiming that Prof Joseph Henry cannot be given credit for inventing the telegraph because he did not invent its most important component, copper wire. It is also wrong to say that Baird's system was 'incapable of anything more than poor quality picture definition'. This was true of the American Charles Jenkins' system demonstrated in Washington in 1925, but not of Baird's system demonstrated in London four months later. Crucially, Baird's system was capable of carrying sound and pictures together. Inventions often depend to some degree on earlier discoveries, but to withhold credit from those who put in place the final pieces is simply churlish.
R. G. Harrold, Shanghai, China.

QUESTION: Assuming that most Saxon, Norman and Medieval communities would have required a varied mix of skilled people in order to survive, why are there so many Smiths in relation to Weavers, Coopers, Bakers and Wrights? And what did Jones do originally?

☐ SMITHS were very good at picking chastity belts.
Brendan Cooper, Hammersmith, London.

☐ HAVING worked all day on something hot and sweaty, it obviously came naturally to continue at night. I realise that this does not explain the relative lack of Rogers but I shall leave this to others more expert than I.
Maurice Childs, Bromley, Kent.

☐ THE prevalence of smiths presumably dates from the many centuries when the only mode of transport was a horse. So every town – however insignificant – would have had its own smithy. Perhaps not everyone had a cart (or the wheel rims didn't wear out so fast); so there were not so many wrights, nor much call for

barrel-makers (coopers), bakers or weavers. As for Jones, this is a shortened form for Johnson – and similar abbreviation applies to Evans, Williams, Hughes, Davis, etc.
Graham R. Jones, Withington, Manchester.

□ IT IS wrong to conclude that there were more Smiths than wrights or coopers. Small variations in the frequency of names, which happen by chance, are magnified as the generations pass. I made a computer simulation of a village of 100 couples, with 20 each of Wrights, Smiths, Jones, Coopers and Weavers. I assumed that every couple makes 10 attempts to reproduce, and that each attempt has a 1 in 10 chance of success. This ensures that the population stays roughly stable. The simulation ran for 50 generations (about 1,000 years). I tried it 200 times, and the results varied greatly. Usually one or more names die off altogether, and it is very common for one or two names to become dominant. If we could wind back to AD 1100 and start again, the dominant name might turn out to be Weaver or any of the others.
Chris Brew, Edinburgh.

□ SMITH is from the same root as Smitan which means 'to smite', and is one of the few Old English bynames to be recorded a century before the Norman Conquest. Smith of the 10th century was a worker in iron, smiting ingots into swords, shields, battle-axes, halberds and ploughshares. But the occupational term 'smith' embraced other workers who smote their raw materials; it lost its precision and new names were needed. They were found in another Old English word *wryhta*, 'wright or craftsman', subsequently dividing into Cartwright, Wheelwright, and Wainwright (maker of wains or waggons). With increasing specialisation, a distinction had to be made between a worker in iron and a worker in tin, so more exact definitions were made, hence blacksmith and whitesmith. The Smith was an important man in medieval times, making and repairing swords, lances, defensive iron-works for castles and manor houses, offensive engines for assaulting enemy castles, and peaceful items such as agricultural implements. He was the technologist and technician, the engineer and mechanic of his day. There are several reasons why Smith is such a widespread surname; it is one of the oldest Anglo-Saxon names, so Smiths have been around longer than most. The Smiths of Old England were a strong, lusty, vigorous people capable of raising large families.

Smiths were much in demand in medieval and later times; every village had its smithy with one or more Smiths working profitably in it, so they and their families are unlikely to have gone hungry in English winters when food was scarce. Because he was not quite so close to the heat of battle in medieval warfare as Archers, Bowman (Bowmen), Knights, and others, Smith probably returned safely to his native village after the war, to resume his work and the care of his family.
Kenneth Allen, Cook, Australia.

QUESTION: What is the highest ever recorded IQ? Does it mean anything?

□ IN THE late 1980s the *Guinness Book Of Records* cited an IQ score of 228 achieved by the aptly named Marilyn vos Savant. IQs used to be calculated by dividing 'mental age', as measured on a standardised test, by actual age and then multiplying by 100. But nowadays it is defined statistically as a normal distribution in which scores are assigned so that 50 per cent of the population score above 100 (the population average), 16 per cent score above 115, 2 per cent score above 130, and so on. This means that about one person in 100 million billion can be expected to score 228 or above. Given the world's population of about five billion, the odds against anyone having such a high IQ are more than 20 million to one. This suggests that either Ms vos Savant's IQ is meaningless, or she is a walking miracle. If she is a miracle, she must have the intelligence to realise that her IQ is meaningless. Even if it were credible, it would not be the highest IQ ever recorded. In *Pygmalion Reconsidered* (1971), Elashoff and Snow reveal that Rosenthal and Jacobson, researching the effects of teacher expectations, recorded IQs of 249, 251, 262 and 300 in a single San Francisco primary school. The meaningfulness of IQ scores is debatable but experts agree that no IQ test can be trusted to measure accurately outside the range 60 to 160.
(Dr) Andrew M. Colman, Department of Psychology, University of Leicester.

QUESTION: What is the origin of circles with arrows and crosses as male and female symbols?

□ THESE symbols are among those that have been used since ancient times to represent the various gods and goddesses. The circle with an arrow means Mars and the circle with a cross underneath means Venus. Later doctors and naturalists began to use them as a shorthand for male and female, apparently in the questionable belief that Mars, the god of war, and Venus, the goddess of love, typified the sexes. The Mars symbol denotes a circular shield resting on a spear; while Venus's vanity about her appearance is represented by a hand-held looking-glass. If the latter interpretation is correct, the symbol's adoption by feminists is one of history's subtler ironies.
John Bryant, London N5.

□ THERE IS more to the signs than offered by John Bryant. Originally the male sign was simply the inverse of Venus's mirror, with a cross over the orb. The cross represents the human situation, the intersection of the horizontal earth line with the vertical heaven line, indicating the equilibrium between our instincts and the rationality of society. The circle represents a further dose of nature, which the male surmounts and controls, while the female learns to carry.
Will Milne, London N4.

QUESTION: Is it possible, anywhere in the world, to buy tinned parrot? If not, what other unusual items can be bought in cans?

□ I THOUGHT that was what tinned Spam was.
G. Campbell, Newtownabbey, N. Ireland.

□ A FRIEND once showed me a tin of elephant chunks in gravy which had been sent to him by a friend in South Africa. However, since he was a vegetarian, the tin is still unopened.
David Harper, London E1.

□ WHILE working at the Savoy Hotel in the 1960s I had to open a tin of chocolate-covered ants for a visiting dignitary. The chocolate provided a sweet contrast to the bitter taste of the ants' formic acid.
Keith Barratt-Smith, Hyde, Cheshire.

☐ MY SON bought canned earthquake for my daughter in Los Angeles.
Dennis Salt, Horsham, W. Sussex.

☐ I HAVE a tin of alligator chowder from Florida.
M. J. Lyons, Lancing, W. Sussex.

☐ WHILE living in North Carolina I discovered tinned pork brains in milk gravy; a true southern delicacy.
(Dr) Dave Richard, Pennsylvania, US.

☐ IN MY kitchen is a tin labelled 'Pacific Northwest Kitchen Sliced Slugs: Cajun Style, in Louisiana Hot Sauce', packed by Slyme Tyme Ltd of Newport, Oregon. I have not yet sampled the contents.
Lawrence Moran, Eugene, Oregon.

☐ IN 1990 in Hungary, I bought two tins labelled 'The Last Breath of Communism'.
David Lewis, Ferney-Voltaire, France.

☐ BACK in the Sixties, my teenage daughter came home with a tin of fried locusts. They were obviously genuine but too oily.
D. H. O'Dell, Hailsham, E. Sussex.

☐ I BOUGHT tins of 'Genuine London Fog' and 'Dehydrated Thames Water' (instructions: Just add Water) near the Embankment many years ago.
A. Liebenthal, Pinner, Middx.

QUESTION: Is it true that even a blind chameleon can change its colour to that of its surroundings?

☐ CHAMELEONS have dedicated a large area of brain to vision. Each eye has colour, 3-D, 180-degree vision. And many of the more than 100 chameleon species have the use of their primitive pineal gland, or third eye, located behind the 'forehead'. A tiny hole in the skull allows the detection of light and heat, making a limited degree of colour change theoretically possible. However, the stress of being

blinded will likely result in dark, 'stressed' colour, whatever the background. Utterly dependent on eyesight to catch prey, a blind chameleon will soon be a dead chameleon!
Ray Cimino, Irish Herpetological Society, Clontarf, Dublin.

□ THE chameleon's colour has nothing to do with vision, but a lot to do with the texture of the surface it is on. You can test this easily by putting a chameleon on a soft red blanket and watch it turn the colour of lush green vegetation, then on a hard green surface like bathroom tiles, and watch it turn the colour of the rock it usually adapts to.
Brian MacGarry, Magunje, Zimbabwe.

QUESTION: What is the origin of the modern usage of the word 'gay'?

□ MELVILLE in *Moby Dick* (1851) uses 'gay' in its slang sense throughout, as he does 'fairy', 'queen' and 'queer'. They can't have been so understood by a mass audience – he wanted to sell books, not go to jail – but since he'd just been four years at sea, it's reasonable to suppose they were sailors' slang. The American whaling industry in which he'd served operated out of the Quaker strongholds of Nantucket and New Bedford. Somewhere in the writings of Bertrand Russell is a story about his first wife, the American Quakeress Alys. She used 'gay' as a disparaging term: to her, 'gay' was anything non-Quaker in lifestyle. Quakers, at least in the US, used it to connote vanity, ostentation, hedonism. Could it be that the sailors from this community, meeting a whole new lifestyle at sea, extended the word to mean something else their community would undoubtedly have despised?
Sheenagh Pugh, Canton, Cardiff.

□ FOR hundreds of years 'gay' referred to casual sex. It once described roués and prostitutes. Victorian rakes didn't flock to Gay Paree because it was a jolly place.
Peter R. Brooke, Straloch, Aberdeen.

□ MEMBERS of The Religious Society of Friends are familiar with the phrase 'gay Quaker' in its non-sexual sense – but the term Quakeress used by Sheenagh Pugh is rarely if ever used. For more

than 300 years Quakers, recognising that all are equal in the sight of God, do not use titles, even Mr, Mrs, Miss or Ms. 'Quaker' derives from the verb to *quake* and has no gender: 'Quakeress' as a means of identifying women from men can only have come from outsiders who felt a need to identify gender.
John Dunning, Hoddesdon, Herts.

□ THE usage derives from demonstrations in America in the early Seventies proclaiming homosexual equality. Demonstrators carried placards with the slogan 'Good As You'. The acronym GAY stuck.
Samantha Hannay, London.

□ SAMANTHA HANNAY is wrong. In its meaning of loose-moralled, 'gay' goes back to the late Middle Ages; when it occurs in old ballads the lady in question is about to do something awful, like commit adultery. 'Dance over, my lady gay!', in 'London Bridge Is Falling Down', is a straightforward reference to women involved in the same profession as the sad little waif in the *Punch* cartoon of the 1840s asking her downcast friend: 'Tell me, Maud, 'ow long 'ave you been gay?' The 1811 *Dictionary Of The Vulgar Tongue* defines 'gaying instrument' as the penis. By the 19th century it had become linked to males with males.
John Brunner, South Petherton, Somerset.

QUESTION: When was the first vending machine used and what did it vend?

□ A COIN-in-the-slot system was used in London during the early 19th century for selling newspapers – not so much a labour-saving device as an ingenious use of the principle that machines (unlike people) can't be punished for breaking the law. To discourage the spread of 'dangerous' ideas, information about parliamentary sleaze, etc., the Government imposed a hefty stamp duty on newspapers, which raised their price beyond the pockets of the masses. The tax was widely evaded, even though it was illegal to sell unstamped newspapers. One solution was the mechanical vendor. Customers entering the shop turned a pointer on a dial to indicate the journal they wanted and inserted their money. An unidentifiable operator concealed behind a screen then slid the

paper down a chute to the customer. (See *Poor Men's Guardians* by Stanley Harrison, Lawrence & Wishart, 1974.)
Tom Watson, London N1.

□ In 215 BC, the mathematician Hero of Alexandria published a method of dispensing holy water through a coin-operated mechanism. The water was contained in a covered urn in which an upright rod balanced on one side a small plate, while on the other side a bell-shaped cap was suspended to fit over and close the water outlet from the urn. The position of the plate under a slit in the top of the urn ensured that when a coin was pushed through the slit it dropped on to the plate, depressing it so as to lift the cap on the other side. The outlet being thus opened, the water flowed freely until the coin slid off the tipped plate, sending the apparatus into reverse to stop the flow. How much water the Egyptian worshipper received for the money was a matter of chance and it is not known whether the device was ever put into practice. In Britain it was not until the 17th century that the first instance of automatic vending was recorded. It was a device known as an honour box, for dispensing snuff or tobacco, which was used in taverns and held about 1lb (450 grams) of tobacco or the equivalent of snuff. An old English halfpenny dropped in the slot and triggered the opening of the spring-loaded lid, but the device was less ingenious than Hero's, for unless the user closed the box by hand, other customers could help themselves to the contents without paying. (Source: *Automatic Vending Machines* by Colin Emmins, Shire Publications.)
Janette Gledhill, Vend Inform, Banstead, Surrey.

QUESTION: Vampires, werewolves and the like are said to be active while there is a full moon. Why? Surely these beasties would prefer to do their worst when moonlight is at a minimum.

□ Only during the full moon can you see at night – and before there was street lighting, most potential victims would stay at home. The werewolf would risk bumping into things in the darkness – and werewolves were especially prone to injury. The likely origin of the werewolf legend, and its vampire variant, is an inherited disease called porphyria. The porphyrin ring is a vital

component of haemoglobin which is vital in carrying oxygen round in our blood. It is also a pigment and the colours it produces are all seen in a bruise as it breaks down. Starting red, it is changed to a yellow-green compound also seen in bile. Porphyria sufferers can't break this compound down and recycle its iron. When the pigment gets into the skin the porphyric gets rashes and scars from sunlight acting on the pigment. The sufferer quickly learns to stay out of the sun. Tender, scarred faces are hard to shave and beards are often preferred. In addition, nails and teeth begin to stain reddish brown and may fall out. Eyes also may look red and victims readily become anaemic. This can, at least partially, be overcome by taking a diet rich in iron. The richest source known is blood. Finally, the abnormal porphyrins can cross into the brain and drive you mad. So an anaemic, hairy madman with red teeth and eyes, who avoids the sun, wandering around when he can see at night seeking to supplement his diet with blood is not too difficult to picture as the werewolf.
(Dr) Steve Seddon, Newcastle under Lyme, Staffs.

QUESTION: Given (a) the velocity of a falling object, (b) the average individual's reaction time and (c) the speed of sound, is there any point in shouting a warning to those below if I accidentally drop a heavy object from a tall structure?

□ FORGETTING about air resistance, the basic difference between the progress of your shout and the heavy object is that the object accelerates progressively, while the shout travels at a constant (though high) speed. If you drop the object from a height of 10 metres and shout immediately, the person has almost a second to get out of the way, increasing to about three seconds if the building you drop the object from is 100 metres high. Eventually, however, the object has long enough to accelerate past your shout, giving the victim no chance to respond, which happens when your building is about 900 metres tall. In that case, you'd best spend the intervening few seconds covering your tracks and preparing an alibi for the unlikely event that the victim survives and decides to sue.
(Dr) Simon Saunders, Cambridge.

□ DR SAUNDERS seems to have his numbers in a twist. Assuming a temperature of around 18°C so that sound travels at a constant

speed of 342m/s; that the acceleration due to gravity is 9.81 m/s; that air resistance can be ignored; that the sound travels unimpeded and is still audible when it reaches the person; then the optimal height of the building is 5.96km. This is the height that maximises the time between the arrival of the sound and the object, with the time interval being 17.4 seconds (should be enough for the slowest of reactions). For heights up to around 23.8km the sound will reach the person before the object. Absurd, perhaps, but that's assumptions for you.
Charles Arthurs, Painswick, Glos.

☐ DR SAUNDERS began his reply: 'Forgetting about air resistance . . .' You can't in this case. Air resistance increases as a falling body's speed increases, eventually equalling the gravitational force. Thereafter, the body will fall at a constant velocity, the terminal velocity. This final velocity depends on the shape and density of the object. Drop a feather from a height and it will reach a very low terminal velocity. Even for objects likely to do serious damage to those below, the terminal velocity will always be far less than the speed of sound.
(Dr) Stephen J. Moss, Sutton Coldfield, W. Midlands.

QUESTION: Which has been the most uneventful day of recent times?

☐ FEBRUARY 29, 1995.
Simon Walsh, Braintree, Essex.

☐ LATE in 1994, Bridgwater must have had a quiet time, since the local paper had a column headlined: 'No more human remains found.'
Paul Bovett, Bridgwater, Somerset.

☐ SOME years ago the South African Broadcasting Corporation reported: 'There is no news tonight.'
Gertrude Cohn, London NW3.

☐ LET us consider that there is such a day. Then we can be sure that on that day, a not insignificant thing occurred: it became the most uneventful day of recent times. Now this is probably

enough for the said day not to be the most uneventful day of recent times. So if there is such a day, then it isn't. Hope this makes things clear.
Felix Salmon, London SE19.

QUESTION: What does OK stand for? Why is it such an internationally understood phrase?

☐ OK's origins are still hotly debated by American professors. Bill Bryson, in his book *Made In America*, lists nine possible derivations, ranging from Only Kissing to *Olla Kalla* – allegedly the Greek for all good – to *okeh*, the Choctaw Indian word for Yes. Some claim that OK was what President Andrew Jackson, who started life in the backwoods of Tennessee, wrote in the margins of documents signifying Orl Korect when he was in the White House in the 1830s. The initials first appeared in print in the *Boston Morning Post* in 1839 as a whimsical shortening of Oll Korrect and were taken up the following year by supporters of Jackson's protégé and successor as president, Martin Van Buren, who set up OK Clubs to help his election prospects. Van Buren was known as Old Kinderhook, after his home town in New York, but that may have been a piece of tidying-up to improve the nickname of a rather fastidious politician.
Steve Bates, London SW1.

☐ ONE theory is that it originated among African Americans. Apparently, in Mandingo *o ke* means 'all right' and in Wolof (Senegal) *wav kay* means 'yes indeed'. Use of the term in New England *c.* 1840 (the first known use was in a Boston newspaper) has been put down to the steady influx of refugees from the Southern slave states. Other suggestions about origins include: the Latin *omnia corrects*; the Southern French dialect word *oc* (*oui*); *aux quais* ('to the harbour') stencilled on casks of Puerto Rico rum specially selected for export; Aux Cayes (a place in Haiti noted for the excellence of its rum); the Scots 'och aye'; and the initials of Otto Kaiser (a German-born US industrialist).
Basil Morgan, Uppingham, Rutland.

☐ IT GOES back much further than either of your correspondents suggest. When the Black Prince married Eleanor of Aquitaine,

he became Henri II of France (which was in fact four different countries in those days). The local dialect of Aquitaine (the south-west of France) was Occitaine – it's still spoken today in more rural parts. 'Oc' is obviously a shortened form of Occitaine and also means 'yes'. Henri brought this word back to England and the rest is history.
Dave Novell, Leeds.

□ DAVE NOVELL'S letter contains historical inaccuracies. First, the Black Prince may have been Duke of Aquitaine (or Guyenne as it was known to the English) but he did not marry Eleanor of Aquitaine – he was Eleanor's great-great-great-great-grandson. Eleanor's husband became Henry II of England, but Henri II of France was the husband of Catherine de Medici and died in a tournament in 1559. France was never four different countries, just one country whose king was so weak that he had magnates who were more powerful than he. Occitaine was never a dialect but a full language, spoken widely across all of what is now southern France, north-east Spain, the Balearics and north-west Italy. From Occitaine are descended Provençal, Mallorquin and Catalan. The great linguistic divide of France was typified by the word used for 'yes'. In the north it was *oeuil*, which has now become *oui* but was then pronounced something like 'aye'. In the south 'yes' was *oc*, hence the alternative name of the heartland of Occitanie – Languedoc. But, if we are genuinely to believe that 'oc' was the origin of the term 'OK', it has even older roots than Mr Novell suggests. Oc itself was derived from the Latin affirmative 'hoc'.
Colin Pilkington, Ormskirk, Lancs.

QUESTION: What is the most (monetarily) valuable object in the known universe in terms of value per unit mass?

□ A SUBSTANCE known as Prostaglandin E2 (used in research into respiratory function) is commercially available at a cost of £17.90 per nanogram. This equates to £3,580 billion per kilogram.
John Peacock, Cardiff.

□ THE *Guinness Book of Records* tells us that, in 1970, the element californium was available for sale at $10 per microgram, approximately £6 billion a kilo. Of course, it's unlikely you could

buy a whole kilogram, but if you did you'd probably get a bulk discount.
Mike Frost, Bilton, Rugby.

□ ATOMS much heavier than uranium do not occur in nature, and have to be made artificially in large accelerators. For the very heaviest elements, literally only a few atoms have been made, with the almost unimaginably small mass of about 0.0000000000000000000002 of a gram per atom. Considering the size of the accelerator and the length of time the scientific teams have worked on it, a million pounds would be a very conservative estimate of their cost, so these atoms are at least five thousand million million million million pounds per gram. This enormously exceeds the annual gross domestic product of the entire world. They only last a tiny fraction of a second before decaying, and for some of them a few grams in one place would cause a nuclear explosion. So if you can afford the price the enjoyment will be short-lived!
(Prof.) Harvey Rutt, University of Southampton.

□ A BIRTH certificate bearing the name House Of Windsor would be worth several millions sterling per gram.
Roger Nall, Worcester.

QUESTION: Is there a Tory equivalent of Clause 4? If not, what would be a succinct statement of the Tories' principles and *raison d'être*?

□ IT COULD be argued that their *raison d'être* is: 'Look after No 1.' However, I reckon it should be: 'Look after No 1 – and No 1's friends.'
Les Brooksbank, Thornton, W. Yorkshire.

□ SINCE 1979, the guiding principle has been: 'Government of the spiv, by the spiv and for the spiv.' What else could be expected from a party whose very name begins with a 'con'?
R. J. Wootton, Aberystwyth, Dyfed.

□ I WOULD suggest Chapter 25 verse 29 of *St Matthew*: 'For unto everyone that hath shall be given, and he shall have abundance:

but from him that hath not shall be taken away even that which he hath.'
K. J. A. Crampton, Brockenhurst, Hants.

□ I SUGGEST the following: 'A party of great vested interests, banded together in a formidable federation; corruption at home, aggression to cover it up abroad; the trickery of tariff juggles, the tyranny of a party machine; sentiment by the bucketful, patriotism by the imperial pint; the open hand at the public exchequer, the open door at the public house; dear food for the millions, cheap labour for the millionaire.' It is taken from a speech by Winston Churchill, in Manchester 1906, when he stood as a Liberal. In the same speech he went on to say: 'We want a government that will think a little more about the toiler at the bottom of the mine and a little less about the fluctuations of the share market.'
Bob Cottingham, London N10.

□ 'TO SECURE for ourselves by hook or by crook the full fruits of everyone else's industry, and the fastest bucks that may be possible upon the basis of running down and flogging off the means of production, distribution and exchange, and to ensure the public are so badly educated that they keep electing us.'
Tom Freeman, Cambridge.

□ 'EAT the poor.'
Peter Donnelly, Berkhamsted, Herts.

QUESTION: What happened to the prototype car that ran on water? Is it still a viable option? Who invented it, and is he/she still alive?

□ IN THE early 1930s there was an experimental steam car on trial at the Sentinel Wagon Works, Shrewsbury. It was a marvellous car to drive but never commercially viable.
A. I. Pottinger, Edgbaston, Birmingham.

□ THE idea of a spark ignition engine running on water is a common legend and was the subject of a film many years ago. After prolonged negotiations, the British Admiralty conducted a test on a small motorboat, but the 'inventor' failed to attend.

The probable basis of the legend is the chemical reaction between water and calcium carbide, producing acetylene gas. Acetylene would probably burn in a suitably designed spark ignition engine, albeit badly. However, I strongly advise any interested persons not to experiment without advice: acetylene is a very unstable compound.
John Nichols, lecturer, Peterborough Regional College.

□ IN 1897, in America, the twins Francis and Freeland Stanley introduced the first commercially successful car powered by a steam engine, the first of a series of 'Stanley Steamers'. In 1906, on a Florida beach, the Steamer achieved a speed of 127 miles per hour. There was at this time real uncertainty as to whether steam, electrical or internal combustion propulsion would win the day; many assumed it would be steam. But an outbreak of foot and mouth disease caused the US government to ban water troughs on the street. The troughs were essential for recharging the Steamers. By this historical accident did the internal combustion engine gain ascendancy.
Michael Glickman, London NW5.

□ YOUR enquirer probably had in mind the car that ran on water with petrol – not mixed in the tank, of course, but in the combustion chamber by a special carburettor. The idea, as I recall, was that the heat of the combustion of petrol turned the water into steam, thus adding to the energy and giving more power and/or less fuel consumption. It created a lot of interest in the Fifties and I believe it was used for a while by the Metropolitan Police.
G. M. Maclean, Market Harborough, Leics.

□ I HAVE always understood this to be a reference to cars running on hydrogen gas, derived from water. An American project, entitled the Hindenburg Project, was carrying out experiments into this some years ago, and so were BMW in Munich, but I do not know if there is any likelihood of commercial production.
Patrick Nethercot, Durham.

□ IN 1903 my grandfather, W. E. Galloway, went to New York and while he was there met the Stanley brothers. He was so impressed with their steam cars that he persuaded them to grant him the agency for the British Isles and the Dominions. The cars were imported direct to Newcastle-upon-Tyne from Boston, US, and the

early models were 10 horsepower and cost £225 or £300 for special coachwork. The American styled body did not prove popular and soon the imports were of the chassis only and coachbuilt bodies were added at Gateshead. Also spares were soon made there too. Later there was a 20hp Gentlemen's Speedy Roadster capable of 90mph. My grandfather took up racing in the North-east and won many trophies, as the steam car was much faster than the ordinary internal combustion engine. The steam car sold fairly well before the First World War. About 360 were sold, but when the war came deliveries were erratic and Stanley boilers were used in conjunction with a pump to pump out the water from the trenches in Europe. Steam cars were fun to drive and easy to operate and little could go wrong apart from the need for a new boiler, which was expensive at £50. However, they needed nearly half an hour to warm up from cold, and even on the 30-mile trip to Gateshead my grandfather had to stop and refill with water. After the war it was decided not to continue with the agency, as by that time it was difficult to sell steam cars against the opposition and vested interests of the internal combustion engine combines.
Michael Armstrong, St Brelade, Jersey.

□ THE only car fuelled solely by water is the 1600cc Volkswagen-engined 'dune buggy', invented by Stanley Meyer in Grove City, Ohio. Water from the fuel tank is converted into an explosive hydrogen gas mixture through very high voltage, very low current pulses. No storage of hydrogen is involved. The exhaust is de-energised water vapour. The car is expected to run at up to 65 mph for 25 miles on 1 pint of water. A prototype was demonstrated to an Ohio TV audience in 1984 and 1985. Since then development has continued and a conversion kit for petrol engines up to 400hp has now been manufactured to a pre-production standard. Further demonstrations await clearance in accordance with the US Clean Air Act.
Anthony Griffin, Bosham, W. Sussex.

QUESTION: When Shelley drowned in a boating accident, his wife Mary and Lord Byron burnt his body on a funeral pyre. Mary rescued his heart from the flames and kept it in a casket for the rest of her life. What happened to the heart when Mary Shelley died and where is it now?

□ SHELLEY'S cremation, stage-managed by his friend of only six months, Trelawny, was attended by Trelawny himself; Lord Byron; Leigh Hunt, who had travelled to Italy to join Shelley and Byron in a publishing venture; and various local officers. Mary did not attend and, according to Trelawny's account, the others could hardly face it; Byron swimming off to his boat and Hunt remaining in his carriage. Trelawny observed that Shelley's heart was not consumed in the fire and rescued it, burning his hand and risking quarantine in the process. Hunt lay claim to it from Trelawny, justifying his action to Mary, who assumed a natural right to possession in a letter: '. . . for [Hunt's love of Shelley] to make way for the claims of any other love, man's or woman's, I must have great reasons indeed brought to me . . . In his case above all other human beings, no ordinary appearance of rights, not even yours, can affect me.' Byron was asked to intervene but flippantly questioned Hunt's need for the heart ('He'll only . . . write sonnets on it') and it was through the efforts of Jane Williams, the Shelleys' friend, whose partner Edward had drowned with Shelley, that Hunt was eventually persuaded to part with the relic and Mary took charge of it. At Mary Shelley's death in 1851, the heart was found in her desk wrapped in a copy of *Adonais*, Shelley's self-prophesying eulogy on the death of Keats. It was kept in a shrine with other relics at Boscombe Manor, the home of Shelley's son, and finally buried in 1889 in the family vault in Bournemouth.
Abbie Mason, Cambridge.

□ AMY WALLACE, in the second *Book Of Lists*, writes: 'There is a peculiar note of irony to the whole affair. The organ that longest survives a fire is not the heart but the liver – and no one present at Shelley's funeral knew enough about anatomy to tell the difference. This theory would explain the legend that the heart was unusually large.'
David Cottis, London SW15.

□ A MORE precise location of Shelley's heart is the graveyard of St Peter's Church, Bournemouth, where it shares a resting place with the remains of other such worthies as Mary Woolstonecraft, 18th-century feminist, and Sir Dan Godfrey, founder in 1893 of the precursor of the Bournemouth Symphony Orchestra.
John Gritten, London.

☐ NO ONE interested in Shelley's heart should omit to read Timothy Webb's 'Religion Of The Heart' (*Keats-Shelley Review*, Autumn 1992). The reader will learn that Shelley's heart was not unusually large, but unusually small – according to Trelawny, who snatched it from the fire. It was Leigh Hunt who changed Trelawny's account probably, as Webb plausibly argued, because he could not face the idea of a Shelley with a diminished organ of benevolence. Hunt himself was well-equipped to know the heart from the liver, having been much struck when young by some preserved hearts among the anatomical specimens of a Lincolnshire surgeon. So we must look for an explanation, other than anatomical confusion, for why Shelley's heart would not burn. A condition leading to progressive calcification is one possibility that has been advanced. The irony of the whole affair might well be that Shelley's heart was becoming literally, though not metaphorically, a heart of stone.
Nora Crook, Cambridge.

☐ ACCORDING to John Gritten, Mary Woolstonecraft is buried in Bournemouth. But while her body may be there, her memorial headstone is still in London's Old St Pancras churchyard, behind the station.
Paul S. Coates, University Of East London.

QUESTION: Why is it commonly recommended that a bottle of red, but not white, wine should be opened and allowed to 'breathe' some time before it is drunk?

☐ THE *Larousse Wines and Vineyards of France* says: 'If a wine is to be served in bottle it does not matter if it is opened three hours before it is served or at the last moment. There can be no evaporation, and oxidisation is minimal. The quantity of oxygen that penetrates the wine after it has been uncorked is very small: it absorbs twice as much while being poured into the glass and three times as much after it has stood in the glass for 15 minutes.' Decanting, on the other hand, encourages oxidisation, which develops the bouquet – but only if the wine's structure can withstand exposure to air. Larousse recommends that a very old wine should be opened at the last moment and should not be decanted.
David Barker, Birmingham.

QUESTION: Whenever I have written to a government department, questioning a decision they have made, I get fobbed off with a bland reply. When I have written back asking what is the basis for the answers, I hear nothing. Do I have a right to a reply?

☐ You could make an application to the High Court for a judicial review of your dispute – but this is an expensive and time-consuming activity (and unbearably dull). You could use clause 5 of the government's insipid *Code of Practice on Access to Government Information* (available by telephoning 01345–223242), which requires responses to be sent within 20 working days from the date of receipt. The code's remedy, if a department fails to supply information within this target period, is for you to refer the matter to the Parliamentary Commissioner for Administration (the Ombudsman) via your MP. I have found an almost foolproof way of eliciting information from most government departments and agencies. Firstly, my headed notepaper reads: 'Author and Journalist'. Anyone can call themselves an author, even if their only literary claim is to have penned letters of complaint to government departments. Secondly, if a reply to your initial request (which should always be polite, lucid and to the point) is not forthcoming within, say, 14 days, then a copy of the original should be sent with a reminder. One can add a suitable caveat along the lines: 'I reserve the right to disclose the content of this correspondence to representatives of the media if this will help to facilitate a public debate on the subject.' If you really want to upset your enemy, you should send a copy to your MP – and mention this in the letter. Forget the Ombudsman; a letter of complaint sent to an MP will usually be channelled directly to the appropriate minister (even if you are represented by the most spineless political toady) and goes straight to the top of the pile. Finally, learn how to write and produce a simple press release. Using these simple skills one can launch a mini lobbying campaign for less than the price of a pint!
David Northmore, London N10.

☐ It is obvious from David Northmore's faith in 'spineless political toady' MPs, that he doesn't live where I do. When enquiring about government plans for education, Eric Forth of the Department for Education sent me a copy of the white paper

'Choice And Diversity'. He invited me to join the consultation process by sending my comments and questions about it through my MP, an invitation endorsed by that same MP. I did so, upon which my MP, after acknowledging that I was an intelligent and articulate person, refused to pass them on as he had promised. His argument was that my comments were hypothetical (as indeed were the policies in the white paper until he voted them into law), and that he preferred to spend his time dealing with constituents who had real problems. My Conservative MP opted out of the democratic consultation process which, of course, raises the question as to whose views he did pass on to education ministers?
Eileen Hathaway, Swanage, Dorset.

□ WHILST I agree with David Northmore that various devices can be used to irritate government departments, the real reason for the bland reply is that the person does not know the answer to the question. This is because he or she works in a customer services department whose mission is to meet some bogus Citizen's Charter target. This requires a response within 'x' working days. The content of the letter is irrelevant. Much better to fob people off on time than take the trouble to give them a proper reply. Anyway, in 90 per cent of the cases the answer is the same: the quality of service has been diminished as a result of government spending cuts or a management reorganisation.
R. M. Hawkes, London N20.

□ IF I fail to get a reasonably quick reply from a business or government organisation, I send a full frontal picture postcard of the Cerne Abbas Giant to the managing director or chief executive. Everyone in the firm sees and reads it before the chief gets it, and a reply usually arrives by return of post.
Richard Harvey, Salisbury, Wiltshire.

□ I WROTE to Tony Blair raising a number of questions about his irrational attack on Clause 4. From an underling I received a bland reply. Is this preparation for government?
Councillor Douglas McCarrick, Moseley, Birmingham.

QUESTION: Is it true the average height of Britons has

increased by a foot or more over the last few centuries? Is this phenomenon caused by improved diet? When will we stop growing?

□ IN 1873, the medical officer and the natural science master at Marlborough College measured the height of 500 or so of the pupils. At 16½ years the average height of the boys was 65.5 inches. When a comparable sample was measured 80 years later, the average was 69.6 inches – equivalent to a gain of half an inch a decade. James Tanner (in *Foetus Into Man*, 1978) makes the point that such trends in children's height are at least partially accountable in terms of earlier maturity. The so-called secular trend at completion of stature in adulthood is in the region of four inches in a hundred years. He did not detect a slowing down in the trend. Although improved standards of nutrition are cited as one possible cause, Tanner also invokes a genetic explanation, which in turn hangs on the increased incidence of marriages and procreation outside the village community. He notes that a key factor in the growth of this 'outbreeding' was the introduction of the bicycle.
Peter Barnes, Milton Keynes.

□ THE study of skeletons from archaeological excavations has shown that the average height of the population within the British Isles (and elsewhere) has varied over time, and there is no doubt that the single most important influence is that of diet. In this present era of food surpluses and balanced diets in Europe, most people will grow to their full genetic potential (unless other factors such as smoking or ill health intervene). But earlier generations were acutely prone to the fluctuations of harvests, poverty and starvation – unless they were members of privileged groups. Skeletons of wealthy lay-people found in excavations I directed at Norton Priory in Cheshire showed their height to be little different in range to that of the present-day population. The peasant population of the same era tended not to grow as tall, and would usually die much younger.
(Dr) Patrick Greene, Director, Museum of Science and Industry in Manchester.

□ AVERAGE young male height around 1750 was about 160cm

(63 inches) and in 1980 it was 176cm (69.3 inches); there is no evidence of growth as large as another 6 inches in earlier centuries. The answer is complex because there has always been significant variation in height between social classes, although the inequality has narrowed over time; it therefore matters whom you measure. The average height of public school boys has risen less than that of working-class children. This fact helps to answer the second question: the primary cause of growth is increased income, which means that people can eat more, although changes in disease and pollution can have effects. But it also means that the increased income inequality since 1979 may be affecting average heights and variation between classes. We do not know when we will stop growing; in Britain we still have a long way to go to catch up with richer nations such as the Netherlands, where young males average over 180cm (71 inches).
Roderick Floud (co-author Height, Health And History, *CUP), London Guildhall University.*

□ LET'S assume that there have been humans or human-like beings for some 2 million years or, say, 100,000 generations. If their average height increased each generation by a mere one-thousandth of an inch we should now be 8 ft 4 inches taller than our remote ancestors. It seems therefore that there are powerful influences restricting humans to a fairly narrow variation in height, even over long periods of time.
Louis Judson, Penrith, Cumbria.

QUESTION: How automatic is the automatic pilot on an aeroplane? And can we do away with human pilots altogether?

□ MAJOR advances are being made with the complexity of computer technology in the civil aviation industry. It is now confidently predicted that the flight-deck crew of large airliners will soon comprise a single pilot, accompanied by a dog. The primary task of the pilot will be to feed the dog. The role of the dog will be to bite the pilot if he or she attempts to touch anything.
M. J. Ingham, Nettleham, Lincoln.

□ THE term Autopilot is rather misleading, being the trade name

for the German control system used in the Graf-Zeppelin L7127 in 1927. Aircraft Flight Control Systems are essential for the safe operation of modern civilian and military aircraft and contribute to an aircraft's stability. No aircraft is 'really' stable in flight, and continuous adjustments have to be made in order to maintain straight and level flight. If a pilot is on a long-haul journey, the continuous manipulation of rudder and flaps (especially in windy conditions) would be exhausting. The AFCS's are designed to make life easier. As for doing away with human pilots altogether, unless an electronic system can be made to anticipate all possible eventualities and to act appropriately then we shall have to stick with humanity. If an airline ever proposes to introduce self-flying pilot-free aircraft then remember – it's your life!
Gregory Slaughter, York.

QUESTION: What is the origin of the expression 'raining cats and dogs'? I note that Thomas de Quincey used it in *Confessions Of An Opium Eater*, written about 1820.

☐ IN THE pre-industrial city, when there was no adequate drainage, but a large population of stray animals, it was not unusual to find drowned cats and dogs in the streets after a violent rainstorm. Hence, 'it's been raining cats and dogs'.
Patrick Hennessy, Paris, France.

☐ YOU might be interested in the German (Austrian) equivalent phrase: 'It's raining cobblers' apprentices.'
Eric Sanders, London W12.

☐ IN AFRIKAANS, the equivalent expression is '*dit reent oumeide met knopkieries*,' which literally means 'it's raining grandmothers with knobkerries.'
Robert J. Newman, Croydon, Surrey.

☐ WHILST not knowing the origin, I am certain it pre-dates the expression 'hailing taxis'.
D. A. Dyer, Mayland, Chelmsford.

☐ IN NORTH Wales the expression is '*bwrw hen wragedd a ffyn*'

– 'raining old women and sticks'; in South Wales it is '*eyllyll a ffyre*' – 'knives and forks'.
R. P. W. Lewis, Earley, Reading.

QUESTION: Who was Hobson and what was the choice he had to make?

□ THOMAS HOBSON (1545–1631) was a well-known Cambridge figure. As the 'University Carrier' he plied his trade for many years, hiring out horses for long-distance travel. The Bull Inn in Bishopsgate was his stopping-place in London. According to Milton, who wrote two epitaphs to commemorate Hobson's death, his business appears to have failed when he was 'forbidden to travel to London by reason of the plague' and he fell ill and died during this involuntary 'vacancy'. The expression 'Hobson's choice' originated in his practice of hiring out hackney horses in strict rotation, making each customer take the horse which stood nearest the stable door (Steele: *Spectator* 509; 14 October 1712).
Kayode Robbin-Coker, Southwark Street, London SE1.

QUESTION: Why is the road surface on French autoroutes and other main roads much smoother and of finer composition than equivalents in Britain?

□ FRENCH road-building contractors are encouraged to innovate, whereas their British counterparts are stuck with Department of Transport specifications which refuse to recognise that new techniques can offer advantages. The best example of this is the use of a paving material called porous asphalt. This allows water to drain through a series of interconnecting voids, rather than sit on top of the road. This greatly increases safety by reducing the risk of aquaplaning, and improves visibility by reducing spray. A spin-off benefit of porous asphalt is that it reduces road noise by about half – the voids serve to deaden the noise which would otherwise be reflected. This in turn improves comfort and reduces driver fatigue – another safety advantage. These qualities have made porous asphalt very popular

in many European countries – in Austria it is called 'political asphalt' because of its reduction of environmental noise. A stretch of the A38 Burton-on-Trent bypass was surfaced using the material over 10 years ago, and is still performing well; but the DoT remains extremely conservative. One reason cited is that the material is slightly more expensive than conventional asphalt, but numerous studies have shown that the savings in accidents more than make up for this. The company which is building the Birmingham Expressway (the first privately-owned toll road in Britain for 200 years) has indicated that it might use the material – so that drivers will get a premium service in return for paying the toll. Paradoxically, porous asphalt is a British invention, developed in the 1950s to improve friction on airfields.
Russ Swan, Editor, World Highways, *Nottingham.*

□ RUSS SWAN rightly points out that the Government has been extremely reluctant to sponsor improved highway standards, the key example being the quiet road surface, porous asphalt. The efforts of myself and others to have the porous asphalt surface laid on the section of the A34 that skirts East Ilsley, near Newbury, came to no avail. Villagers now have to put up with incessant road noise, made more intolerable by the fact that it was avoidable. Work on the A34 Newbury by-pass is due to commence during the winter. There is again a glaring need for the new road to feature porous asphalt. The Government could at least show that it is capable of understanding public fears. A quiet road surface on the by-pass would be a good start.
David Rendel MP, London SW1.

□ THE surface of our main roads is made deliberately rough to provide more grip between the tyre and road surface when travelling at higher speeds. In the wet this roughness plays an important role by preventing water building up in front of the tyre, which could otherwise cause aquaplaning and loss of control. As a result we have one of the lowest levels of people killed on our roads per head of population both in Europe and further afield.
Nigel Organ, Head of Road Engineering & Environmental Division, The Highways Agency.

□ THE ANSWER given by Nigel Organ is indicative of the Highway Agency's casual attitude to road safety. By permitting vehicles to travel faster on rougher road surfaces, the more vulnerable road users, such as cyclists and pedestrians, are forced off the road and into using cars themselves. In countries which have a smoother road surface, traffic travels slower, road noise is reduced, and cyclists are encouraged to use the road both by the reduced vehicle speeds and the smoother riding surface, which incidentally is much kinder to a cyclist's skin if he/she falls off.
Tim Chamberlain, Bristol, Avon.

□ THE REAL reason our roads are so bad is that they are laid with the cheaper wheel-suspended surface-laying machines and not the tank-like track-laying machines that used to be used. The tracked machines perform a better averaging of the surface than the wheeled machines, leading to a much better macro surface.
A. A. Brodie, Finchley, London.

QUESTION: A friend carries an organ donor card to which he has added the words: 'My organs are not to be used for a member of the Conservative Party.' Would his wishes be respected? Would his estate have any recourse if not?

□ EVEN though I agree entirely with the sentiment expressed, we do not retrieve organs from anyone who puts conditions on their use. Once removed, donor organs are placed with recipients who have, in the opinion of the transplant team, the best chance of success, both short-term and long-term. This is regardless of race, colour, religion or indeed political views. Your friend should either tear up his donor card, or remove this clause. The card has no legal status, and therefore no recourse could be taken.
Deirdre M. Westwood, Transplant Co-ordinator, Nottingham.

□ IF ANY one of my bits and pieces are ever transplanted into a Conservative, it would reject them.
Allan Davies, Grimsby, S. Humberside.

☐ I WOULD hope that the carrier of this card (or his estate) would have no legal recourse whatsoever for this ludicrous action. Since the holder dislikes Conservatives so much he is, presumably, a socialist. Is he therefore advocating a medical system whereby patients are asked their political affiliations before being treated? This is clearly some new and exciting form of socialism I was not previously aware of. I personally am proud that my regard for human life extends beyond my party-political beliefs. Anyone (even Tony Blur) is welcome to my organs after my death if it will help to save a life.
Tim Walls, London SW7.

☐ LIKE Tim Walls, I would be happy to let a member of the Conservative Party have any of my organs – at the current market rate, of course.
Richard Towers, Lymm, Cheshire.

☐ MY LIVER is in an advanced state of cirrhosis, my pancreas rotten with paracetamol and my kidneys pickled in alcohol. My lungs are all glued together with the tar from 30 years of 60 cigarettes a day; my stomach and duodenum are riddled with ulcers; my eyes almost closed with cataracts; and my optic nerves wasted with worry about the rest. My heart only continues to beat with the aid of a plastic contraption which holds the mitral valve together. I absolutely insist that upon my demise every one of my organs is transplanted in different members of the Conservative Party, whether they like it or not. There is no charge.
Gerard Mulholland, Chevilly-Larue, France.

QUESTION: Descartes said that the only thing that is certain is the existence of doubt. How could he be so sure?

☐ HE WASN'T. That's why he was.
David Boland, Wanstead, London E11.

☐ DESCARTES didn't say this. At an early stage of his antisceptical project, after subjecting all his beliefs to an artificial and exaggerated doubt, he realised that he could at least be certain of his own existence. One reason for this was that if he doubted that he existed, then he must exist in order to do the doubting. He went on to try to

re-establish all of his former beliefs as certain in which he thought he'd succeeded. Descartes thus believed that a vast number of beliefs are certain. The question as asked seems to assume that there is a contradiction involved in doubting everything except doubt itself. Does the questioner think that doubtful doubt is the same as certainty?
Peter J. King, St Hilda's College, Oxford.

□ DESCARTES' residual certainty was 'thinking': '*Cogito, ergo sum*'. The fallacy was that Descartes thought he had reduced his sceptical investigation to one element only, and he overlooked his assumption that there was a second: the 'I' in 'I think, therefore I am'. He fails to subject 'I' to his own sceptical process. This 'I' led to dualist philosophy and the soul in the pineal gland, but he never proves that 'I' is an entity rather than a generalised term for consciousness.
Karl Heath, Coventry.

□ 'I AM confused, therefore I am' might be a more relevant argument for Karl Heath. He suggests that for Descartes the soul is in the pineal gland, whereas Descartes concludes that the soul has no spatial location, being neither in nor outside nor above nor below the pineal gland. Descartes usually is uncertain about those beliefs which he could conceivably doubt or over which he could make a mistake. So, when Peter King tells us that Descartes realised that he could be certain of his existence because, in doubting, he must exist in order to do the doubting, there is some confusion. It is impossible both for Descartes to believe he thinks or exists and be mistaken in his belief; but it looks as if this is being confused with the mistaken claim that it is impossible for Descartes to doubt or make a mistake about these matters. His reflections on the possibility of an evil genius, for example, could lead him into mistakenly thinking that he does not exist or is not thinking. Heavy alcoholic consumption could have the same outcome. As it is, it seems as if he thinks he cannot make a mistake about his existence, thus making a mistake.
Peter Cave, Hampstead, London NW3.

QUESTION: Is it morally right for a lawyer to defend a client despite knowing that the client is guilty?

□ YES – although the nature of the defence must be clarified. If the client tells us that he/she is guilty, there are two ways of 'defending' the case. The first is upon a guilty plea, defending a client's interests by way of mitigation. Secondly, a client may be defended by getting the prosecution to prove its allegation. It is morally right that the state should be required to prove its case against those whom it seeks to prosecute. To allow anything less than proof would be wholly unacceptable. This process of 'putting to proof' is closely connected to the issue of the right to silence. Any legal right or freedom is a building block in the overall morality of a society, even when such a right or freedom may enable the individual to act with something short of full personal morality.
Tim Rose (defence solicitor), Douglas & Partners, Bristol.

□ NO. The principles under which I have operated as a criminal defence lawyer for the last 24 years have been as follows: If the client says that he is not guilty, then I accept at face value his instructions, and I will 'defend' him to the best of my ability. If the evidence against him is so overwhelming that he will be convicted in any event, I will always point out clearly the risks that he faces, but the decision must always be that of the client. If he persists in his denial, then I will continue to defend him. If a client tells me that he is guilty, but he is going to put forward a defence, I will show him the door forthwith. If a client admits to me his guilt and subsequently admits it to the court, I have no moral qualm at all about representing him (not 'defending him'), so that all that is good about him (if anything) can be said to the court.
Roger Corbett, Russell Jones & Walker, Birmingham.

QUESTION: Which is the safest method of transport (i.e. ship, bus, train, car)?

□ THE Department of Transport's annual publication, *Transport Statistics Great Britain*, gives this information. Different modes of transport are used for different purposes, but the overall averages show that air has the lowest fatality rate at 0.3 per billion kilometres travelled. This is followed by bus and coach at 0.4, rail 1, car 4, ship 6 and motorbike 100. Figures are for travel in Britain, except for air and water which are for travel in UK-registered aircraft or vessels.

If account is taken of serious injuries also, rail is safer than bus or coach.
D. W. Flaxen, DoT, London SW1.

☐ THE figures given, based on a common mileage, indicate that air travel is the safest mode of transport. However, if the calculation were based upon a common *time* (e.g. an hour in a plane, an hour in a car, etc.) the same figures would yield a rather different order of safety: bus/coach 0.25 units; rail 1; air 2.25; ship 2.25; car 3; motorbike 75. On this basis a day's flight is nine times more likely to prove fatal than a day's coach journey. Who is to say which criterion is the more valid?
P. W. French, Farnham, Surrey.

☐ WALKING. Last year pedestrians killed no one in a bus or a lorry. But buses and lorries, the most dangerous form of road transport, killed 195 pedestrians; cars and vans killed another 1016. D. W. Flaxman of the Department of Transport answers from the perspective of the motorist demonstrating, despite some recent green rhetoric, where the Department's heart is still to be found. But statistics can tell only part of the story. There were fewer than half as many children killed in road accidents last year than in the early 1920s. This does not prove that it has become twice as safe for children to play in the street; it suggests that parental appreciation of the threat of traffic is now so great that they don't allow their children out any more.
John Adams, Geography Dept, University College London.

QUESTION: UK bank notes are merely IOUs, since they carry the words: 'I promise to pay the bearer on demand the sum of . . .' signed by the Governor of the Bank of England. How can I cash this IOU, and in what form would it be paid?

☐ THIS wording is simply a relic of the days when the country was still using the gold standard. The pound note was supposed to represent a pound's-worth of gold deposited in the vaults of the Bank of England for which, in theory at least, it could at any time be exchanged. But nowadays, if money no longer represents an entitlement to a given quantity of gold, then precisely what is it? Conventional economists say that money cannot be accurately

defined, which is distinctly odd since money is an artefact, entirely a creation of man. Bankers on the other hand seem to take a different view. In his book *Money In Britain*, R. S. Sayer tells us that money has no intrinsic value and that we now have a commodity-based currency instead of one based on gold. That is, the value of money lies in that it can be exchanged for the commodities and services which the real economy produces. But if the value of money is dependent upon the productive capacity of the real economy, then financial or fiscal measures designed to impair the productive capacity of the real economy to preserve the value of the currency must, in reality, be self-defeating.
T. W. Parsons, Twickenham, Middlesex.

□ T. W. PARSONS'S reply omitted two points.
1. Bank notes are not IOUs, which are merely records of debts, but are promissory notes, promising specific repayment as stated.
2. The Catch 22 is that you could sue the Governor for the amount on your bank note, and win. But he will legally redeem his promise with another bank note for the same amount.
W. W. Bloomfield, Camberley, Surrey.

□ THE IOU on the currency notes can be redeemed in whatever form you wish. If you want it in gold then the man at Threadneedle Street could direct you to a jeweller or bullion dealer who would be only too happy to complete the transaction. Alternatively, you can convert it into company shares, Big Macs or whatever takes your fancy. You can even cut out the middleman and go directly to the traders without bothering the Bank of England at all. The promise on the note should mean that the Bank will maintain the value of the currency. Whether or not it does that is another matter entirely.
Derek Middleton, Swinton, S. Yorkshire.

QUESTION: What area of land given over to wind farming would produce the power-generating capacity of each of the four main fuels: coal, gas, oil and nuclear?

□ WIND FARMS in the UK are typically based on separation distances of between five and 10 times the diameter of the turbine rotor. A wind farm of 10 turbines with typical rotor diameters

could extend over about 50 hectares (e.g., a rectangle of 100 metres by 500 metres). The precise spacing depends on the wind regime over the site. But this represents purely the external boundaries of the wind farm. The actual land 'given over' to the turbines (and the accompanying access roads) is much less than this – typically only 1 or 2 per cent of the area of the wind farm – because normal agricultural activities can continue right up to the base of the turbines. A crude assessment, looking at just the amount of land required by wind farms to match the output of other power stations, would yield the following: the average rated capacity of coal-fired plants in England and Wales is 1,164 MW (which would supply about 4 per cent of the UK's electricity demand). This could be matched by about 180 wind farms occupying about 270 hectares but extending over some 27,000 hectares. To put this into context, there are some 18,500,000 million hectares used for agriculture and the Government estimates that it is reasonable for the UK to get some 10 per cent of its electricity from the wind by the early part of next century.
Michael Harper, Director, British Wind Energy Association, London WC2.

□ WHY use land? With the construction technology used to build oil rigs in the sea, we could site all the windmills we need in mid-Atlantic, where there's plenty of wind and no one to complain about the noise or view.
Rachel Johnston, Keighley, W. Yorks.

□ IF THERE were a day with little or no wind, the entire area of the British Isles and associated territorial waters would have to be given over to wind generators to produce nothing. Hence wind power is prohibitively expensive, except as a minor adjunct to an already complete and self-contained electrical system. Power stations must be ready to supply electrical energy when required irrespective of whether the wind be blowing or not, and so any number of wind generators can never be used as a replacement for even a single power station. The only savings that can be made are on the power station fuel costs, but these are significantly less than the total electricity costs, typically 2–3p per unit (kWh), which should be compared with the 11p per unit given to the wind generators; quite a subsidy.
W. M. Nelis (C. Eng., MIEE), Porthmadog, Gwynedd.

☐ MICHAEL HARPER'S answer contains dubious figures. The wind farms in Cornwall have shown that each 400kW turbine (a typical size) produces about one million units per year. The total UK electrical power consumption was 280 TWh (280,000 million units) in 1992. Therefore to produce just 4 per cent of this (i.e. 11,200 million units) will require 11,200 wind generators, and at the rate of 50 hectares per 10 generators will extend over an area of 56,000 hectares (i.e. 216 square miles). The 'reasonable estimate' of 10 per cent from the wind by the early part of the next century will require 28,000 turbines covering an area of 540 square miles – a mile-wide swathe of wind generators stretching 500 miles from Cornwall to Cumbria!
E. W. Luscombe (C. Eng., MIEE), Stoke, Devon.

QUESTION: When did the western world start using 'Anno Domini' to show which year it was; what form of registering years was in common use before then?

☐ THE way of registering years in most places was to count from the accession of the king or, in a republic, to give the names of annual officials (archons in Athens, consuls in Rome). Civilisations covering large areas for long periods also adopted eras, counting from some mythical or historical event: the four-year cycle of Olympic Games from 776 BC; the foundation of Rome in 753 BC; the establishment of the Seleucid dynasty in 312 BC. The early Christians adopted the Roman system, using years of Emperors, Olympiads and the foundation of Rome, and also the 15-year cycle of tax indictions established in the Roman Empire in AD 297 (still used in the Church). They also added years of Bishops and in some places adopted the era of Martyrs from AD 284. But as Christianity lasted and expanded, several scholars tried to compile universal chronologies, dating from the Creation of the World (between 6000 and 4000 BC) or the calling of Abraham (about 2000 BC). In the early 6th century, the Roman scholar Dionysius Exiguus suggested counting years from the Incarnation of Jesus, fixing the Conception on 25 March and the Nativity on 25 December AD 1 (four years after the death of Herod and five years before the Census in Judea). This system slowly spread through Western Europe, taken on by Bede in the early 8th century and officially adopted by the Emperor Charlemagne in the 9th century. It then

spread throughout the world, becoming the Common Era with years counted as CE or BCE. The Jewish era counts from the Creation in 3761 BC, and the Muslim era from the Hijra in AD 622. The Renaissance scholar Scalliger collated all chronologies in a Julian era from 4713 BC (used by astronomers and historians), and the French Revolutionaries tried to establish a Republican era from 1792.
Nicolas Walter, Islington, London N1.

QUESTION: By what right can the British state require me to observe its laws and accept its institutions, given that I have never been asked to signify my assent to arrangements which include ones negotiated in previous generations by tiny elites?

□ IF YOU have ever made use of the provisions of British law yourself, it could be argued that you have implicitly consented to comply with the entire body of it. But it is easier to argue that you imply consent when you participate in the democratic process by voting. This may also be the principle that leads opposition parties to withdraw from elections when they think they will be rigged; by not putting up candidates, and by asking their supporters to abstain, they presumably hope to invalidate the government's claims on them for compliance, freeing them and their supporters to oppose the government both within and outside the law. But even this latter argument for compliance seems rather stretched; many people comply but don't vote; and many people who vote are nonetheless outraged at some of the legislation they are asked to comply with. Rights are things you get when they are granted to you. You have no rights (in law) other than those granted to you, and conversely the state's rights over you can only be the rights you have granted to it.
John Cleaver, London.

□ JOHN CLEAVER'S answer is not entirely satisfactory. If the state has no rights over an individual without their consent, then it can have no right to control the actions of most people under the age of 18, since it does not allow such people to vote, nor does it ensure that they have the opportunity to consent in any other way. This would imply, for instance, that the only reasonable way to remove

a 12-year-old playing on a railway line would be through impact with a train. Any answer to the question should take into account that a state is not only an abstract entity: it also implicates huge numbers of individuals, in part through the existence of consensus. For example, when police officers restrict an individual's liberty by preventing him or her from driving the wrong way up a motorway, their action frequently draws the approbation of a majority of onlookers. These onlookers wish this aspect of state activity to continue. There does not seem to be any reason why their wishes should not be accorded at least as much respect as the wishes of dissidents who would prefer to be free to drive on the right if they want to, like other Europeans. Readers might conclude that while the majority is perhaps not always right, doing what it wants – obeying the state, for example – does violate the wishes of fewer people.
Hudson Pace, Teddington, Middlesex.

☐ TOM PAINE, in his *Rights Of Man*, 1791, supplied an answer to this question. 'There never did, there never will, and there never can exist a parliament, or any description of men, or any generation of men, in any country, possessed of the right or the power of binding and controlling posterity to the 'end of time', or of commanding for ever how the world shall be governed, or who shall govern it; and therefore, all such clauses, acts or declarations, by which the makers of them attempt to do what they have neither the right nor the power to do, nor the power to execute, are in themselves null and void. Every age and generation must be as free to act for itself, in all cases, as the ages and generations which preceded it. The vanity and presumption of governing beyond the grave, is the most ridiculous and insolent of all tyrannies. Man has no property in man; neither has any generation a property in the generations which are to follow.'
John Davies, History Department, Liverpool Institute of Higher Education.

☐ QUESTIONS on the nature of the individual, their moral fibre and their rights were argued about at length during the 18th and 19th centuries. John Stuart Mill argued for utilitarianism, of which the founding principle was that 'society' was more important than any one person or group of individuals. So individuals had the right to do as they pleased, provided they did not impinge upon the

rights of others. There was also a theory that just and otherwise law-abiding people, of suitable moral rectitude, were within their rights to disregard laws they considered inherently unjust. This presupposes that 'good' citizens do not need laws to keep them in check. Thus, individuals are not going to object to a directive or law which prohibits something which they would never dream of doing anyway. All the theories on law and moral development were developed when the law was so draconian that society was effectively lawless – if you are going to hang, you may as well commit a big crime. Today we may consider that some laws which exist from those times are petty, but they rarely result in conviction. And we may think that some sentences passed by judges are ridiculous, or that their comments show a lack of understanding, but this does not necessarily undermine the authority of the law or our obligation to obey it.
Graham R. Jones, Withington, Manchester.

□ MANY are the political philosophers who have tried to turn the fact that humans are social animals into some ethical or pseudo-scientific basis for the injunction to observe laws. But as any good anarchist knows, by the right of might is the true answer to this question. The fact that it is sensible or desirable to have some rules and to obey them such as traffic rules, does not give generalised grounds for observing all laws. Each of us has the right, even the duty, to question the laws imposed on us. In some forms of direct democracy, individuals have the chance to acquiesce deliberately in the rules that are generated to govern the society to which they belong, and to argue for changes or new ones. In the so-called representative so-called democracies, we are powerless and allow institutions to frighten us into obedience. Their 'right' is our 'duty'. While the sanction of punishment for breaking laws is undoubtedly one reason why many people are law-abiding, the really clever bit is the fear that is conditioned into us – a fear that makes us delegate our power as individuals to the state, and lets us duck the moral responsibility for our actions.
Maurice Herson, Oxford.

QUESTION: The term 'Jim Crow' refers to the social, political and educational segregation of the races in 19th- and early

20th-century America, particularly in the southern states. Can anyone tell me who Jim Crow was?

□ THOMAS Dartmouth 'Daddy' Rice (1808–1860) is given credit, if such it is, for establishing the black-face characterisation that became the mainstay of the black-face minstrel show. The generally accepted version, which appears in Sigmund Spaeth's *A History Of Popular Music In America* (Random House, New York), is that Rice, an actor, heard a Black street entertainer hopping and skipping down the street, singing: 'Wheel about an' turn an' do jis so, An' ebry time I wheel about I jump Jim Crow.' Rice added some words of his own, put on a black face and some ragged clothes and introduced the song and character as a major part of his act (*c.* 1829). It was an immediate success. He took the act to England where he appears to have made a great impact. Philip Howe wrote in his diary on 4 August 1837: 'Rice, the celebrated Jim Crow . . . entertains nobility at their parties; the ladies pronounce his black face "the fairest of the fair" . . . and the wits of London have established the Crow Club in honor of the Yankee buffoon.' Thus this crude comic black figure, created for the entertainment of white audiences, provided the label for the race segregation laws.
D. H. Palmer, Macclesfield, Cheshire.

□ THE song 'Jump Jim Crow' popularised the use of the name as a synonym for any black male. But the phrase has been dated back to 1730 when black people were first described as crows (*Dictionary Of Eponyms*: Martin Manser).
Keith Cook, Manor Park, London E12.

□ THE origins of the phrase in 18th-century plantation culture may have some connection to the legendary West African chieftain, John Canoe (or Jim Kano), who is celebrated to this day in the annual Junkanoo carnival in the Bahamas.
Martin Walker, Washington DC.

QUESTION: My father is deaf, but when he goes to the swimming pool there is something in the water that makes him hear. What is it?

☐ THE water makes him hear better. Water is a more dense fluid than air and as such transmits the sound vibrations more efficiently. When the head is immersed these vibrations are transmitted directly to the bones of the skull. This causes the bones of the middle ear to become excited to a greater degree than air-borne vibrations which affect the eardrum, and this increased vibration is sensed by the nerves situated in the cochlea, in the inner ear. In addition, when the head is raised from the water it is placed in a highly reverberant sound field. This causes the intensity of the sound to be raised.
Steven Payne, Frecheville, Sheffield.

QUESTION: When a fly is making its approach to land on a ceiling, does it fly upside-down or does it flip over in the last micro-second before landing?

☐ THIS question was asked on the *Brains Trust* programme on the radio a few years ago when Commander Campbell, Dr C. E. M. Joad, and Sir Malcolm Sargent treated it as a joke, but Professor Julian Huxley was quite angry that he didn't know what he thought he ought to have known. The following week, I believe, he returned to say that he had conducted experiments which showed that the fly flew closer to the ceiling until its first two legs could be put over its head to touch, and adhere to, the ceiling, bringing the rest of its body up to leave the creature on the ceiling and facing in the opposite direction.
V. Beilby, Fareham, Hants.

☐ THIS question was the subject of intensive study by an American convict. After many years of observation he said that, in the process of landing on the ceiling, flies always perform a half-upwards loop. To start flying again, they have to complete this loop. To prove it, the convict invented this way of catching flies: nearly fill a glass with soapy water, beat up a bit of a foamy head on the surface and raise the glass slowly from directly beneath the fly. Once the surface of the foam is about an inch and a half from the fly, it is doomed. In completing the interrupted loop, the fly cannot but dive into the foam.
Dulcie Kirby, Franschhoek, South Africa.

☐ PROFESSOR Joad, in the *Brains Trust*, 1941, said: 'It all depends on what the fly had for lunch. Normally it lands on the ceiling by a loop-the-loop, but if it had too much to drink it does a roll.'
Peter Helsdon, Chelmsford, Essex.

QUESTION: TV documentaries on the moon-landings have compared today's computer technology with that available to NASA a quarter of a century ago. It has been claimed that a modern lap-top is as powerful as the whole of Apollo's mission control. Can anyone give definitive figures?

☐ THE first mainframe computer I worked on was an Elliott 4120. It had 32k words of memory (we didn't have bytes in those days). One word was 24 bits long and held four 6-bit characters, so I suppose it could be taken as four bytes to the word. This made the computer's total memory 128k bytes. My present 486-based PC has 4 megabytes of RAM; 32 times as much. Mass storage on the 4120 was magnetic tape. Disc drives did exist but we didn't have one. Our usual reel of tape was 1,200 feet long and information was stored at 200 bits to the inch. At eight bits to one byte, 1,200 feet of tape would hold 360,000 bytes. This is roughly equal to 350k bytes; my PC has diskettes holding 1.44 megabytes. Not only that, the magnetic tapes were about 9 inches in diameter, compared with 3.5 inches for the diskettes. If that wasn't enough, the magnetic tapes were serial devices (that is, if the data to be read was at the end of the tape, it was necessary to read right through to find it); the diskettes have almost instantaneous access to any part of the data. Speed of operation of the PC is greater by a factor of thousands; the mainframe occupied a room 25 feet by 10 feet while the PC sits on a desk; the mainframe cost £90,000 at 1967 prices while the PC cost about £1,500 at 1994 prices. Add to that the incredible range of cheap software and the modern PC has computing power only dreamed of in 1967.
Dudley Turner, Westerham, Kent.

QUESTION: Do diet drinks which contain no sugar still cause dental decay?

☐ DIET colas are highly acidic – the pH of Diet Coke is 2.89.

A few years ago, when my children were small, we put one of their teeth in a glass of diet cola. In the morning the tooth had dissolved. Cola drinks contain a large amount of phosphate and on Radio Four's 'Food Programme' last year an eminent US professor stated that these drinks may be responsible for osteoporosis in humans because they replace bone calcium. Diet cola is also a better spermicide than old 'Classic', 'New' and 'Caffeine Free'.
John McGarry, Barnstaple, N. Devon.

□ DIET drinks do not usually contain sugar, and so cannot cause dental decay. However, soft drinks, especially carbonated ones, are generally acidic and can cause dental erosion. This is a progressive loss of enamel and dentine resulting from chemical attack. Some 'no added sugar' drinks contain hidden sugars such as fructose and these can cause decay, so it is important to check the label. The advice of the dental profession is to keep consumption of all soft drinks, including sugar-free varieties, to a reasonable level and preferably to meal times. The more often you consume sugary foods and drinks, the higher the number of attacks to the tooth enamel and the more damage is done.
Sara Morris, British Dental Association, London W1.

□ THE phosphoric acid which rots teeth is largely neutralised by saliva. In the few studies done, the main problem appears to be cavities in the front teeth as the cola washes past them into the mouth. Putting teeth in glasses of Coke might scare children, but it is hardly a scientific experiment. The studies suggest that colas should be drunk with a straw so that the cola misses the front teeth. Incidentally, orange juice is just as acidic as cola.
Mark Lee, Sheffield.

QUESTION: Was Asclepius, the ancient Greek physician said to appear in his patients' dreams and administer healing (often by performing 'surgery'), man, myth, or both? And what is the explanation for the numerous 'offerings' (in the form of inscriptions on tablets or terracotta models of the healed body part or organ) supposedly left by grateful patients?

□ ASCLEPIUS was a myth, said to be the progeny of Apollo, a God, and of Coronis, a mortal woman. Apollo's sister Artemis killed the pregnant Coronis but Asclepius was saved by post-mortem

Caesarean section. Asclepius became a great healer. After he had been struck dead by Zeus he was resurrected as a God. His tale inspired Greek healers for centuries. The healing temples originated about the 6th century BC. Many healing techniques were used including magic, drugs and surgery. One sleeping method was preceded by elaborate ritual and sacrifices. Grateful patients then made offerings to the temple of terracotta. These were models of the part which had been healed, and common examples include limbs, breasts, ears and genitals. The magic was effective for the same reason that almost any therapeutic procedure, orthodox or unorthodox tends to help, especially if the patient has faith in the treatment. There is a placebo effect, a well recognised psychosomatic phenomenon which should not be decried. In addition, time cures many diseases. This explains many cures claimed by healers of all kinds down the ages.
(Dr) Michael L. Cox, Higham-on-the-Hill, Warwickshire.

□ ASCLEPIUS may have been a myth, but the Egyptian Imhotep, who was identified with Asclepius, was definitely historical. Imhotep is recorded as holding the high offices of chief executive and master sculptor during the reign of King Zoser of the 3rd Dynasty (*c.* 2650 BC). It is likely that he was the architect of the king's tomb, the Step Pyramid at Saggara – the first large building in the world to be built entirely of stone. After his death he was deified, and during the Graeco-Roman period (*c.* 332 BC – AD 395) he was worshipped as a god in cult centres and temples throughout Egypt. Imhotep's posthumous reputation as a healer at a time of Greek rule over Egypt led to the identification with Greek Asclepius.
(Dr) Piotr Bienkowski, Curator of Egyptian and Near Eastern Antiquities, Liverpool Museum.

QUESTION: Was there ever really a phrase-book containing the sentence: 'My postilion has been struck by lightning'?

□ A COLLEAGUE of mine has just left for Vietnam armed with a copy of *How To Speak Vietnamese*, which was originally a phrase book for missionaries in past centuries. In the section at the railway station you can learn '*Có vé cho chó không?*' (Are there tickets for dogs?)
Martin Nugent, Augsburg, Germany.

☐ MANY years ago I bought a second-hand *Baedeker* of, I think, 1882. Unhappily the book has gone missing but, as I recall, the full phrase was something like: 'Driver – stop the coach! The postilion has been struck by lightning.' Another phrase which sticks in my memory was in the section on crossing frontiers: 'Do not keep me waiting, my good man! Do you not realize that I am the holder of Her Britannic Majesty's passport?'
Peter James, East Malling, Kent.

QUESTION: Are humans the only animal species to have pudding?

☐ IMMEDIATELY after his main meal, my Jack Russell terrier goes to his biscuit bowl and consumes three or four of his dog biscuits. They are always there for him, but the only time he ever eats them is after his main meal. As yet he has not developed the sophisticated human habit of having custard with his pudding.
Ruth Harvey, Pontefract, W. Yorks.

☐ I ONCE watched a hedgehog and a slug drinking from a bowl of milk. When the hedgehog finished the milk it ate the slug.
John Malcolmson, Sheffield.

QUESTION: Whatever happened to the 'Bermuda Triangle'?

☐ THE Bermuda Triangle, a vaguely defined area in the North Atlantic supposedly associated with a number of unexplained crashes, disappearances and other 'paranormal' phenomena, reached the height of its popularity between 1965–75. Its demise followed the realisation that the number of reported sinkings and other accidents was not at all exceptional for the amount of sea and air traffic that normally passes through the area. Careful analysis of individual incidents showed that logical and familiar explanations could be found for almost all of them, and that there was no more reason to search for a single cause than there would be for all the road accidents in Southern England. In what is probably the definitive book on the subject, *The Bermuda Triangle – Mystery*

Solved by Lawrence David Kushe, the author concludes: 'The legend of the Bermuda Triangle is a manufactured mystery. It began because of careless research and was elaborated upon and perpetuated by writers who either purposely or unknowingly made use of misconceptions, faulty reasoning and sensationalism. It was repeated so many times that it began to take on the aura of truth.' The Bermuda Triangle may no longer be with us but, for those who need such things, psychic surgery, alien abductions, spoon bending and corn circles seem to have proved more than adequate substitutes.
Michael Hutton, Camberwell, London SE5.

☐ AS EVERYONE who lives and works in west London will know, this has shifted to west London. It is now known as the 'Southall Triangle' and is located near Hayes Bridge. In spite of a clearly illuminated display, indicating the time of arrival of the next bus, 207 buses frequently disappear a minute or so before they are due. Many will also be aware that all planes approaching or departing from Heathrow carefully avoid this area.
Eric Parsons, Southall.

☐ IT DISAPPEARED without trace in mysterious circumstances.
Peter Sommer, London N4.

QUESTION: I suffer from large dark spots, lines and splodges floating across my eyes, which impair my otherwise good, glass-corrected sight. Can you tell me what causes this condition and if there is any cure for it?

☐ ACCORDING to Traditional Chinese Medicine, 'floaters' are caused by 'blood deficiency', which means that one's blood lacks vitality or '*Qi*'. Other signs and symptoms commonly seen alongside floaters are a dull pale face, pale lips, difficulty in getting off to sleep, dizziness and poor memory. Blood deficiency is more common amongst women than men owing to the strain placed upon the blood by the menses. One of the traditional remedies for blood deficiency in China was to eat more meat and fish, and it is true that one commonly sees blood deficiency in vegetarians and vegans in

this country. Acupuncture and herbs are the main remedies, used for at least 2,000 years to treat blood deficiency. You should be careful, however, to ensure that you consult a properly trained practitioner.
Peter Mole, College of Integrated Chinese Medicine, Reading, Berks.

□ I TOO suffer, except that my splodges are more like fairy lights. Perhaps, like me, the questioner has, in the past, digested several large quantities of a certain kind of mushroom and can still see the after-effects.
Sadie Atkins, Bradford, W. Yorks.

□ PETER MOLE rightly advises a consultation with a trained practitioner. The symptoms described are probably caused by a posterior vitreous detachment. At birth the vitreous is a homogenous gel filling the space between the lens and the retina. With time the vitreous partially liquefies. The remaining gel portion separates from the retina and moves around in the liquid. Thickenings in the gel occur wherever the vitreous was strongly attached to the retina, in particular around the optic disc or blind spot. Before the gel liquefies, the thickenings are not noticeable. Once the vitreous becomes mobile the thickenings or floaters come into the line of sight. An uncommon risk is that the mobile gel may only partially separate from the retina and pull on it, so causing a retinal tear or detachment. Traction on the retina causes the patient to experience flashes of light, often noticeable in low-light conditions. Anyone with recent onset of symptoms of floaters or flashes should be seen by an ophthalmologist to exclude a potentially sight-threatening problem.
(Dr) Mark Wilkins, Ophthalmologist, London SW7.

□ PETER MOLE may be correct in offering 'blood deficiency' as an acupuncture explanation for floaters in the eye. His corollary concerning vegetarianism, however, does not match my experience in acupuncture practice. Surveying recent years, the majority of patients with floaters have been meat-eaters. An interesting side issue is that most of those with floaters have either been smokers or have lived with smokers.
Joseph Goodman, Chairman, Council for Acupuncture, London NW4.

QUESTION: Is it possible to get tanned through glass?

☐ NO. To get a tan requires exposure to ultraviolet radiation, whether from the sun or any other source. Glass is effective in screening out ultraviolet radiation.
Peter Hughes, London E17.

☐ HOW come, Mr Hughes, that my arm was tanned on a coach journey from Liverpool to Manchester? I've even got the white bits to prove it!
John Cole, Liverpool.

☐ YES, most definitely. Many people with curtains will notice that they tend to fade where sunlight has fallen through a glazed window directly on to the fabric. The fabric not directly exposed to the sunlight fades at a much slower rate. The bleaching of curtains is a result of mainly ultraviolet B (UVB) light that the glass cannot block. UVB is the main cause of sunburn, although UVA used in sunbeds will tan but not burn. 'Laminated glass' as used in car windscreens and 'risk areas' in buildings is made of a sandwich of glass and Polyvinylbutaryl (PVB). Manufacturers of PVB claim that this can block up to 99 per cent of UVB. Use of laminated glass in windows will certainly reduce fading in curtains and help reduce sunburn of those who wish to sunbathe in the comfort of their own living room.
Noah Shepherd, Phuket, Thailand.

☐ PETER HUGHES says it is not possible. So, if they don't use glass to make the fluorescent tubes for sun beds, what do they use?
Ian Joyce, Furzton, Bucks.

QUESTION: If all people worldwide were to stop eating meat and become vegetarian, would there be enough non-meat products available to feed the world's population?

☐ IF MORE people became vegetarian, a larger number could be fed. If everyone in the world were to give up meat in favour of a grain-based diet – and food evenly distributed – the world could support 6 billion people at the UN recommended calorie level. If Americans were to reduce their meat consumption by 10 per cent

they would each year free over 12 million tons of grain for human consumption – enough to feed adequately all the 60 million people who will starve to death this year.
Anne Benewick, London W1.

☐ THE food would be fairly dull and basic, but variety could be achieved by industry producing synthetic and manufactured products. The world would also have to allow food to be grown instead of housing development, and farming might need to become less aggressively exploitative. We should note that two-thirds of the world's surface does not grow vegetation fit for human consumption, i.e. the sea, the mountains, and the polar areas. These areas do yield animals fit for human consumption, though, so it would be unreasonable for all the world to become vegetarian. In areas where both animals and vegetable crops thrive we would need to kill the rabbits, hares, marsupials, birds and other competitors in order to preserve the vegetation for ourselves. Apart from the morality of this, if we are going to kill them, why not eat them? They make very good food.
Diana Sandy, Food and Nutrition Information Service, Cottingham, E. Yorkshire.

☐ EITHER out of necessity or because they follow the tenets of their religion, the great majority of the world's population is already in the non-meat-eating category. It is only the richer third who at present depend on the intensive rearing and slaughter of the animal kingdom – 5 million cows, 14 million pigs, 20 million sheep, 600 million chickens. Contrary to the myths peddled by certain food and nutrition experts, vegetarian food can be as varied, exciting and appetising as anything achieved by *haute cuisine*. Chinese, Mexican, Greek, Indian, Middle-Eastern and French culinary skills can transform even the humble tofu or the versatile Quorn and any conceivable vegetable into unforgettable mouth-watering delights. Much more satisfying than the prosaic meat and two veg.
Ifor Rhype, Millend, Glos.

QUESTION: What is the youngest age at which the cause of death can be registered as 'old age' by a doctor?

☐ THE Registrar-General's guidance – in *Forms For Medical*

Certificates of The Cause Of Death Under The Birth And Deaths Registration Act 1953 – states: 'In some elderly persons there may be no specific condition identified as the patient gradually fails. If such circumstances gradually lead to deterioration and ultimately death, "Old age" or "senility" is perfectly acceptable as the sole cause of death for persons aged 70 and over.'
(Dr) C. J. Tierney, Widnes, Cheshire.

□ DR C. J. TIERNEY correctly quotes the age of 70 from current guidance in the death certificate booklets used by doctors. But while the doctor certifies the death – stating his/her medical opinion of the cause(s) of death – it is the registrar of births and deaths who registers the death (officially recording the fact and cause from the death certificate and from information provided by the relatives). Registrars have instructions not to accept a death certificate on which 'old age' or 'senility' appears as the sole cause unless the dead person was 70 or over. Old age is not a 'perfectly acceptable' cause of death. It is extremely vague, and in the vast majority of cases the doctor can specify the cause of death more precisely. This is desirable, because detailed and continuous monitoring of mortality is the most precious tool we have for the long-term surveillance of public health. Recent data show, for example, a fall in lung cancer mortality for men but an increase for women, and a rise in mortality from Creutzfeld-Jakob disease. Fortunately, very few death certificates for persons aged less than 85 specify simply 'old age' – the numbers for 1995 were 34 at 70–74 years (0.04 per cent of all deaths in this age group); 201 (0.23 per cent) at 75–79 years; 936 (0.90 per cent) at 80–84 years; and 7,381 (4.8 per cent) at age 85 years and over. Even so, I shall be updating the guidance on medical certification of the cause of death during 1996, in an effort to reduce these numbers still further.
(Prof.) Michael P. Coleman, Deputy Chief Medical Statistician, Office for National Statistics.

QUESTION: What was the last recorded instance of a duel being fought with seconds, at 10 paces and using pistols?

□ MY ANCESTOR, Captain George Cadogan, avoided the police to

fight a duel with pistols and seconds on Wimbledon Common on 30 May 1809. His opponent, Lord Paget, had seduced George's sister Charlotte, who was married to the Duke of Wellington's brother. The duel was fought at 12 paces, not 10, and they both missed (in Lord Paget's case this was deliberate).
David Colombi, Angmering, W. Sussex.

□ THE Duke of Wellington fought a duel with pistols, and seconds, on 21 March 1829. His opponent was Lord Winchilsea, who had cast a public slur on Wellington's political honour. They met at Battersea Fields. The seconds were Sir Henry Hardinge and Lord Falmouth respectively. The duel was fought at 12 paces, and as the command 'Fire' was given, Wellington noticed that Winchilsea kept his arm close to his side. The Duke fired wide, accordingly, and Winchilsea fired in the air. A brief letter of apology was presented by Hardinge, and the matter was deemed concluded. (Source: *Wellington, Pillar Of State*, by Elizabeth Longford 1972.)
Carol Ball, Aylesford, Kent.

□ ON 19 October 1852, in a duel with seconds, Emanuel Barthelemy shot and killed Frederic Cournet on Priests Hill, Egham, Surrey. The full ceremony was observed, with the combatants standing back to back and walking 20 paces before turning and firing.
Duncan Mirylees, Surrey Local Studies Library, Guildford.

□ A CONFRONTATION involving Marcel Proust, the author of *À La Recherche Du Temps Perdu*, and his literary contemporary Jean Lorrian, took place in France at Bois de Meudon as recently as 6 February 1897. The clash was occasioned by Lorrian accusing Proust of plagiarism and referring to him as 'one of those pretty little society boys who have succeeded in becoming pregnant with literature'. Two shots were fired, but – to quote *Le Figaro* – nobody was hurt and the seconds declared that the dispute was ended. (Source: *Fights, Feuds And Heartfelt Hatreds*, by Philip Kerr, 1992.)
Bob Hays, Ripponden, Halifax.

□ IN DECEMBER 1971 a duel was fought between a Uruguayan field

marshal and a general, after the former had dubbed his colleague 'a socialist'. The protagonists met at dawn in a Montevideo public park and, from 25 paces, fired 38 rounds at each other. Neither was hurt. According to the field marshal's second, the men did not put on their glasses before commencing the back-to-back walk. (Source: *The Book Of Heroic Failures*, Stephen Pile, 1979.)
Dominic Gould, Hull.

QUESTION: A government with a majority in both Houses of Parliament and acquiescent civil servants announces at the end of its five-year term that it is going to stay in office, and not call a general election. It would then have no legality, but how would it be ousted from office?

□ STOP sending the chauffeured cars round!
Jan Appleton, Bramhall, Stockport.

□ GIVEN that Britain does not have a written constitution and that, for all practical purposes, the sovereignty of Parliament is limited only by Acts and Treaties which Parliament itself can abrogate or alter, there is no constitutional check on Parliament's extending its term. In fact Parliament did precisely this in 1716. In 1694 a Triennial Act was passed requiring elections to be held at least once every three years, establishing formal terms for Parliament for the first time. Following the election of 1715, Parliament repealed the Triennial Act and replaced it with a Septennial Act requiring elections only once every seven years. As a result, this Parliament sat until the general election of 1722. There is no constitutional bar on a modern Parliament's similarly prolonging itself. Indeed elections due by 1915 and 1940 were postponed as a result of war.
(Prof.) David Eastwood, University of Wales, Swansea.

□ THE Queen as Head of State can dissolve Parliament at a time of her own choosing and does not have to be asked by a prime minister (although this is generally the case). If the Parliament/government continued to disobey the Queen's dissolution, the House of Commons Police force, Metropolitan Police and armed forces (all of whom owe allegiance to her) could be called in to remove and, if necessary, gaol the dissenters

(Representation of People Act). This is perhaps the only credible argument for having a monarchy.
S. Mahoney, Manchester.

☐ ALAS, S. Mahoney, the Monarch's ability to dissolve Parliament in person died with George III. Nowadays, Parliament may only legally be dissolved (and writs issued for a fresh election) by means of a proclamation under the Great Seal, exercised through the Lord Chancellor at a meeting of the Privy Council – and the Lord Chancellor and Lord President of the Council, as government ministers, are unlikely to co-operate. So a Parliament *cannot* legally be prevented from voting to extend its life beyond five years – although dissolution could only be deferred for a stated period, not abolished altogether. An Act to forbid all subsequent parliamentary elections – or to forbid all subsequent Acts of Parliament – would have no legal force, as a Parliament may not bind itself or its successors. In time, even the largest Commons majority can fall through defections and by-elections.
Tom Hennell, Withington, Manchester.

☐ USING her prerogative power, the Queen would dismiss the despotic government, an act requiring no help from anyone else and no more formality than just informing the prime minister that he no longer held office. She would then appoint the leader of the opposition as prime minister, on condition that he recommended an immediate dissolution of Parliament. He would be more than happy to accept on that basis.The new government would then carry out the formalities outlined by Tom Hennell to bring about a general election.
Rodney Brazier, Professor of Constitutional Law, University of Manchester.

QUESTION: How has the word 'loo' become a British euphemism for water closet?

☐ THIS is the shortened version of '*Le oo*', as used in France in the days when two holes were cut in the door of the WC so that you could see if it was occupied.
Joan Ireson, Harold Wood, Essex.

□ ONE of the most widely-accepted explanations is the warning cry, in pre-seweraged Britain, of 'gardy-loo!' (from the French '*garde à l'eau*' – watch out for the water) as 'slops' were thrown out of upper-storey windows into the open sewer that was the street. Another version has it that we abbreviated an old French euphemism for lavatory, namely '*lieu d'aisance*' (place of easement).
Philip J. Evison, London SW15.

□ IT COMES from the Eskimo '*igloo*' where the 'ig' is at the front and the 'loo' is at the back.
Garry Chambers, London N3.

□ DESPITE the previous responses, the true reason a loo is known as a loo is because in continental hotels with door numbers, it was traditional that the first room, numbered 00, was the toilet. Instead of being called *le zero-zero* or some other cumbersome term, it became known as '*l'oo*'. Note also that the colloquial German term for the toilet is '*der Null-Null*', i.e. 'the zero-zero'.
Cie Sangster, University of Leeds.

□ THE most likely explanation comes from the sea. There was a small platform on each side of the bow on the old sailing ships which was used for swinging the lead. It was known as the heads. Sailing ships had little in the way of lavatory accommodation and the heads were normally used instead. The lavatory on a boat is still called 'the heads'. When the ship was heeled to the wind the leeward side was obviously the most practical side to use. Leeward in nautical language is pronounced 'looard'. Hence 'I'm just going to the looard head' later became 'I'm just going to the loo'.
Donald Edwards, Cotobro, Granada, Spain.

QUESTION: If Essex, Sussex, Wessex and Middlesex belonged to Saxons in the east, south, west and middle respectively, what happened to the Saxons in the north?

□ THEY lived in Nosex, so they all died out.
Malcolm Brown, Glasgow; Peter Mair, Netherlands; Helena Corran, Bath; and many more . . .

☐ THE questioner is overestimating the importance of the South Saxons. In the historic period after the initial Anglo-Saxon invasions, Sussex was largely ignored as an unimportant back-water. After an initially fierce invasion which led the South Saxon king Aelle to be recognised as overlord of all the English, Sussex seemed to have been rigidly contained within not very extensive boundaries and rapidly sank from sight – the Anglo-Saxon Chronicle does not mention Sussex between 491 and 675. By the time Sussex was conquered by Offa of Mercia in the 8th century the South Saxons were divided up and owing allegiance to at least three local kinglets. At the time the Anglo-Saxon kingdoms were being formed in the middle of the 6th century, the Saxons were basically divided into the West Saxons and the East Saxons. At some earlier point there had been a people occupying the land to the west of London who, from their position between the West and East Saxons, were known as Middle Saxons. But, by the late 6th century Middlesex north of the Thames had been absorbed with London into Essex, while Middlesex south of the Thames (southern district, Surrey) was disputed between Wessex and Kent. The 'middle' in Middlesex therefore refers to midway between east and west. In any case, the Angles of Mercia began beyond Watford.
Colin Pilkington, Ormskirk, Lancs.

QUESTION: How should we define working class, middle class and upper class?

☐ PAID by the week, rent your house – working class. Paid by the month, own your own house – middle class. Don't have to work, inherited your house, plus estate – upper class.
Eric Robbie, Stroud, Glos.

☐ THE difference between the classes is in their relationship with society's institutions. The working classes do what the system sets out for them. The middle classes invent, operate and belong to the system. The upper classes tolerate the system but know the right people to speak to if they feel the need to bypass any part of it. The underclass (often overlooked) don't have any relationship with the system at all. Similarly, for example, working-class attitudes on

school are: 'Keep your head down and your mouth shut – if they don't notice you, then you can't get into trouble.' Middle class on school: 'Your school is there to help you learn, and teachers are there to answer your questions.' Upper class on school: 'It's a pity you have to spend your time with second-rate people but you'll get the real lessons of life here, when you come home for the hols.'
J. Nieman, Muswell Hill, London N10.

☐ Rich Hall, a US stand-up comic explained: when you go to work in the morning, if your name is on the front of the building, you're upper class; if your name is on your desk, you're middle class; and if your name is on your shirt, you're working class.
Bill Harvey, Edinburgh.

☐ The last two of these three terms are confusing. The important division is between working class and owning class. Members of the owning class own enough so that they do not have to work to stay alive, while members of the working class have to sell their work to survive. The point about the owning class is not that they are richer than the rest of us, but that they own the things that generate wealth without them having to work: essentially, land and buildings (giving them income from rent) and businesses (giving them income from the sale of goods or services). The only sure way to ensure your place in the owning class is to choose your parents carefully.
Raphael Salkie, Brighton.

QUESTION: Assuming the likelihood of at least one other planet in the universe with animal life on the surface, what physical characteristics would the inhabitants be most likely to exhibit?

☐ By far the most likely sort of extra-terrestrial life would be based on carbon compounds and liquid water – just like life on Earth. This is not parochialism, but based on fundamental and universal properties of matter. If, as is very likely, planets with such life are abundant in our galaxy, then the physical characteristics will depend on the physical environment during

the evolution of the extra-terrestrial life. At a cellular level, the life could well be fairly similar to life here over a wide range of physical environments. At the level of multicellular creatures, such as animals and plants, the life might well be similar if the physical environment has been similar to that on Earth. This does not mean that, for example, anything resembling a horse would roam on anything resembling grassy plains. But there could well be two- or four-legged creatures, with eyes at the top of the body adapted to the wavelengths of light emitted by the planet's star, etc., and it might have as food some plant-like surface growth that built its own tissue by some local version of photosynthesis.
(Dr) Barrie W. Jones, Physics Department, Open University.

QUESTION: Why is Saint George the patron saint of England? And why is he the patron saint of Catalonia?

□ In his *Oxford Dictionary Of Saints*, David Hugh Farmer explains that St George was adopted as patron saint in the Middle Ages by England and Catalonia, as well as by Venice, Genoa and Portugal, because he was the personification of the ideals of Christian chivalry. St George had been known in England since the 7th–8th centuries but his cult gained new impetus in England during the Crusades. A vision of George and Demetrius at the siege of Antioch preceded the defeat of the Saracens and the fall of the town on the first Crusade. Richard I placed himself and his army under George's protection, and St George was subsequently regarded as the special patron of soldiers. Edward III founded the Order of the Garter under St George's patronage in 1348. In 1415 – after the battle of Agincourt, when Henry V invoked George as England's patron – St George's feast was raised in rank to one of the principal feasts of the year. St George remained popular in the post-medieval period, but as there is considerable doubt about the historical veracity of his legend, his cult was reduced to a local one in the reform of the Roman calendar in 1969.
Katherine Lewis, York.

□ By the time George took over from Edward the Confessor as patron of England – at the founding of the Order of the Garter – he had already been guarding Doncaster for over 400 years. In the East he was generally held to protect the armies of Byzantium,

and is claimed as national saint by both Georgia and Ethiopia. In Germany he is one of the '14 Saints' who are considered particularly receptive to prayers for help – and in this century was to become the favourite national image of Nazi propaganda. George's attraction was originally as a martyr in the persecution of AD 303. Tradition elaborated his death into a highly imaginative and varied list of tortures, offering church artists a complete iconographic programme – as at St Neots in Cornwall. At the time of the crusades he also begins to be shown as a mounted dragon-slayer – a depiction probably borrowed from late Egyptian carvings of the god Horus.
Tom Hennell, Withington, Manchester.

QUESTION: Why is it that lots of people used to be very leftwing when they were young and are now quite rightwing; but hardly anyone goes the other way?

☐ PEOPLE take ideological stances out of either high-minded principle or materialistic self-interest. The former rarely change; they merely sophisticate their views. The latter change when their circumstances change. In recent times most UK citizens have become more prosperous with age; they find they have more to lose as they grow older; their views become more conservative out of greed and fear. However, in the next decade or so, as more and more elderly people descend into poverty and misery, you will find more and more examples of right-to-left movement.
D. Hartridge, Yate, Bristol.

☐ AS PEOPLE get older their stomachs broaden and their minds narrow.
Kevin Buckley, Kingsley Green, Cheshire.

☐ THE political spectrum established at the French Revolution has been moving steadily leftwards. This is why Thatcher, who in 1800 would have been described as a 'Jacobin' on the extreme left, is now regarded as on the far right. Liberalism, the belief in personal and economic freedom, is now on the extreme right. Hence, people whose political ideas remain unchanged find themselves on the 'right' as the political spectrum moves leftwards.
H. M. Lowry, Marlborough, Wilts.

☐ OLDER people grow more conservative, not Conservative. Electoral studies show that they become less volatile as voters – rarely, for instance, changing their voting intention during an election campaign. Lifelong Labour voters are extremely likely to continue in that mode; the imbalance of rightwing voting is chiefly explained because well-to-do people, who tend to vote Conservative, also tend to live longer.
(Prof.) Eric Midwinter (co-author of Polls Apart: Older People And The 1987 General Election*), Harpenden, Herts.*

☐ IN 1947 Bertrand Russell argued that Russia should be coerced into accepting international control of atomic energy; in 1961, aged 89, he was jailed for organising an illegal sit-down against nuclear weapons. In 1936 Jean-Paul Sartre did not bother to vote; in the early 1970s he sold revolutionary papers on the streets of Paris. Those who move leftwards may be few in number but they are the clever ones.
Ian Birchall, London N9.

QUESTION: Were native Americans' smoke signals myth or fact? If fact, what range of information could they convey?

☐ THE book *Indian Sign Language* by William Tomkins (Dover) uses as its source the Museum of the American Indian in New York City. 'Inasmuch as they aimed to transmit secret knowledge, most or many of the signs were devised privately and to suit a particular purpose or the caprice of the transmitter. There were, however, certain more or less recognized abstract smoke signals . . . One puff meant "Attention". Two puffs meant "All's well". Three puffs of smoke, or three fires in a row, signified "Danger", "Trouble" or a call for help.'
Margaret B. Brooks, Pittsburgh, US.

QUESTION: Why is a capital 'S' with two vertical lines running through it used as the dollar sign?

☐ BILL BRYSON in *Made In America* refers to two theories. The first is that it originated as the letters 'U' and 'S' superimposed on each other. Bryson explains, however, that the symbol itself

predates its application to US dollars, being used much earlier as a symbol for '*peso*'. A more likely explanation, he says, is that it is a modified form of the pillars of Hercules, wrapped around with a scroll, found on old Spanish pieces of eight.
David Handley, Whale Beach, Australia.

□ DAVID HANDLEY was way out with his explanation. The real reason for the sign is that the Spanish doubloon was a rather large value coin and as there were no smaller denominations it was difficult to trade. Therefore the doubloon was cut into eight pieces – marked with the figure eight with a vertical line each side – to show that it originally came from a doubloon. Hence 'Pieces of Eight'. Over a period of time, the eight became abbreviated to the capital letter S, with the two vertical lines running through the middle.
Larry Spector, Dagenham, Essex.

QUESTION: What is a continent? Is Europe a continent or just the western part of the Asian landmass?

□ EUROPE and Asia have been welded together for at least 300 million years. Geophysically, continents are defined by the thickness and composition of their crust, which (unlike oceanic crust) is silica-rich and thick. There are seven patches of continental crust, but it makes sense to subdivide them where they are cut by tectonic plate boundaries, because the fragments are in relative motion. This makes 14 continents in all: Jan Mayen, the Rockall Plateau, the Agulhas Plateau (south of South Africa), the Seychelles, New Zealand, Antarctica, South America, Central America, North America (including a large chunk of Siberia), Eurasia, Australia, India, Arabia and Africa.
Graham Cogley, Professor of Geography, Trent University, Peterborough, Canada.

□ CONTINENTS are pieces of physical geography that we think have some cultural unity. The Greeks began this by calling the different shores of the Mediterranean (Mid-Earth Sea), Europe, Asia and Africa. But they settled all three and Alexander the Great's conquests began a unification completed by the Romans, whose empire encircled *Mare Nostrum* (Our Sea). Europe re-emerged

when the Islamic conquests stopped at the Mediterranean, which became a moat around Christendom. Only from the 16th century onwards did Europeans impose the idea of continents on the world. Missionary-educated 'Asians' and 'Africans' learned to accept these definitions. Everywhere except Antarctica is just a 'peninsula of Asia' in strict physical terms.
John Newson, Birmingham.

QUESTION: What phenomena might one observe if the Earth were to slow down, come to a dead halt and then reverse the direction of spin on its axis?

☐ WHIPLASH.
Brendan Quinn, Manchester.

☐ THE circulation of the Earth's atmosphere and the weather systems that form in it are strongly influenced by the Earth's rotation. This constrains the major wind systems, such as the trade winds and the mid-latitude westerlies, to blow largely along latitude circles. As the Earth slowed down, these winds would become more sluggish and would adopt a more north-south orientation. The atmosphere would become much less efficient at transporting heat from the equator to the poles so the climates of the tropics and the polar regions would become much more extreme. I suspect that the resulting climatic chaos would put an end to all human life but, should anyone survive to witness the second half of the experiment, they would see the old atmospheric circulation patterns re-establish themselves with one crucial difference – the directions of the major wind systems would be reversed, with the trade winds blowing from the west and easterlies prevailing over Britain and Europe. Similar changes would take place in the flow of the ocean currents and in motions within the Earth's liquid core. The latter are responsible for generating the Earth's magnetic field – as this changed there could be dramatic changes in the amount of cosmic radiation reaching the Earth's surface which, again, might have fairly dire consequences for life on Earth. We can get some idea of the changes that might occur on a slowly-rotating Earth by studying the atmosphere of Venus, which takes 243 days to rotate about its axis. Interestingly, the Earth's rotation has slowed down significantly over geological time. The consequences of this for the

evolution of life on Earth are speculated on by John Barrow in his book *The Artful Universe* (Oxford, 1995).
(Dr) John King, Cambridge.

☐ For the Earth to behave in this way would involve the suspension of all physical laws. Hence, one might experience virtually anything. Perhaps astrology might become scientifically valid.
(Dr) Steven Hall, Leigh, Lancs.

QUESTION: The word 'cleave' has two opposite meanings – either to stick together or to split apart. Are there any other words that do the same thing?

☐ There were originally two quite separate words, with distinct etymologies, the Old English forms being *cleofian* or *clifian* (to adhere) and *cleofan* (to split). During the medieval period, inflexional endings largely disappeared and the Anglo-Saxon vowel system was simplified. The present tenses of the two verbs came to be spelt and pronounced more or less the same – for example, cleve in Chaucer could indicate either word. The past tenses and past participles were still distinct (cleaved and cloven) but, in practice, there was a lot of confusion. (Sources: *Oxford English Dictionary; Origins* by Eric Partridge.)
Alan Clarke, Bristol.

☐ Another possible example is 'let', which means both permit/enable and forbid/obstruct (as in 'without let or hindrance').
Deborah Cameron, Glasgow.

☐ The word 'sanction' can mean either to approve or permit, or to punish – as in trade sanctions against Serbia. In the UK, to 'table' a bill or proposal, means to bring it forward or put it on the agenda. In the US, it means to take it off the agenda, to kill it.
Marjorie Lister, Bradford.

☐ Left can be interpreted as 'departed' or 'remaining'.
Luke Williams, Sydenham, London SE26.

☐ Others are 'to dust', and 'to draw' (curtains). Similar curiosities are words which appear to be opposites but which share the same

meaning: flammable and inflammable; bend and unbend; passive and impassive.
Margaret Diamond, Coventry.

□ HOW about the word 'conserve': to save or protect (the countryside) as in conservation; or to destroy or dismantle (the country) as in Conservatives.
Guy Johnston, Kirchhundem, Germany.

□ IN CANADIAN military parlance, the verb 'to secure' has three meanings. If you tell the Army to secure a building, they'll surround it, kick in the doors and clear it room by room. Tell the Navy to do the same thing and they'll lock all the doors and go home. The Air Force, however, would secure a building by taking out a three-year lease with an option to buy.
Dominic Rossi, Halifax, Canada.

□ INFLAMMABLE and flammable do not have the same meaning. An inflammable substance, like petrol, is liable to catch fire easily; a flammable substance, like wood, burns once it is set fire to. The 'in-' in inflammable is a Latin intensitive and not a negative.
Jon Almond, Colchester.

□ I MUST correct Jon Almond when he said inflammable and flammable have different meanings. The *Oxford English Dictionary*, *Webster's Third New International Dictionary* and *Collins English Dictionary* all state the same meaning for both words.
John Graham, Armagh, N. Ireland.

□ THE *Oxford English Dictionary* defines 'chuffed' as: 'pleased, satisfied'; and 'displeased, disgruntled'.
A. W. Rowe, Huddersfield.

□ JON ALMOND was making a more subtle point than John Graham realises about the distinction between 'flammable' and 'inflammable'. *Cassell's Latin Dictionary* connects the verb '*flammo*' to 'flame, blaze and burn', but '*inflammo*' to the activity of 'lighting up, kindling and setting fire to'. The distinction is that inflammable substances are more likely to burn than flammable ones.
Will and Joe Brooker, Woolwich, London SE18.

☐ A CONSCIOUS decision to replace 'inflammable' with 'flammable' as the label for petroleum products, etc., was taken in the US in the 1930s on the recommendation of a linguist, because of the danger that the prefix 'in-' might be taken as a negative. Until then 'flammable' was rare. So, as a replacement, it was obviously intended to have the same meaning. Etymology cannot determine the present-day meaning of words.
F. R. Palmer, Winnersh, Berks.

☐ 'SEEDED' has three contrasting meanings. It can mean that seeds have been put in, taken out, or left in (in the case of non-seedless grapes).
Colin Bootle, Aylesbury, Bucks.

QUESTION: Has there ever been a scientific study of astrology with regards to its ability or otherwise to define personal characteristics?

☐ THE French statistician Michel Gauquelin conducted studies on some 15,000 subjects on astrology applied to eminent professionals. He established strong correlations between profession and the appropriate prominent planet in the birth chart (Mars for athletes, Saturn for scientists, Moon for writers, etc.). He attempted to show that the personal characteristics of his professionals (via published biographies) corresponded to prominent planets but these findings have been criticised as arising from personal bias. More recently there has been a personal characteristics study of 'ordinary people' which appears to confirm the Gauquelin results (*The Astrology Of Time Twins*, Roberts and Greengrass, 1994). Additionally, a large study of personal characteristics and astrology is currently being carried out by a research group of the Astrological Association.
(Prof.) P. C. Roberts, Chalford, Glos.

☐ WHAT about the *Guardian*'s Zodiac test in 1984? This showed that while occupation varied with birthdate, it had more to do with season than astrology. There were also some patterns linking personality to astrology, but this seemed to be due to people

reporting themselves in terms of their star signs rather than any direct effects of the cosmos.
Alan Smithers, School of Education, University of Manchester.

□ QUITE apart from the experimental evidence, there are at least two reasons for scepticism. First, China and India have ancient astrological systems that are just as influential as ours but are based on quite different star patterns. The three systems contradict one another, so at least two of them must be wrong. Second, because of the precession of the earth's axis, the constellations have all slipped out of place since western astrology was devised by the Babylonians. At the Spring equinox, for example, the sun used to be in Aries but is nowadays in Pisces, yet the astrological charts have not been amended accordingly.
(Dr) Andrew Colman, Department of Psychology, University of Leicester.

□ PROFESSOR P. C. ROBERTS ignores the many scientific studies that contradict astrology, in favour of the few that are supportive. He cites the work of Michel Gauquelin as providing 'correlations between profession and the appropriate prominent planet in the birth chart'. But Gauquelin's evidence refuted such tenets as the planet Jupiter being high in the sky at birth being an 'indication of success'; and it showed that for murderers the distribution of the planet Mars among the astrological houses is consistent with chance. The remaining examples Roberts mentions have been criticised because of the poor sample size or inability to repeat the results.
Bill White, Bucks.

QUESTION: French onion men were a feature of my 1950s childhood. They rode around on bicycles selling strings of onions. Where did they come from, and what's happened to them?

□ THE onion sellers hailed from the Roscoff region of Brittany. Spending the growing season in France they would travel to Britain during the autumn and winter because the British were said to pay more for their onions than the French. During their

heyday the sellers would charter their own boats to carry the crop to Britain. On arrival, they lived in hovels surrounded by mountains of onions to be threaded on raffia strings. Each team of men (and women) would travel to the same area of Britain each year. They were particularly numerous in all areas of Wales, where they were often called *Sioni Winwns* (Johnny Onions). Some still travel from Brittany but they are few in number.
Eryl Crump, Bodorgan, Gwynedd.

□ FURTHER to Eryl Crump's contribution, Roscoff was a particularly good area for vegetable growing but the large markets were too far away to sell the produce profitably. In 1828, Henri Olivier, a 20-year-old vegetable grower, hired a sailing barge and, with three friends and a load of onions, crossed the Channel. Their success was such that, at the peak of the trade, in 1928–29, over 9,000 tons of onions were imported to Britain from Roscoff, mostly sold from door to door by some 1,400 Johnny Onions. The trade declined during the Thirties, partly because of a 'buy British' policy, partly as a result of fluctuations in the exchange rate, and then because of the outbreak of the war. Because of the affinity between Celtic peoples, the Breton onion sellers were particularly welcome in Wales and Scotland, and many were able to conduct their trade in Welsh. As they were the only foreign visitors to penetrate many parts of Britain, the bike-riding onion sellers became everyone's idea of the typical European – even though they were virtually unknown on the Continent. The trade has almost disappeared now, thanks largely to the improvement in living standards in Brittany (the successful Brittany Ferries company was set up in the early 1970s originally to transport vegetables to the UK).
Rhys Lewis, Cyncoed, Cardiff.

□ THE book *Goodbye, Johnny Onions*, by Gwyn Griffiths, published by Dyllansow Trosan from Redruth, Kernow, gives a history of the onion sellers.
Cen Llwyd, Llandysol, Dyfed.

QUESTION: When I die, I do not want any memorial or final resting place. I also don't want to burden my dependents with the unnecessary expense of a funeral. What is the cheapest, legal, way to dispose of a human body in England?

☐ You could leave your body to a medical school for dissection by students. The snag is that they tend to accept only bodies that are unautopsied after death, non-cancerous and within easy range of a school. If your next of kin are receiving either income support, housing benefit, disability working allowance or council tax benefit, the local Social Security will pay for a basic funeral. If not, your relatives can refuse to arrange for disposal of your body, in which case the local authority is legally obliged to register the death and carry out the funeral, with reimbursement from the estate or next of kin where possible. Your body can be buried by friends and relatives in a garden or farm with the permission of the landowner, without permission from the council planning department or the environmental health department. It is advisable for the burial to be 250 metres from any human-consumption water supply or well or borehole, 30 metres from any other spring and 10 metres from any field drain, with no water in the grave when first dug. But a garden burial could severely reduce the value of a property. In my view, the most satisfactory option is burial organised by the relatives in a nature reserve burial ground run by a farmer, local authority or wildlife trust, where a tree is planted instead of having a headstone.
Nicholas Albery, Director, Natural Death Centre, London NW2.

☐ Become the owner of a privatised mine.
Henry Hubbal, Redditch, Worcester.

☐ The body should be giftwrapped and left overnight on the back seat of an unlocked car. It will be gone by morning. Failing that, try mailing it Recorded Delivery. This guarantees it'll be lost forever.
Garry Chambers, London N3.

QUESTION: Why do we 'pull someone's leg'? Why not an arm?

☐ Thomas Hood wrote in his poem *The Last Man* (1827):

I must turn my cup of sorrow quite up,
And drink it to the dregs,
For there is not another man alive,
In the world to pull my legs!

He was referring to the fact that, before the invention of the long drop in executions by hanging, the friends of the criminal were permitted to pull his legs in order to shorten his suffering. This developed into a sick joke that one's friends would always be around to pull one's legs if needed.
Brian Palmer, Noke Side, Herts.

QUESTION: In this age of electronic communication, why do British banks still require at least four working weekdays after a cheque has been paid in for the money to be available?

□ THE banks have made significant and ongoing investments in cheque processing technology. However, the Bills of Exchange Act 1882 requires a bank to return every cheque to the branch address on the cheque prior to the cheque being paid. For a cheque paid in on, say, a Monday, this would occur on the Wednesday. The bank receiving the payment (the collecting bank) will not know until Thursday at the earliest whether the cheque has bounced. It is for this reason that the bank would not normally allow its customer to withdraw funds prior to Day 4 (Thursday in this instance). On a separate but related issue, most banks now pay customers interest on the value of the cheque on Day 3, i.e. when they themselves receive the proceeds of the clearing settlement. Where speed is of the essence in making a payment, all banks now offer electronic services to provide same-day transfer of funds across the UK.
Richard Tyson-Davies, Association for Payment Clearing Services, London EC2.

QUESTION: What was the single most profitable financial transaction in the history of civilisation?

□ ON 2 MAY 1803, President Thomas Jefferson offered to buy from France the whole of the Louisiana Territory which was so vast that its acquisition more than doubled the size of the United States. It was later divided into 12 separate states: Arkansas, Iowa, Kansas, Louisiana, Minnesota, Missouri, Montana, Nebraska, Oklahoma, Wyoming, and the two Dakotas. The price paid was 15 million dollars – working out at less than 5 cents an acre.
Idwal Walters, Cardiff.

☐ THE scramble for Africa, in which colonialists paid nothing but continue to reap billions in 'invisible' profits to this day.
Nana Asare Yeboah, Tsuchuria, Japan.

☐ WHILE 5 cents an acre is not a bad price for the Louisiana Purchase, it was only 64 years later, in 1867, that US Secretary of State William Seward negotiated the purchase of Alaska from Russia and got almost 600,000 square miles for about 2 cents an acre ($7.2 million). It was referred to as Seward's Folly at the time but the wealth that came out of Alaska in the gold rush of 1898 alone would have covered the purchase price tens of times over. And even that amount pales by comparison to the revenues generated by the largest oil field in North America, at Prudhoe Bay on Alaska's northern coast.
John C. Logsdon, Juneau, Alaska.

QUESTION: According to Suetonius, Caesar Galba introduced 'the spectacular novelty of tightrope-walking elephants' at the Floral Games. Is this really possible and, if so, has it ever been performed since?

☐ THE activity is more like tightrope roller-skating. There are two wires, not one, arranged in parallel, and separated by the width of an elephant – around eight feet off the ground. Sturdy rollers are attached in the manner of horseshoes to the elephants' feet, and after having been hoisted aloft by crane and aligned with the high wire, the animal is pulled along by several groundlings using ropes. This is possible because, when suspended in space, elephants become paralysed and rigid. (The phenomenon was first discovered by Romans when they were loading their cattle on to cargo ships.) This might sound complicated, but it's a thin feat compared to other Roman entertainments, such as the re-enactment of sea battles in the middle of a city. The feat has been attempted since, in the freakshows of 19th-century American circuses. In Lexington, Virginia, in 1862, an elephant fell from the wires, slicing off a leg in the process. A bill was passed through Congress after this which formed the basis for modern animal welfare legislation in the US.
Robbie Fraser (author, Packing The Trunk), *Kilburn, London NW6.*

QUESTION: Some posters around the time of the *Titanic* launch also advertised its sister ship, the *Olympic*. Was this ever built? If so, what happened to it?

□ THE *Olympic* was launched at Belfast on 20 October 1910. She began her maiden voyage on the day her almost identical sister, the *Titanic*, was launched on 31 May 1911. *Olympic* almost sank a tug on her first arrival in New York, hit a naval cruiser in September 1911, lost a propeller blade in February 1912, rammed and sank a U-boat in April 1918 while serving as a troopship, hit a freighter in 1924 and crushed the Nantucket lightship, killing seven men, 10 years later. It is not clear how she earned the nickname 'Old Reliable', which she bore until paid off in 1935. She was scrapped in 1937, but her dining-room panelling adorns the restaurant at the White Swan Hotel, Alnwick, Northumberland, to this day. The third and last in the class, *Britannic*, was launched in February 1914, completed in November 1915 and sunk by a mine in the Aegean a year later, while serving as a hospital-ship. She never carried a fare-paying passenger.
Dan van der Vat, author, The Riddle Of The Titanic, *Twickenham, Middlesex.*

QUESTION: I understand that under the Vichy regime in France, the game of Rugby League (but not Rugby Union) was outlawed. Why?

□ THE Vichy government saw professional sport as having contributed to the decadence which led to France's defeat by Germany in 1940, and as being antithetical to the moral and physical regeneration which the regime sought to bring about. The government department headed by the Wimbledon champion, Jean Borotra, a torch-bearer for amateur ideals, drew up plans to make all sport non-professional, including football, cycling and tennis, within three years. Rugby League, however, which was deemed to be merely a professional version of Rugby Union, was banned immediately, its funds confiscated and its players made to play the 15-a-side game. It was not until after the Liberation that Rugby League was able to be played again in France.
Mike Rylance, Wakefield.

QUESTION: Why 'spitting image'?

☐ THE idea behind the expression is that the progeny is so like the parent that it is as if it had been spat out by them, i.e. a very part of them. It dates from the early 17th century: 'He's e'en as like thee as th' had'st spit him' (Source: Eric Partridge's *Dictionary Of Historical Slang*).
Adrian Murphy, London SE16.

☐ THE theory cited in Partridge's by Adrian Murphy is a load of cobblers. Spitting image predates the 1600s by centuries, and is to the phrase 'spirit and image' as 'good-bye' is to 'God be with you'. In remote pockets of the Appalachians in the US it can still be heard in full, as in 'he's the spirit and image of his father', i.e. a chip off the old block.
J. Brener, London NW6.

☐ J. BRENER'S explanation that 'spitting image' evolved from 'spirit and image' may be wrong. In Brazil there is a corresponding expression, *cagado e cuspido*, and *cuspir* means 'to spit'.
Severino Toscano Melo, São Paulo, Brazil.

☐ THE phrase is a corruption of 'spit and image'. According to the *OED*, there are other similar phrases such as 'spit and fetch' and 'spit and picture'. All of them refer to exact likenesses, as seen in other phrases such as 'the very spit of your father'.
David Lane, Wakefield.

☐ IN MY childhood in County Durham the expression used in my family was 'splitten image'. The derivation was from splitting something symmetrically in half so that the two parts would be similar in all respects but be mirror images of one another.
G. M. Berriman, Wakefield.

☐ ADRIAN MURPHY'S explanation is correct, but image itself doesn't spit – it is spit, normally by the man who fathers the child who so resembles him. The correct term is therefore 'spitten image', where 'spitten' is the old past participle – I have spitten. Nowadays I have spit is more common, and the term 'the spit image' is also heard.
Stanley Mason, Effretikon, Switzerland.

QUESTION: If you strap a piece of toast, buttered side up, to the back of a cat, and throw the cat out of a window, will the cat land on its feet or will Sod's Law apply?

☐ IF THE cat lands on its feet, you've obviously buttered the wrong side of the toast.
Len Feltham, Keynsham, Bristol.

☐ THE cat will land on its feet, but then roll on to its back before the toast can be retrieved.
Howard Partridge, West Bridgford, Nottingham.

☐ SOD'S Law goes on to state that toast will fall buttered side down *unless* it has been dropped as part of a scientific attempt to prove Sod's Law. In this case Murphy's Law applies to Sod's Law and it falls buttered side up. The cat is therefore safe!
T. A. Jones, West Dulwich.

☐ SOD'S Law will apply. The cat will land on the head of a passing RSPCA official.
Len Clarke, Uxbridge, Middx.

QUESTION: We have the Twenties, Thirties, etc., right up to the Nineties. But what do we call the first two decades of a century?

☐ FOR the forthcoming one I suggest the Noughties (spelling optional) because the celebrations of the millennium will lead to a prolonged bout of hedonism; to be followed by the Tenties, because we shall all have had so much expensive fun we shall be forced to sell our houses and live under canvas.
Adam Horner, Roath, Cardiff.

QUESTION: Humpty Dumpty is usually portrayed as an egg, but I can find no evidence in the nursery rhyme to support this. Are there other now-obscure verses, or are we just following the assumptions of illustrators like Tenniel?

☐ HUMPTY Dumpty was taller than a house, he was made of wood,

probably had a coat of hides, and sat on little wheels. When he was built, over 300 years ago, he was one of a pair, but his brother did not even get to the wall. Humpty Dumpty was not an egg – he was a siege tower (probably one of the last ever built in Britain). These wooden structures were pushed against a castle or town wall by besiegers in an attempt to gain entry by storm. The biggest problem was getting them close enough to the wall: they were big, clumsy, top heavy (especially when they had troops on board) and had to be moved by hand on ground that was sometimes neither level nor firm. The whole procedure was very precarious and prone to accidents. Humpty Dumpty was constructed during the English Civil War by Royalist forces ('all the King's horses and all the King's men') while they were besieging a town held for Parliament. We know Humpty got to the wall and that he fell with such power as to make it impossible to put him together again. But did he fall or was he pushed?
Roy Palmer, Dimlock, Gloucestershire.

☐ WHEN Alice first sees Humpty Dumpty in Lewis Carroll's *Alice Through the Looking-Glass*, she says: 'How exactly like an egg he is.' Humpty Dumpty replies: 'It's very provoking to be called an egg!' (Later he says, 'My name means the shape I am, and a good handsome shape it is too.') Tenniel's illustration simply uses Lewis Carroll's text. There is a belief that the verse was originally a riddle, and the answer is 'an egg'. This pre-dates the publication of *Alice Through the Looking-Glass*, and Lewis Carroll made use of a common tradition. However, eggs are not normally placed on walls (although this may have been to make the riddle more confusing), and the verse has never appeared in a book of riddles. The *Oxford English Dictionary* records that the expression 'Humpty Dumpty' was the name of an ale and brandy punch in the late 17th century. The use of the expression 'Humpty Dumpty' to describe a short or unattractive person first occurs in Grose's *Dictionary of the Vulgar Tongue* in 1785. The rhyme itself is not recorded before the 19th century, when several variants were published in Britain and the United States, although these may have been of earlier origin. All evidence suggests that 'Humpty Dumpty' has always been a self-contained four-line verse. Some differences in the final two lines are recorded (for example 'Threescore men and threescore more,/Cannot place Humpty Dumpty as he was before'), but all versions follow the same

basic pattern. Continental versions are also recorded in the early 19th century. For example, 'Runtzelken-Puntzelken' and 'Humpelken-Pumpelken' in Germany, 'Boule Boule' in France and 'Thille Lille' in Sweden. Efforts to explain Humpty Dumpty as a siege tower are not wholly satisfactory, as the verse makes it clear that Humpty Dumpty could not be repaired by human agency. An army could repair a damaged siege tower or build a new one, but human science cannot fully repair a broken egg. Of course, this ignores the possibility that the verse may have been devised for no other purpose than to amuse.
Robert Halliday, Bury St Edmunds, Suffolk.

□ THE theory that the verses refer to a siege engine used at Gloucester in 1643 is merely a *jeu d'esprit* contrived in 1956 by Dennis Daube, and popularised subsequently by Richard Rodney Bennett in the opera, *All the King's Men.*
Roy Palmer, Dimlock, Gloucestershire.

□ IT WAS 'a short clumsy person' who had a great fall – the sort of fall (into pregnancy) that the French, Swedish, Danish, Finnish, Swiss and German versions of the rhyme warn their daughters about. This meaning is confirmed by the game played while reciting this verse. The girls 'sit down holding their skirts tightly about their feet. At an agreed signal they throw themselves backwards and must recover their balance without letting go their skirts' (*Oxford Dictionary of Nursery Rhymes*). In the 1846 version it's the '40 doctors and 40 wrights' who 'couldn't put Humpty Dumpty to rights'. But I prefer the restored version in Norman Iles's *Who Really Killed Cock Robin* (published by Robert Hales, 1986): 'Plumpty-Dumpty sat on a wall. Plumpty-Dumpty had a great fall. All the king's doctors, all the king's laws, Couldn't put Plumpty back as she was.' Adult rhymes were censored into childishness, as Iles's book explains.
S. Makepeace-Brown, Llandyssol, Dyfed.

QUESTION: Is a severed head briefly aware of its fate after the blade has dropped?

□ THE answer, however appalling to contemplate, is yes. Consciousness is a function of the cortex, the outermost region of the

brain, and requires a constant supply of oxygen from the blood. If that blood supply is interrupted by some outside agency, such as an axe through the neck, then the reserve of oxygen will very rapidly run out, and the brain will first stop functioning, and then die. This process starts with the cortex, causing loss of consciousness in about 20 seconds, and gradually goes through all regions of the brain, producing irreversible brain death in about four minutes. The brain will therefore be aware of its fate for those 20 seconds. There is some evidence that after Marie Antoinette was guillotined, her lips moved in an attempt to speak. The length of time involved has almost certainly been exaggerated in the retelling of this tale. However the blade that separated the brain from its blood supply would also have separated the mouth from its source of vocalisation – the lungs and larynx – so speech to discuss the subtleties of decapitation from the recipient's viewpoint would be impossible.
(Dr) Steve Seddon, Sandyfields, Newcastle, Staffs.

☐ I THINK Dr Seddon has forgotten two facts. The first is that the instant outflow of blood from the head equally instantly collapses its blood pressure and thus the brain's consciousness. This is proven by pilots 'blacking out' to very rapid unconsciousness if pulling out of a powered dive too fast, despite the fact that their head blood pressure is only slightly lowered. The second point is that if the minor impact to the neck vertebrae of a knock-out punch instantly produces unconsciousness, then I suspect that the somewhat larger shock of actually severing the spinal cord would be even more efficacious. Perhaps Madame Guillotine was quite merciful, after all.
Len Clarke, Uxbridge, Middx.

☐ MR CLARKE implies that the processes of decapitation necessarily lead to immediate loss of awareness. While his points are valid, the question asks whether or not a head is aware, and perhaps the answer is rather less clear cut. The point is that it may be aware. A blow to the head or back of neck can violently shake the brain, and produce a knockout. So indeed can severing the spinal cord. If the executioner was a rotten shot, he might KO the victim, but the guillotine or a good axeman are unlikely to be so inaccurate. A clean severance will only reduce the blood flow, and unconsciousness will take the usual 20 seconds to occur. If there is indeed spinal shock, it may or may not produce unconsciousness;

but some unfortunate people who do suffer accidental transection of the spinal cord live to tell the tale, and the details of the event (i.e. they were not rendered unconscious by the trauma). Pilots suffering severe G-forces in pulling out of a dive may also become unconscious, but not necessarily instantly. They may faint, or simply be exposed to a downward pull of the G-force in excess of their blood pressure, but the brain, being fluid in a rigid box, will not be drained. Neither is likely to happen in the snap of a finger, but while the blood supply is failing, the pilot is conscious, and will not necessarily be aware of the imminent blackout. In the same way, someone being strangled will suffer compression of the neck arteries, but does not become unconscious immediately. So while decapitation may render the head unconscious, the possibility and indeed probability exists for a brief period of awareness. No doubt it would suffer from a splitting headache. But who knows, it may be able to remain slightly detached about it all.
(Dr) Steve Seddon, Sandyfields, Newcastle, Staffs.

QUESTION: What exactly *are* the odds of being run over by a bus?

□ VERY few people are literally 'run over'. In 1991 there were 1,651 pedestrians injured when they were hit by a bus or coach; that is three per 100,000 population per annum or, roughly, two per 1,000 people in a lifetime.
Barbara Preston, Marple Bridge, Stockport.

□ THERE are 2,000 pedestrian fatalities each year, of which approximately 250 are 'bus related', say around five per week. If we assume that the population is 50 million, then the odds (of being killed by a bus) are one in 10 million.
Gordon Joly, London E14.

□ ONE can lie in the road for hours without being touched but then be run over three times in a row.
Paul Newstead, Hertford.

QUESTION: What event happened on the earliest precisely known date in history?

□ THE earliest event which we can accurately date was an astronomical one recorded by the Chinese on 6 September 775 BC. Chinese eclipse records began in 720 BC, but the Babylonians recorded an eclipse in 763 BC. Modern estimates of the exact dates of these events could be made. A better candidate, however, for a real historical date is 28 May 585 BC. On that date the battle between the Lydians and Medes was suddenly called off when a solar eclipse occurred. Both armies were too worried to continue. The eclipse had been predicted by Thales of Miletus.
Frank Large, Blundellsands, Merseyside.

□ THE earliest known viable record of an eclipse was found on a clay tablet from the city of Ugarit (in present-day Syria). This was analysed as referring to an eclipse on 3 May 1375 BC. The transcription of the tablet reads: 'On the day of the new moon, in the month of Hiyar, the sun was put to shame, and went down in the daytime, with Mars in attendance.' When computing ancient eclipses it is vital to take into account the slowdown in the earth's rate of rotation. By 1000 BC, the difference between civil time, measured from noon to noon on earth, and the time measured by uniformly running mechanical clocks would be more than 7½ hours. This difference must be taken into account when computing where an eclipse might be seen and its date. Any newly-discovered reports of ancient total eclipses, where the location of the observer was known, would still be of great scientific importance for measuring the long-term variation in the earth's rate of rotation, an outstanding problem in geophysics.
(Dr) M. Houlden, Department of Physics, University of Liverpool.

QUESTION: Why is a sporting match between two geographically close teams known as a 'Derby'?

□ ACCORDING to the *Wimbledon Football Supporters' Handbook*, Shrove Tuesday games began in the 18th century. The most famous took place in Derby when the young men of the parish of All Saints challenged those from nearby St Peter's. All men over the age of 18 took part, trying to force the ball from one parish into the other. In 1731 the mayor made an unsuccessful attempt to suppress the game, repeated every year by his successors until 1848, when troops were called in. From then on the name 'local Derby' was

attributed to any football match played with fierce partisanship between neighbouring clubs.
A. G. Fayers, Stanford-le-Hope, Essex.

QUESTION: What is the best thing to do if one is attacked by an aggressive dog? Once they've got their teeth into someone, how can they be persuaded to get them out again?

☐ IMMEDIATELY drop on to all fours, put your head close to the ground, wave one leg in the air and make soft whimpering noises, thus imitating the behaviour of a submissive dog. Do not smile while doing this as it will be interpreted as a snarl. I myself have never tested this method – running as fast as possible in the opposite direction has always seemed to me to be the most appropriate action.
J. C. Hawke, London SW11.

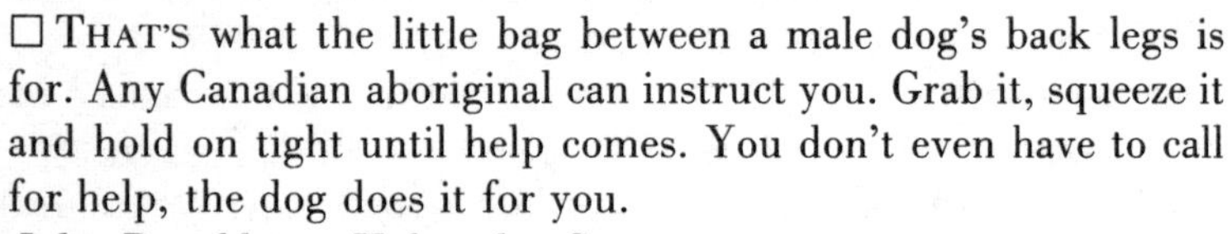

☐ THAT'S what the little bag between a male dog's back legs is for. Any Canadian aboriginal can instruct you. Grab it, squeeze it and hold on tight until help comes. You don't even have to call for help, the dog does it for you.
John Bauckham, Holcombe, Somerset.

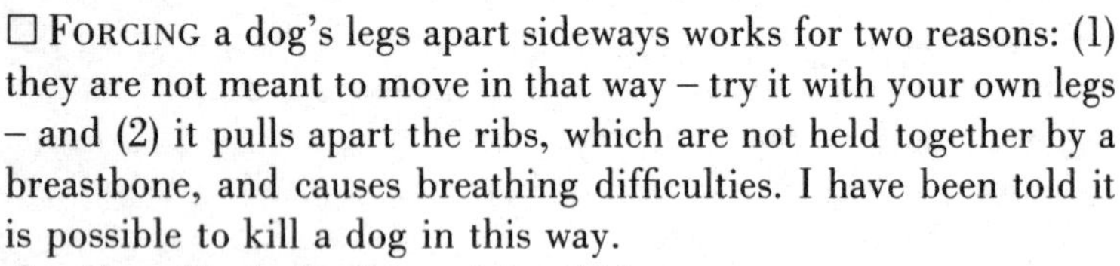

☐ FORCING a dog's legs apart sideways works for two reasons: (1) they are not meant to move in that way – try it with your own legs – and (2) it pulls apart the ribs, which are not held together by a breastbone, and causes breathing difficulties. I have been told it is possible to kill a dog in this way.
Geoffrey Clark, Bradden, Isle of Man.

☐ I HAVE an answer inspired by a short but instructive spell as an employee of the Royal Mail in the suburbs of north London. After a painful experience involving a border collie, my index finger and a letterbox, I was informed that the most effective procedure for declamping oneself from the jaws of an attacking canine is to deftly plunge one's thumb into the back passage of the offender. The shock (I am told) of the unwelcome intrusion initiates a slack-jawed temporary paralysis and a mightily surprised expression on the face of the formerly angered and attacking beast.
Dan Budden, Primrose Hill, W. Yorkshire.

☐ THE question prompted me to recall the action of a colleague in the Northern Rhodesian police some years ago. When his leg was gripped by a crocodile, he ran his hand down the creature's snout, located its eyes and removed them. There seems every reason to believe the same ploy would succeed in the case of an attack by a ferocious dog.
A. N. Joseph (OBE), Garstang, Lancs.

QUESTION: 'As happy as Larry'. Why Larry?

☐ THE term is probably derived from 'As happy as a Lark' where lark is a recent adaptation of the dialect 'lake' meaning sport, and Old English 'lac' meaning contest. According to Brewer's Dictionary, Larry comes from the Australian word Larrikin, meaning a street rowdy, which in turn derives from the Irish pronunciation of 'larking'. Brewer also suggests that the original Larry may have been Larry Foley (1847–1917), a noted Australian boxer.
Brian Palmer, Noke Side, St Albans.

QUESTION: Why is it that the keys on push-button telephones are numbered from the top downwards, but vice versa on computers?

☐ RESEARCH as far back as 1955 showed that the 1–2–3 arrangement conforms to people's expectations better than the 7–8–9 arrangement, but the same research also showed that people did not expect there to be any performance difference between the two layouts. In 1963, the 7–8–9 arrangement was adopted as the British Standard (BS 1909) and the first research on performance with the two arrangements was conducted in Cambridge. Unfortunately the research demonstrated that the 1–2–3 layout led to significantly better performance than 7–8–9. This research has been replicated on a number of occasions. Companies designing numeric keypads therefore had two conflicting pieces of information and I do not know how their decisions were made. However, whatever the issues were then, the problem now is that neither industry can easily change without upsetting many experienced users. The same problem occurs for alphanumeric keypads, where we now know that QWERTY is not the best arrangement, but the major

difficulties of changing to better keyboards (e.g., the Dvorak keyboard) are deemed to outweigh the benefits.
David Gilmore, Psychology Dept, University of Nottingham.

QUESTION: How does a seedless grape reproduce itself?

□ GRAPES do not reproduce if left to their own devices. However, sections of cane can be taken in autumn, stored in cool temperatures over winter and placed outside in an appropriate soil medium during spring to allow root and shoot development. Commercial growers usually encourage root production by treating the canes with chemicals. A second technique is 'embryo rescue'. Seedless fruit plants have a genetic mutation in which seeds fail to reach maturity. The embryo is a pre-seed stage of development still present in the seedless grape at the site where the seed would have been. Embryos can be removed from the grape and placed in tissue culture medium. Under certain conditions the embryo will now develop into a new plant.
(Dr) Jamie Day, Dunedin, New Zealand.

INDEX